Revitalizing Federal Education
Research and Development

Revitalizing Federal Education Research and Development

Improving the R&D Centers,
Regional Educational Laboratories,
and the "New" OERI

Maris A. Vinovskis

Ann Arbor

THE UNIVERSITY OF MICHIGAN PRESS

2004   2003   2002   2001   4   3   2   1

A CIP catalog record for this book is available from the British Library.

Library of Congress Cataloging-in-Publication Data

Vinovskis, Maris.
    Revitalizing federal education research and development : improving the R&D centers, regional educational laboratories, and the "new" OERI / Maris A. Vinovskis.
        p.   cm.
    Includes bibliographical references and index.
    ISBN 0-472-11210-4 (cloth : alk. paper)
    1. Education — Research — United States.   2. Federal aid to research — United States.   3. Federal aid to education — United States.   4. Education and state — United States.   5. United States. Office of Educational Research and Improvement.   I. Title.

LB1028.25.U6 V57   2001
379.1'21'0973 — dc21   2001027375

For Jeffrey Mirel and Gerald Moran,
valued colleagues and cherished friends

Contents

Acknowledgments

This book owes much to a large number of individuals — more than can be fully thanked in a short acknowledgment. My greatest debt is to former Assistant Secretary Diane Ravitch, who brought me to the Office of Educational Research and Improvement (OERI) as the research adviser to her agency. Diane also assigned to me the task of assessing the quality of work produced by the research and development (R&D) centers and the regional educational laboratories. When Diane returned to academia in January 1993, acting Assistant Secretary Emerson Elliott allowed me to continue this project; and Assistant Secretary Sharon Robinson, Diane's successor in the Clinton administration, supported the completion of that endeavor in mid-1993.

Throughout the writing of this book, the OERI staff, other federal officials, and many other scholars and participants in Washington, DC, provided me with indispensable assistance. Among the many individuals who helped were Clifford Adelman, Francie Alexander, Jan Anderson, Judith Anderson, Margo Anderson, David Angus, Sue Betka, Eve Bither, Sharon Bobbitt, David Boesel, Carolyn Breedlove, Thomas Brown, John Burkett, Ron Cartwright, Ned Chalker, Carol Chelemer, John Christensen, Joseph Conaty, Christopher Cross, Blane Dessy, Hal Dick, John Egermeier, Lee Eiden, Chester Finn Jr., Pascal Forgione Jr., Edward Fuentes, Paul Gagnon, Sandra Garcia, Milton Goldberg, Vance Grant, Jeanne Griffith, Charles Hansen, Maggie Hatton, Dick Hays, Eunice Henderson, Thomas Hill, Harold Himmelfarb, Stephen Hunt, Gregg Jackson, Carl Kaestle, Naomi Karp, Sally Kilgore, Sue Klein, Ellen Lagemann, David Mack, Kent McGuire, Hunter Moorman, Lana Muraskin, Martin Orland, Elizabeth Payer, Ronald Pedone, Laurence Peters, Gary Phillips, Ivor Pritchard, Theodor Rebarber, Nina Rees, Wayne Riddle, Marian Robinson, Jeffrey Rodamar, Michael Ross, Robert Rothman, Joe Schneider, Don Senese, Steve Sniegoski, Gerald Sroufe, Nevzer Stacey, Charles Stalford, David Stevenson, Robert Stonehill, Dena Stoner, Keith Stubbs, Anne Sweet, David Sweet, Robert Sweet, Ricky Takai, Tommy Tomlinson, David Tyack, Richard Venezky, and Jerry West.

Chapters 1 and 2 originally were issued as Maris A. Vinovskis, "Analysis of the Quality of Research and Development at the OERI Research and Development Centers and the OERI Regional Educational Laboratories," Final Report, OERI, June 1993. I am especially indebted to the staffs of the R&D centers and the regional educational laboratories for their invaluable assistance in providing me with appropriate materials and in hosting my visits to those institutions. I considerably revised and updated chapters 1 and 2 to reflect the additional information that has become available.

The third chapter was written with the support of a small research grant from the Spencer Foundation. I want to thank Patricia Graham and her colleagues at the Spencer Foundation for their financial assistance as well as their interest and encouragement for the overall project.

The fourth chapter is based on an essay commissioned by the OERI's National Educational Research Policy and Priorities Board (NERPPB). Eve Bither, the executive director of the OERI Policy Board, and her staff were instrumental in facilitating the project. And NERPPB members as well as many others provided useful comments and additional perspectives. The essay was originally published as Maris A. Vinovskis, *Changing Federal Strategies for Supporting Educational Research, Development, and Statistics* (Washington, DC: National Educational Research Policy and Priorities Board, 1998) and has been considerably revised and updated for this volume.

Chapter 5 was orginally presented as a paper at a Brookings Institution conference on education in May 1999. I am grateful to the conference participants for their comments on that essay — especially the two formal commentators, Carl Kaestle and Thomas Glennan Jr., who later also provided thoughtful written comments. The chapter was first published as Maris A. Vinovskis, "The Federal Role in Educational Research and Development," in *Brookings Papers on Education Policy: 2000,* ed. Diane Ravitch (Washington, DC: Brookings Institution Press, 2000), 359–96. It is reprinted in this book, in a revised form, with the permission of the Brookings Institution Press.

Many of the research materials were generously provided by the centers, labs, and many others — especially the unusually comprehensive collections of former OERI staff member John Egermeier. Special thanks go to the National Library of Education, which has important collections of documents relating to these issues. That agency has been extraordinarily helpful to me. Unfortunately, neither the U.S. Congress nor the Department of Education has provided the National Library of Education with adequate resources or space.

The preparation of the manuscript was facilitated by the help of several dedicated and talented individuals. Tanya Hart provided unusually comprehensive and perceptive editing — much as she previously did on a manuscript edited by David Featherman and myself. Colin Day, my editor at the University of Michigan Press, was helpful throughout the entire process; and when he retired, Mary Erwin continued to provide similar, excellent assistance. Janet Opdyke, the copy editor at the University of Michigan Press, did a first-rate job.

I also want to thank Sandra and Ginger Gardei for their hospitality and friendship during my frequent stays in Washington, DC. Sandra's experiences with the federal government have provided me with a fuller understanding of the challenges in working in Washington; and Ginger's experiences in school have documented the opportunities and problems facing our educational system today.

Finally, my wife Mary and my son Andris have provided loving comfort and encouragement in Ann Arbor. When I often have thought of abandoning the crises and difficulties in Washington, DC, they have convinced me of the importance of trying to reform and improve federal educational research and development in order to help all students learn.

The book is dedicated to Jeffrey Mirel and Gerald Moran, two of my closest colleagues, who exemplify the best in academia and our society. Their friendship and help over the years have made my life not only more enjoyable, but more interesting and challenging. I only regret that Jerry's tennis game has gradually improved while mine has deteriorated; and that I have not been able to see all of the movies Jeff has recommended.

Abbreviations

ACES	Advisory Council on Education Statistics
ADA	Americans for Democratic Action
AEL	Appalachia Educational Laboratory
AERA	American Education and Research Association
AIDS	acquired immune deficiency syndrome
ALS-EL	Apple Learning Series: Early Language
CEDaR	Council for Educational Development and Research
CELA	National Center for English Language Learning and Achievement
DDPD	Development and Demonstration Programs Division of ORAD
DHHS	Department of Health and Human Services
DIR	Decision Information Resources
END	Educational Networks Division
ERIC	Education Resources Information Center
ESEA	Elementary and Secondary Education Act
ESSI	Education Statistics Services Institute
FIRST	Fund for the Improvement and Reform of Schools and Teaching
FOIA	Freedom of Information Act
FTE	full-time equivalent
FWL	Far West Lab
FY	fiscal year
GAO	Government Accounting Office
IASA	Improving America's School Act
IGE	Individually Guided Education
IPI	individually prescribed instruction
IRS	Internal Revenue Service
KAD	Knowledge Applications Division of ORAD

LAB	Northeast and Islands Laboratory at Brown University
LESCP	Longitudinal Evaluation of School Change and Performance
LSS	Mid-Atlantic Laboratory for Student Success
LTD	Learning Technologies Division of ORAD
MACOS	Man: A Course of Study
McREL	Mid-continent Lab
MDRC	Manpower Demonstration Research Corporation
NAE	National Academy of Education
NAEP	National Assessment of Educational Progress
NAGB	National Assessment Governing Board
NAS	National Academy of Sciences
NCED	national center for evaluation and development
NCEDL	National Center on Early Development and Learning
NCER	National Council on Education Research
NCES	National Center for Educational Statistics
NCSALL	National Center for the Study of Adult Learning and Literacy
NDN	National Diffusion Network
NEA	National Education Association
NEA	National Endowment for the Arts
NEGP	National Education Goals Panel
NEH	National Endowment for the Humanities
NERPPB	National Educational Research Policy and Priorities Board
NIE	National Institute of Education
NI/E	Northeast and Islands Lab (Northeast Lab)
NIH	National Institutes of Health
NPTA	National Parents-Teachers Association
NPR	National Performance Review
NSF	National Science Foundation
NWREL	Northwest Lab
OAPP	Office of Adolescent Pregnancy Programs
OAS	Office of the Assistant Secretary
OERI	Office of Educational Research and Improvement
OFP	Office of Family Planning
OGC	Office of Grants and Contracts

OPE	Office of Postsecondary Education
OR	Office of Research
ORAD	Office of Reform Assistance and Dissemination
OTE	Onward to Excellence
PAD	Planning and Dissemination
PCAST	President's Committee of Advisors on Science and Technology
PES	Planning and Evaluation Service
PIP	Programs for the Improvement of Practice
PMIS	Project Management Information System
PREL	Pacific Region Educational Laboratory
RAL	regional assistance laboratories
RBS	Research for Better Schools
RFP	Request for Proposals
R&D	research and development
SEDL	Southwest Lab
SERVE	SouthEastern Region Vision for Education
SES	senior executive service
SFA	Student Financial Aid
SLSD	State and Local Support Division of ORAD
SSRC	Social Science Research Council
TQM	total quality management
USOE	U.S. Office of Education

Introduction

Although periodic concerns are expressed about educational research funded by the federal government, it is nearly impossible to locate in-depth assessments of federally funded research. Government employees usually focus on identifying appropriate research topics, ensuring a fair and impartial review of the proposals, and funding the best ones. Additional efforts are made to monitor the progress of grants and contractors, which may or may not include inspection of research under way. The grant and contract procurement process is closely supervised by both program and budget specialists within the Department of Education. Much less attention is given to a systematic assessment of the quality of the commissioned work after the research project is completed. Perhaps it is assumed that the funding of a well-designed project undertaken by a competent scholar requires little scrutiny of the final product. Whatever the reason, few, if any, thorough investigations exist that detail the quality of educational research submitted by federal grantees and contractors.

Infrequent systematic assessment of the quality of final research produced is not confined to the Department of Education; it tends to occur throughout much of the federal government. For example, the Office of Adolescent Pregnancy Programs (OAPP) in the Department of Health and Human Services (DHHS) often failed to seriously consider the final research or evaluation reports submitted by grantees or contractors or to examine carefully and critically the quality of those final products on a regular basis.[1] Unfortunately, little has been done during the past three decades to examine and address the widespread, though often erroneous, perception among many policymakers and the general public that the quality of most educational research is particularly weak.[2]

Much of the rather small amount of research and development undertaken by the Department of Education is funded by the Office of Educational Research and Improvement (OERI) — successor to the National Institute of Education (NIE), which was created nearly thirty years ago. Despite sporadic calls to examine the quality of work funded by NIE/OERI, the agency had never commissioned a detailed examination of the research and development it sponsored. This reflects its lack of concern about the quality of research and development and the extremely short tenure of most of its politically appointed leaders. Even outside analysts, such as the National Academy of Science panel convened in the early 1990s to study OERI, have not explored the quality of work funded by that federal agency (Atkinson and Jackson 1992).

It has been all too easy to forget the importance of considering the quality of research and development produced by the labs and centers. Neither NIE/OERI nor Congress has given it sufficient thought in the past, despite the occasional and prophetic warnings of experts such as Sam Sieber, who stated a quarter of a century ago:

> In the context of current pressures for dissemination, it is easy to forget that not all information or innovations are really worth disseminating. Obviously, if information or innovations are *unreliable, misleading, or unsuited* to the situation, they can have repercussions which are altogether harmful. And even if not harmful, an *accumulation of futile experiences* with information or products might create an attitude of skepticism toward R&D of all kinds. Further, even when an innovation is workable and effective, the *opportunity cost* of this particular innovation rather than another might be undesirable. Although these points are obvious, it would seem that we are still wedded to the notion of "the more utilization the better." (Campbell et al. 1975, 90, emphasis original)

Diane Ravitch, an accomplished scholar and determined school reformer, was appointed assistant secretary for OERI in mid-1991. Much of her personal focus in that office centered on the development of world-class curriculum standards and assessments, but she was also deeply concerned about the general quality of educational research — perhaps reflecting in part her previous experience as codirector of the National Academy of Education's study, *Research and the Renewal of Education* (NAE 1991).

Ravitch contacted me in September 1991 and inquired whether I might be available and willing to come to OERI on a temporary excepted service appointment. While there, I would examine the nature and quality of work supported by that agency and offer suggestions for improving it.[3] Originally I was scheduled to join OERI full time in January 1992, but delays in completing the paperwork meant that I served as a part-time consultant for the first six months. My official title, Research Adviser to the Office of the Assistant Secretary, permitted me to range broadly across programs within OERI, pursuing different research-related assignments. The primary and initial task assigned to me was to analyze the nature and quality of OERI-funded research and development and to make specific recommendations for improvement.

Since a major portion of the research and development funds of OERI are expended on the centers and laboratories, I explored these areas first.[4] Ravitch wanted an examination of the nature and quality of research and development and also expected specific recommendations on how to improve the overall system. As research adviser to the Office of the Assistant Secretary (OAS), I quickly began to work with the Office of Research (OR) and the Programs for the Improvement of Practice (PIP) to enhance the quality of research and development at the centers and laboratories.[5] A preliminary draft of the center report was completed in July 1992, but the laboratory report was not finished until January 1993; thus, I had a greater opportunity to influence the changes in the operation of OR than PIP. In each case, however, I was expected to work closely with the staffs of both programs to help implement changes or recommendations seen as desirable by their OR leader or the assistant secretary.

My work focused primarily on the nature and quality of research and development at the centers and laboratories, but I also include more comprehensive observations and recommendations on the role of the centers and laboratories. These larger findings flow not only from my specific research on the centers and laboratories but from my experiences with research-related activities in OERI and from the writings of other analysts about NIE and OERI.[6] Most of the analyses and recommendations in the first two chapters of this book focus on the nature and quality of the research and development at centers and laboratories. Some broader suggestions of the role of these institutions within the overall OERI context are also found in these introductory chapters.

Because I had been appointed to a three-year, renewable term at OERI, the change in administrations would not have necessarily affected the status of my employment there, but it could have altered my ability to complete work on the laboratories and centers had the new leadership been opposed to my analysis. Thanks to the continued open, friendly cooperation from Emerson Elliott, the acting assistant secretary, and from Sharon Robinson, the new OERI assistant secretary, the transition from the Bush to the Clinton administration did not impede the writing of my report. Moreover, the three assistant secretaries, together with other OERI staff members, offered extensive constructive comments and criticism about the draft reports, but none of them ever attempted to insist upon a particular interpretation of data or to censor any specific findings or recommendations.[7]

The usefulness and quality of my analyses of the centers and labs were usually acknowledged, although some government employees and outside education advocates were less than eager to document and publicize the problems inherent in these institutions. Apparently, some inquiries were made to determine whether the release of the centers and labs report could be suppressed upon my departure from government service. However, I had already deposited the report within the Educational Resources Information Center (ERIC) system, and there was thus no way to prevent public access to the information. The Department of Education, however, did not widely publish or circulate the report at the time of its submission.[8] During the reauthorization of OERI (and its centers and laboratories) in 1993 and 1994, members of the congressional education committees did not receive copies of the centers and laboratories report; nor did administration witnesses mention the existence or availability of that document during the extensive reauthorization or appropriations hearings on the agency.[9] The existence of the report was widely publicized in a lengthy *Education Week* news story in mid-1993, but I was never invited to testify before the 103d Congress during its reauthorization of OERI (Rothman 1993).

My earlier analysis of the centers and laboratories indicated significant shifts in federal expectations of these institutions and in funding and monitoring procedures. Because my investigation centered on an analysis of the nature and quality of research and development at the centers and laboratories, I did not have the opportunity to examine the role of Congress in guiding and overseeing these institutions. The relative neglect of the role of Congress was due in part to time constraints and in part to the fact that my position in OERI did not provide me with direct access to the legislators.

I found it unfortunate that I was unable to systematically examine the role of Congress in the development and functioning of the centers and laboratories because I noticed ample evidence that members of the Congress played a periodic but key role in defining the perception and treatment of these organizations. For example, many OERI career bureaucrats, after working for many years with the centers and laboratories, believed that congressional intervention in the operation of these institutions was a major factor in OERI's ability to deal with them. Unfortunately, a systematic analysis of the long-term congressional involvement with the centers and laboratories did not exist.

Upon returning to the University of Michigan, I was free to turn to the issue of congressional involvement in centers and labs. My work in this area was financed by a small grant generously provided by the Spencer Foundation. The result of this research, a summary of the changing role of congressional oversight of the centers and laboratories from 1965 through 1992, is analyzed in chapter 3. Citing published and unpublished documents as well as interviews with some key participants in the relationship between OERI and Congress, the chapter explores the complex and often changing interplay among Congress, NIE/OERI, the R&D centers and regional education laboratories, and key groups such as the Council for Educational Development and Research (CEDaR) in the creation and evolution of the centers and labs.

Both policymakers and the general public often ignore or underestimate the role of individual members of Congress in influencing educational research and development. Most observers comprehend the importance of legislators in creating and reauthorizing agencies such as OERI. However, they infrequently appreciate the way in which individual senators and representatives can affect research and development by earmarking monies for specific types of entities such as the regional education laboratories or by inserting legislative directives into appropriation bills or reports, thereby restricting the ability of the federal government to oversee grantees and contractors. The ability of lobby groups such as CEDaR to influence not only key members of Congress but the operations of federal agencies has been neither adequately documented nor understood. Indeed, federal education research and development appear to be more constrained and shaped by political considerations than by comparable work both in related disciplines and at agencies such as the National Institutes of Health (NIH) or the National Science Foundation (NSF).

Several individuals suggested that my analysis of OERI, which ostensibly ended in 1992, be updated to reflect major changes in OERI resulting from the agency's 1994 reauthorization and the arrival of its new leadership team. One reason for the earlier primary focus on laboratories and centers was the considerable continuity (as well as some important changes) extant in their structure and monitoring processes within NIE and OERI.[10] However, the major reorganization of OERI into five national research institutes, together with the creation of a new policy board, made imperative a review of the recent developments in the laboratories and centers within the context of the larger changes in the agency as a whole. Therefore, when the newly created National Educational Research Policy and Priorities Board (NERPPB) asked me to provide a historical and policy perspective on the recent changes in OERI, I welcomed the opportunity to update and expand earlier analyses of the centers and laboratories.

Chapter 4 addresses the changes in OERI from 1993 through 1997, focusing on the reauthorization and restructuring of the agency. My extensive participant observations and subsequent in-depth interviews with staff members and other knowledgeable individuals contribute to a discussion of the agency's evolution under the leadership of Sharon Robinson. Particular attention is paid to reconfiguration of the R&D centers within the five national research institutes and alteration of expectations for the regional education laboratories to an emphasis on "systemic reform" and "scaling up" existing proven practices.

With the election of a Democratic president and Congress in November 1992, many observers hoped for a more harmonious and productive future for OERI. The new education secretary, Richard Riley, was considered a strong, longtime supporter of educational research and development; Marshall "Mike" Smith, the influential undersecretary, was an NIE policymaker during the Carter administration and an active, accomplished, social science researcher. Yet OERI lost more than 25 percent of its employees, including some of its more capable and experienced researchers, during the first term of the Clinton administration. In addition, the agency neglected to replace departing professionals with highly trained and renowned researchers.

While the agency enjoyed an unusual period of stability in leadership under Assistant Secretary Robinson, most analysts now acknowledge, at least privately, that only limited scientifically sound, important research or development was produced. For example, a conference of research leaders convened by OERI and the agency's planning board in July 1998 concluded that its centers and labs "are not preeminent in the field" (Timpane 1998, 8). The Senate Budget Committee Task Force on Education in 1998 indicated little confidence in OERI's ability to commission and monitor high-quality research and development. As the task force stated, "There seems to be little faith in our current education infrastructure to produce the needed research on policies and programs that work" (U.S. Senate Budget Committee, Task Force on Education 1998, 25). Why? Chapter 4 investigates these and other issues in the so-called new OERI, assessing the strengths and weaknesses of its 1994 reauthorization and the operation of the agency during the Clinton administration.

The final chapter discusses the federal government's historical experiences in educational research and development, paying particular attention to the creation and evolution of the OERI laboratories and centers. This chapter also addresses the broader issues facing OERI as it undergoes yet another reauthorization. Much of the material in this chapter stems from my five years of experience as a member of the congressionally mandated Department of Education's Independent Review Panel as well as my recent studies of the effectiveness of federal compensatory education programs.[11] Many of these ideas have also been shared in testimony before both the House and Senate during the reauthorization of Title I and OERI.[12] In contrast to the scant interest shown in my detailed analysis of the quality of work produced by the centers and labs during the OERI reauthorization hearings before the 103d Congress in 1993 and 1994, the 105th and 106th Congresses have shown much more interest in hearing constructive criticism of these institutions and listening to recommendations for improving educational research and development.[13]

The concluding chapter offers final observations about strengths and weaknesses in the current system of educational research and development at OERI, providing suggestions for possible future improvements. Historically, the relationship between NIE/OERI and the labs and centers has been strained and contentious. Perhaps now is the time for all parties to set aside past acrimony and work together to develop an effective and useful system for educational research and development that adequately considers the quality of work commissioned and produced.[14]

At the same time, the opportunities and problems involved in producing systematic development and rigorous research are broader than an analysis of the activities of the labs and centers. An understanding of these problems also necessitates a reconsideration of the organization and operation of OERI and the Department of Education during the 1990s. As a result, chapter 5 considers (1) the relative independence of OERI, (2) program evaluations and large-scale development efforts, (3) the agency's research staff, (4) its funding and flexibility in allocating resources, (5) the fragmentation of research and development, (6) the quality of research and development, (7) its intellectual leadership, and (8) the role of politics. These structural and procedural barriers to the production of high-quality research and development must be addressed candidly and expeditiously, although it will mean reorganizing the current system and instituting and enforcing more rigorous quality standards. Otherwise, the research community will continue to waste the scarce federal resources available to help children receive the high-quality education they need and deserve.

CHAPTER 1

Analysis of the Quality of Work Produced by the OERI Research and Development Centers

The research and development centers of the Office of Educational Research and Development have been a primary source of federally supported educational research since their inception more than three decades ago. From the 1964 fiscal year (FY64) through FY98, approximately $1.16 billion (in constant 1996 dollars) were expended on these centers.[1] Despite the large amount of funds expended, almost no effort has been made to analyze the research produced — although individual observers occasionally offer comments on its quality and usefulness.

This study of the OERI research and development centers focuses on the nature and quality of research produced by these institutions. Some budget and staffing analysis is included, but little specific attention is devoted to an evaluation of their other important activities such as dissemination of information or an assessment of research effects.

Beginning with an examination of the major trends and changes in policy toward R&D centers since the early 1960s, this study reviews five current and two former centers during 1992–93. Included are detailed analyses of the amount and types of research conducted, the quality of research products, and the manner in which OERI staff members interacted with the centers. Although the necessity of focusing attention on a small number of centers somewhat limits the extent of the generalizations drawn from this study, the sample is nonetheless larger than those assessed by other, individual reviewers. It is my hope that the issues raised and the recommendations made in this investigation will contribute in a modest way toward improving the overall quality of the research produced by such centers.

I. Historical Development of the R&D Centers

Although the federal government established a Bureau of Education after the Civil War, federal involvement in research was sparse until the 1950s. The Cooperative Research Act of 1954 (P.L. 83–531) authorized the establishment of research and development activities in universities and state educational agencies. Yet the total amount of money allocated for federal education research was limited; indeed, most of the initial grants were quite small. For example, although the 1956 budget appropriated approximately a million dollars for educational research, two-thirds of this amount was earmarked for research on the education of the mentally retarded.[2]

During this time, concern mounted among members of the research community that many of the federally funded educational research projects were uncoordinated and unrelated and had led to no significant, cumulative advances in the field. Francis Chase summarized these earlier efforts at education research in one of the first comprehensive analyses of the federal educational laboratories and centers.

> Our older educational institutions were not well adapted to provide continuous development based on research. Because of this, we have had a history of erratic innovation in education. All too often, heralded innovations have meant the introduction of partially worked out ideas and systems without adequate provisions either for continuing refinement or for modification of other elements with which the new components must interact. The result frequently has been failure to achieve the expected benefits and consequent discard of theories and technologies before full exploration of their usefulness. In other words, we are suffering in education not so much from lack of innovation as from arrested development. The educational landscape is littered with bright ideas which once evoked high hope and with technologies and systems imperfectly adapted to educational use. (1968, 8)

In response to this fragmentation of federal education research, the first R&D centers were created in 1964 under the authorization of the Cooperative Research Act and were administered by the U.S. Office of Education (USOE). The passage of Title IV of the Elementary and Secondary Education Act (ESEA) of 1965 authorized the establishment of more R&D centers and the creation of new regional educational laboratories.[3] By FY67, a total of ten R&D centers, each affiliated with a major university, had been established (U.S. House 1967a, 224).

The early centers were intended to be large, national institutions, each focused on a specific problem area in education. The Office of Education permitted each university desiring R&D centers to exercise discretion when specifying in the application the problem area on which its research would focus. Among the R&D centers created between 1964 and 1966, the average annual funding per center for the first three years was approximately $2.9 million (in constant 1996 dollars) — considerably larger than the $1.2 million (in constant 1996 dollars) average annual funding available to centers created between 1990 and 1992.[4] As evidenced by the preceding figures, the average cost per center diminished over time. This trend continued until the mid-1990s when the size of the centers increased substantially.

Despite general agreement that the early R&D centers should be large national institutions organized around a specific educational issue or problem, there was little consensus about the exact nature of the work to be performed.[5] Title IV of the Elementary School and Secondary Education Act of 1965 did not specify the exact activities that R&D centers should undertake. Nor did the influential 1964 John Gardner Task Force on Education provide much concrete guidance for the centers, although it did offer more detail on expectations for the new educational laboratories (Gardner 1964).[6] Directives from the USOE, together with several assessments of the centers and laboratories, provide some clues about the intentions of educational laboratory founders as well as the ideas of the early USOE administrators. Jerry Walker, a researcher who consulted the relevant founding documents and interviewed many of the participants involved in the founding process, noted,

> From a review of documents which discuss the origins of labs and centers, and a review of subsequent documents produced by, or about, labs and centers, it is evident that while the initial expectations for their roles and functions were obscure and shifting, they did differentiate labs from centers in terms of fundamental roles and functions. . . . The initial expectations appeared, amid the flux and flax from which they emanated, to differentiate labs from centers primarily in terms of the extension beyond research expected of labs; the problem foci expected of both were to be attacked more by the research of centers and the developmental efforts of labs; and the independent regionality of labs was in contrast to the university-based and administered R&D center. (1972, 10–12)

In principle, centers and labs have remained distinct over the years in terms of their relative emphasis on basic and applied research, development, and dissemination. However, tension continued both within these two institutions and between them regarding the proper balance of these activities. Indeed, observers have frequently charged that the distinctions between centers and labs have often disappeared in practice, if not in theory (Walker 1972, 19). Despite the blurring of expectations between the centers and the laboratories, most participants and outside observers believe that some distinctions in emphasis continued to exist between these two institutions. Most outside reviews of centers and laboratories reaffirm the importance of this distinction.[7]

In terms of the activities of the centers, one major difference of opinion among analysts stemmed from a discussion regarding the amount of effort that they should devote to basic research. Although the distinction between basic and applied educational research was often difficult to specify or identify in practice, there was general agreement that most R&D centers produced little basic research. Initially, the lack of research occurred in part because the USOE separated its commitments to fundamental research from its efforts to improve education through research and development (Chase 1968, 17).

The National Academy of Sciences' analysis of fundamental research in 1977 concurred with Chase's opinion that most of the centers conducted relatively little basic research. Rather than accepting this as either inevitable or desirable, Chase and the NAS urged the National Institute on Education, the successor to the USOE, to emphasize the importance of fundamental research in the centers' programs, pointing out that one of NIE's four stated goals was support for fundamental research (Kiesler and Turner 1977).

The NAS's 1992 analysis of the Office of Educational Research and Improvement reiterated the call for a more balanced portfolio of activities, including an expansion of support for basic research. To quote the NAS, "the centers should undertake considerable [sic] more basic research than they currently do" (Atkinson and Jackson 1992, 150).

Tension within the centers sprang not only from discussions over how much funding should be devoted to basic, applied, or developmental research but from how much effort should be devoted to the dissemination of findings. While precedent dictated that the labs would devote more attention to dissemination than would the centers, that distinction in practice has often eroded, as have many other activities in which the labs and centers participate.[8]

Indeed, Congress and OERI have placed continued pressure on the centers to devote more effort to disseminating research findings to teachers, the public, and interested scholars. While the value and importance of dissemination remained undisputed, there was some question as to how to most effectively and efficiently share the information.

Some felt strongly that centers and researchers should disseminate their own materials, while others have had doubts about the recent emphasis on dissemination. Many who questioned the emphasis on dissemination by the R&D centers in recent years did so believing that it came at the expense of the quality and quantity of research supported by the centers.

One fundamental change in the centers' operation is a significant reduction in the total amount of money available (in constant dollars), despite the fact that the centers consume an increasingly large proportion of the NIE (or OERI) total research budget. The expenditure on centers (in constant 1996 dollars) rose from $5.0 million in FY64 to $65.7 million in FY68 — the high point in center funding. It then plummeted to $50.4 million in FY69 and continued to drop, reaching a low of $21.3 million in FY90. Since then, the budget has increased, with centers receiving $31.1 million in FY98 — still less than half the total budget of thirty years earlier.[9] Moreover, as the overall research budget for NIE/OERI dropped more dramatically than that of either the centers or the labs, the percentage share of total resources for the centers and labs grew significantly. This growth often took place to the dismay of other researchers who preferred to preserve more funds for field-initiated research. As a result of this substantial shift in funding, the R&D centers, though with significantly reduced funding, carried even greater expectations because centers and labs received most of the remaining NIE/OERI research dollars.

While the centers' total funding in real dollars was drastically cut, OERI decided to increase the number of centers — especially in the late 1980s and early 1990s. Because fourteen of the centers were slated to expire in 1989, the OERI Office of Research initiated a series of activities intended to identify the most useful areas of inquiry and to determine how many centers OERI should support. OERI initially called for the establishment of twelve centers, later submitting another seven projects for consideration.[10] Finally, Christopher Cross, assistant secretary of educational research and improvement, recommended funding eighteen new centers, for a total of twenty-five (Cross 1990).[11]

As a result, the ten to twelve centers extant during the 1970s doubled by the early 1990s. Thus the average amount of funding (in constant 1996 dollars) per center dropped significantly — from $3–$5 million in the early 1970s to about $1–$1.5 million in the early 1990s. Consequently, the nature of a national center changed over time due to the decrease in funding to a point lower than envisioned or provided for in earlier decades.

The National Academy of Sciences's recent examination of OERI bemoaned the small amount of funding for the centers, recommending a substantial increase (Atkinson and Jackson 1992, 150–51). Given the surprisingly small amount of money actually invested in research (as we shall later see), the National Academy of Science's recommendation of a $3 million annual budget for minimum-sized centers may have been too scant to fully complete the task envisioned for each of the centers created in the early 1990s.[12]

Shifting expectations of centers' longevity and stability provided an additional, constant source of change for the centers. Originally, the centers were envisioned as institutions to be reviewed and renewed on a long-term basis. OERI instituted a "three-five plan," indicating that the office would evaluate each center in its third year to determine if it should be funded for another five years (Mason 1983).

With the establishment of the National Institute of Education in 1972, support for institutions such as the centers was reconsidered. Center and laboratory activities continued, but the authorities endeavored to introduce more competition through a "program purchase" policy. That is, labs and centers were required to compete both with each other and with similar organizations for NIE project funding—a situation made more difficult by sizable decreases in the overall NIE budget. To counter this move toward competition during a period of total budget decreases, the labs and centers banded together in an effort to persuade Congress to earmark special funds within the NIE budget for the exclusive use of labs and centers (Sproull, Weiner, and Wolf 1978).

In 1975, Roald Campbell headed a group of consultants that analyzed, among other things, NIE's policies toward the centers. Campbell's group rejected the idea of the program purchase for the R&D centers and recommended "stable funding for three to five years, at a level of at least $3 to $4 million per year" (about $8.7 to $11.7 million in constant 1996 dollars) (Campbell et al. 1975).[13] The National Council on Education Research (NCER), the policy-making advisory group for NIE, accepted the recommendations of this report and began to implement them (Mason 1983), abandoning NIE's earlier "program purchase" policy.

As part of NIE's 1976 reauthorization, Congress called for yet another panel of educators to review and make recommendations for the improvement of R&D centers and regional laboratories. The fifteen-member panel endorsed the continuation of these institutions (Panel 1979, iii–iv).[14] The panel explicitly repudiated the program purchase approach and returned to the original concept of five-year agreements renewable after a favorable third-year review (iv, vi).

The early 1980s ushered in major changes in the structure and function of NIE regarding the centers and labs. First, a separate Department of Education was created and OERI was given oversight of NIE, the National Center for Education Statistics, the Library Programs, and several other small programs (NIE did remain a semiautonomous entity until the 1985 reorganization of OERI). Center programs continued to be monitored by the relevant unit within NIE, but each center was now assigned an individual program monitor. Moreover, a laboratory and center coordinator oversaw the operations of these entities within NIE (Mason 1983).[15]

Second, the election of Ronald Reagan in 1980 heralded major changes in the centers' role in educational research and development. The ongoing effort by some to reverse the policy of almost indefinite support for the labs and centers (no center or lab had lost its NIE funding since 1976) appeared successful when Congress inserted in its report for the Omnibus Budget Reconciliation Act of 1981 that "the Regional Educational Laboratories and Educational Research Centers shall, upon completion of existing contracts, receive future funding in accordance with government-wide competitive bidding procedures" (Zodhiates 1988, 81). In March 1982, Edward Curran, the new director of NIE, announced that it planned to terminate the existing five-year contracts for fifteen of the seventeen labs and centers one year ahead of schedule. His actions provoked immediate and angry responses from the centers and labs as well as from other influential educators and some members of Congress. While most did not challenge the principle of competition for the refunding of these institutions, they questioned the legality and wisdom of unilaterally terminating the funding for the existing centers and labs (Zodhiates 1988).

Curran's attempt to quickly terminate the existing labs and centers had failed, but the idea that such institutions would have to compete openly in the future did succeed. Beginning in 1985, a competition was established for future labs and centers with the clear understanding that all would have to face another open competition five years later (assuming that OERI continued support for their particular area of research). Indeed, of the thirteen centers operating during the late 1980s three were terminated and only five successfully competed for continuation in 1990 (of eight that applied) (Atkinson and Jackson 1992, 124). Thus, centers came to be seen as temporary, five-year institutions required to recompete for continued funding every five years should OERI decide to support future research in that particular area of investigation.

While not arguing against the principle of competition for center selection, the National Academy of Sciences lamented the instability resulting from the requirement to recompete frequently, stating that "the 5-year cycles are inconsistent with the need for the repeated iterations of research, development, demonstration, and evaluation, which often require a decade or more" (Atkinson and Jackson 1992, 151).[16]

Instead, the NAS envisioned centers created for ten or fifteen years and terminated only for inadequate performance (ibid.).

Certainly, the National Academy of Sciences was correct in arguing that some educational ideas and innovations required more than a decade to be fully researched and developed. However, the OERI administration faced practical difficulties in not requiring centers to recompete more than every ten or fifteen years. First, if the overall number of centers were reduced as the NAS suggested, it might frustrate a new administration, which would be unable to fundamentally redirect major center-based research activities during its four- or eight-year tenure. Second, if centers were funded for ten or fifteen years a gradual phase in would have been important, providing an earlier opportunity for the creation of at least one new center than would be the case if all centers were established simultaneously. Third, the NAS's recommendation depended, as it acknowledged, on the ability of OERI to closely monitor and influence the quality and direction of a center's activities — a qualification not always true of OERI's supervision of the existing centers.

Throughout the past three decades, the quality of educational research has often been regarded by both the general public and policymakers as inadequate and second rate compared to applied science or other social science research. While these observations and impressions are not necessarily accurate, they have seriously damaged the image of OERI and have minimized support for institutions such as the R&D centers.[17] Given the long-standing federal and public concern about the quality of the research sponsored by NIE/OERI, I was surprised and disappointed to discover that almost no earlier major evaluation of the centers attempted to investigate the quality of center-based research.

Early center assessments did not closely examine the research because these institutions were newly created at the time of these evaluations. Thus, an early congressional study of the U.S. Office of Education explained that "an in-depth evaluation of the work of the Centers was not undertaken by the subcommittee as most of the Centers are only 12 to 18 months old." Nevertheless, the subcommittee, on the basis of discussions with USOE and a reading of some center evaluations, concluded that "the Centers vary widely in quality" (U.S. House 1967a, 224).

Most other major evaluations of the centers simply did not attempt to assess the quality of the research. For example, the large-scale analysis of the labs' and centers' publications in the early 1980s focused on a content analysis of the types of publications produced rather than an assessment of the quality of the work (Price 1984).

Although the recent National Academy of Sciences analysis of OERI initially planned to review the quality of research produced, time and financial constraints compelled it to omit this phase of the investigation altogether.[18] As a result, while the NAS panel concluded that "OERI has a checkered history in respect to quality assurance," it did not attempt to ascertain how this statement translates with regard to the quality of research produced at the R&D centers (Atkinson and Jackson 1992, 126).

Finally, it should be noted that no evaluation of the centers has ever examined closely the budgets of those institutions. Although several reports have commented on the diminishing amount of money (in constant dollars) available at the centers, they have not attempted to ascertain what proportion of the funds were allocated to activities such as research or dissemination. Nor have investigators attempted to determine what variations exist among the centers at any given time in the amount of funding for these activities. Thus, despite the fact that centers have been in operation for nearly three decades, both the quality of research and the amount of funds expended remain unanalyzed and unevaluated.

II. Assessment of the Research and Development Centers in 1992–93

To analyze the quality of recent research produced by OERI's research centers, I examined five current and two former centers in considerable detail in 1992–93. The five current centers studied were:

1. Center for Research on Effective Schooling for Disadvantaged Students (primary site at Johns Hopkins University)
2. Center for Research on Evaluation, Standards, and Student Testing (primary site at UCLA)
3. National Resource Center on Student Learning (primary site at the University of Pittsburgh)
4. National Center for the Study of Writing and Literacy (primary site at the University of California, Berkeley)
5. Policy Center of the Consortium for Policy Research in Education (primary site at Rutgers University).[19]

The two former centers were:

1. National Center for Improving Science Education (primary site at Andover, Massachusetts)
2. National Center on Education and Employment (primary site at Teachers College, New York City).

The seven centers were suggested by members of the Office of Research staff at OERI because they exemplified the variety of activities in the research centers and displayed considerable variation in the type and quality of research produced. Although they were by no means intended to be representative of the other twenty research centers in existence at the time, they undoubtedly reflected some of the strengths and weaknesses of those institutions.[20] As we shall see, the five current centers investigated were significantly larger than those not analyzed in more detail. Therefore, while the specific assessments of these particular centers cannot and should not be applied carte blanche to all centers, it is unlikely that a more extensive study of all twenty-three centers would have altered the overall conclusions of this analysis significantly.

A tremendous amount of time was devoted to understanding the scope and work of the centers. These steps included scrutiny of published and unpublished materials submitted to OERI by each of the seven centers since 1985,[21] examination of center budgets with particular attention given to the information for FY92 for the five continuing centers,[22] careful review of the original center proposals together with comments of reviewers who evaluated centers for funding,[23] an examination of third-year renewal applications and reviewer comments, and an analysis of written comments from the OERI center monitors and corresponding center responses. However, personal visits to each of the five ongoing centers proved invaluable since they enabled me to discuss with center employees their research work and other activities.[24] During the course of these interviews, I was able to speak with OERI center monitors for these seven centers several times.

OERI staff members received copies of an earlier version of this chapter, and the Office of Research held a staff seminar devoted to a discussion of the contents of this report. The center and laboratory directors received a revised version of this report for further comments. Mary Kennedy, chair of the Organization of Research Centers, provided extensive comments on the draft report.[25]

Distribution of Center Research Activities

As previously mentioned, the centers have greatly diminished in size over time. In constant dollars, the funding for the average center in FY92 was about one-third its counterpart in the 1970s. Most were no longer the originally envisioned large-scale national institutions. Twenty-three centers operated in FY92; combined funding totaled $26.8 million (in current dollars) or, on average, an annual rate of about $1.2 million per center. Only five of the twenty-three centers received at least $1.5

million, and four were funded at less than $1 million. The Center on Assessment, Evaluation, and Testing (UCLA) received the most support from OERI — $2.7 million.

Although an annual funding rate of $1.2 million appears at first glance to be a large amount of money, it is important to realize that it was not all funneled directly to research. Instead, a substantial portion of the funds was allocated for expenditures such as overhead, administration, and dissemination. Therefore, a more in-depth analysis of the FY92 budgets from the five current centers was necessary in order to examine the amount and distribution of funds expended for research.

The Berkeley, Johns Hopkins, Pittsburgh, Rutgers, and UCLA centers received more funding than the others. The average annual funding for these centers in FY92 was $1.7 million, while the comparable figure for the remaining eighteen centers was only $1 million.[26] Four of the five centers investigated received at least $1.5 million and the other only $1 million.[27]

OERI gave indirect cost funds to research institutions to defray such expenses as building maintenance and administrative assistance. Varying from one university to the next, those indirect costs were usually a set, negotiated percentage of a project's direct costs. Considerable variation existed among institutions regarding how much, if any, of the indirect costs were directly returned to the unit doing the actual research. For these five centers, indirect costs represented a substantial expenditure. Of the $8.5 million provided by OERI to the five continuing centers in FY92, approximately $2.35 million, or 27.6 percent of the total funding, were earmarked for indirect costs.[28] The proportion of money spent on indirect costs varied considerably among the centers, ranging between 22 and 36 percent of the total funds.

Administrative expenses and the costs of information dissemination also proved to be major expenditures for most centers. As noted earlier, OERI often emphasized the importance of dissemination, expecting centers to play an important role in this process. Since the budget reports of some centers did not always clearly differentiate between the costs of administration and dissemination, it was necessary to group these expenses together in this study.[29] Overall, 19.6 percent of the funds for these five centers were allocated for administration and dissemination. Variation among the centers in administration and dissemination expenditures was even more marked than variation in indirect costs. Whereas the Johns Hopkins Center spent only 5.3 percent of its total funds for these activities, the Berkeley Center spent 51.3 percent of its budget on them.[30]

One interesting but difficult policy issue concerned how OERI should interpret the indirect and administrative costs of the centers. The indirect rate for each university was negotiated prior to the establishment of a center and covered the overhead expenses involved in maintaining research activities — including some funds designated for general administrative purposes. The questions OERI faced, therefore, were how much additional funding was needed to cover the centers' operating expenses and whether centers with considerably higher indirect costs, such as the one at Johns Hopkins, should be expected to charge less for administrative costs than centers at other institutions such as the Berkeley Center.[31]

The net result of overhead, administration, and dissemination expenditures was a markedly smaller amount of money available for research. Overall, only 52.9 percent of the total money allocated to these five centers was devoted to research. Centers varied widely on the amount of money each invested in actual research. Whereas the Berkeley Center spent only 26.0 percent of its overall funds for research projects, the Pittsburgh Center devoted 62.5 percent of its budget to research. Thus, whereas the average annual grant for these five centers was $1.7 million, the average amount spent on research was only $890,991 (ranging from $260,262 at the Berkeley Center to $1,501,441 at the UCLA Center).[32]

How did the five centers invest the rather modest amount of money available for research? They could choose to concentrate the funds on a few large projects or spread them among several smaller ones. Although the definition of an individual research project was not identical among the centers, analysis suggested that most chose to fund multiple projects. The number of separate research projects for these five centers ranged from nine to twenty-five (most reported about ten) — and in practice some of these were even further subdivided.[33] Thus, total annual funds available for any given project were modest and in effect usually precluded large-scale research undertakings. Only 30 percent of the reported individual research projects in FY92 received more than $100,000 in direct costs; almost half of the projects were funded at less than $50,000 a year.[34] Moreover, given the substantial salary costs for many academics and professionals (including fringe benefits), most researchers were paid to devote only a comparatively small fraction of their time to a project — often just one or two months during the summer.[35] Although the pressure to function as national research institutions contributed to the centers' desire to provide broad coverage through multiple projects, limited funding meant that most research funded by the centers could not adequately and systematically address many of the larger questions in the field.

Research Topics of Centers

Historically, centers have varied in the types of research conducted. As mentioned earlier, a long-standing tension continues in the centers between conducting basic and applied or developmental research. Therefore, it was useful in analyzing the centers to consider the distribution of the research genres of the five centers. According to the project input forms for FY92, research was subdivided into seven categories: policy studies, evaluation, basic research, applied research, development, statistics, and dissemination. Naturally, considerable overlap occurred within these categories, and centers appear to vary among themselves on how to classify similar types of research.[36] Since the dissemination activities were considered earlier, this analysis investigated the first six categories.

Given the nature of the categories and the method of assembling information, it was not sensible to analyze the results too closely. It was clear that these five centers paid very little attention to assembling statistics. Almost half the research projects were designated as applied (43.3 percent), and evaluation and development were closely split (11.3 and 13.5 percent, respectively). Marked differences existed among the five centers in the distribution of research within the six categories. For example, the Rutgers Center for Policy Research in Education, not surprisingly, devoted 38.0 percent of its research effort to policy analysis, while the Berkeley Center for the Study of Writing and Literacy classified 76.5 percent of its research work as applied.

Interestingly, centers devoted very little effort to basic research. Among the five centers, only 18.7 percent of the research was basic — ranging from 4.0 percent at the UCLA Center to 37.7 percent at the Rutgers Center. While the distinction between basic and applied research, for example, was not always clear-cut, there is little doubt that these centers did not conduct much basic research — a criticism also offered in the recent NAS study of OERI (Atkinson and Jackson 1992). Of the $8.5 million in total funds allocated to these five centers, $841,103 was invested in basic research.[37] One might argue that basic research is better done in settings (such as field-initiated research) outside the centers. However, the fact that so much of OERI's research funds were allocated to the centers and labs resulted in relatively little basic research being funded.[38]

Development at these five centers was relatively neglected. Only 13.5 percent of center research dollars was expended on development — even though the formal title, Research and Development Centers, suggested that development deserved a more prominent role than it appeared to receive. The relative lack of attention to development was illustrated by the fact that some members of the OR staff were uncertain as to whether the word *development* actually appeared in the centers' formal designations. Moreover, several individuals at the centers suggested that the word *development* be dropped from the formal title since they felt little pressure from OERI to prioritize development.[39]

But the concept and practice of development had not altogether died at the centers. For example, the Johns Hopkins Center had previously developed the teaching strategy of cooperative learning and now employed it in its Success for All program (Balkcom 1992). Similarly, the Pittsburgh Center had developed its Math[3] Program (Making Mathematical Meaning), which drew upon their long-term, pioneering work in the area of cognition.[40]

The range of topics covered by the 1992–93 centers was very large. Indeed, OERI's stated reason for expanding the number of centers was to provide research on more issues than would be possible with fewer centers. Indeed, almost any imaginable educational issue or problem could have found a place in one of the existing twenty-three centers.[41] Ivor Pritchard, director of the Education and Society Division in the Office of Research, acknowledged that the set of centers proposed in 1990 was based upon a fragmented and incoherent view of educational development and needs (Pritchard 1990).

Another characteristic of many centers was the broad definition and description of research agendas as opposed to the more limited, focused scope of the actual research. The disparity between the broad project titles and mission statements and the narrower research efforts was not unique to the centers; this was very common in the social sciences in general. Indeed, a frank acknowledgment of the limited generalizations possible on the basis of specific research projects undertaken was lacking in many of the center descriptions and discussions. It is important to note this distinction because anyone reading only project titles and broad project descriptions would have overestimated just how many educational problems were effectively and systematically addressed by the research undertaken in the centers.

If the research conducted at the five relatively large centers seemed limited, it was sometimes entirely absent in the smaller, three-year centers with annual budgets of about $500,000. For example, in their successful 1987 grant application, the National Center for Improving Science Education explicitly renounced the effort to conduct research.[42] Thus, while OERI believed that small centers should and could produce useful original research, at least one candidly admitted that research was neither feasible nor desirable.

Although the center project titles and mission statements often seemed to present a coherent and coordinated conception of their activities, in practice the projects sometimes appeared to be more of a collection of loosely related research undertakings. Some centers lacked a coherent and detailed research agenda as opposed to providing a broad framework and funding for the individual interests of the faculty. Although one can obviously value and appreciate the diversity of research activities supported by the centers, given the limited funding available perhaps a more focused approach might have been more desirable.[43]

Some activities may not have had an implicit overarching theory, but the plan was often neither explicit nor discernible in the individual publications of a center.[44] Therefore, someone who read the products of a particular center without reviewing its grant application or discussing the matter with a center's researcher might not have seen the coherence or relevance of the entire research project under examination. Quite frequently, individual pieces of useful research did not appear to be an integral part of an ongoing research strategy.[45] Moreover, some centers conveyed the impression that certain portions of research were a more integral part of an overall, ongoing systematic research effort than others.

Sometimes researchers did not adequately follow up on otherwise well-designed and thoughtful research projects; thus, the data were unable to provide the needed information for educators and policymakers. For instance, the Rutgers Center studied differential treatment of school districts by states. They chose four states (Kentucky, New Jersey, South Carolina, and Washington) that were either assuming control of deficient school districts or easing state education regulations for districts with exemplary performance.[46] Unfortunately, researchers did not plan to follow up on the effects of takeover actions in the school districts, thereby neglecting the opportunity to sufficiently assess the effects of state policies on education practices and outcomes.[47]

Given the large number of R&D centers and the broad mandate that each enjoys, some overlap in their activities was not surprising. The Berkeley, UCLA, and Pittsburgh centers evaluated the teaching of history in schools, UCLA and Berkeley assessed writing, and several centers were concerned with the diffusion and implementation of educational reforms at the state level. Although OERI tried to improve communication among the centers, it conveyed the impression that closely related research projects conducted in different centers had little interaction.[48] Often there was even a lack of communication and coordination among individual researchers within a center.[49]

When embarking on a new project, a researcher usually develops a synthesis and critical review of existing scholarly literature in order to ascertain remaining research needs. In field-initiated grants, this synthesis is usually part of the normal grant application process since such information is essential in convincing outside reviewers of the feasibility and desirability of any proposal. Many center grant applications, however, did not provide a thorough, critical review of the existing literature when proposing research activities — perhaps in part because researchers sometimes devoted more energy to perfecting mission statements and broadly describing research plans and dissemination activities than to developing a detailed research design. Moreover, the maximum page limit for applications discouraged thorough literature reviews. Therefore, the initial task of many center research projects was a synthesis of the existing literature on a topic.

Although a synthesis of existing literature is an essential step in the research process, especially as research introduces new perspectives,[50] occasionally the reviews of existing literature appeared to consume a large part of a particular project rather than a small, useful portion of the research process. Moreover, centers sometimes hesitated to develop and provide detailed research designs of some projects while awaiting a researcher's synthesis of existing research. As a result, new research in a given area might have been significantly delayed while centers waited for completion of these reviews. While most reviews proved useful, some seemed to only slightly improve or expand existing literature reviews. Many literature reviews were never published — perhaps due to limited utility to a broader audience or duplication of previously published materials.

Another problem with some centers was that they sometimes seemed too eager to produce and distribute materials of limited interest and utility. The Berkeley Center, for example, produced nearly 150 articles and essays in a seven-year period — some too preliminary to be of significant use to others. Similarly, the UCLA Center generated some excellent papers but also printed a set of overheads from an assessment workshop that perhaps could have been more effectively and efficiently distributed as a photocopy rather than as part of the official deliverables (Herman 1991). Not only were scarce resources earmarked for dissemination expended on materials of limited utility, but the uneven quality of center products did little to enhance the reputation of sponsoring institutions and raised questions about their publication standards and review processes.

Quality of Research

The quality of research produced by the centers has been a topic of much discussion but almost no analysis. A fairly extensive and systematic reading of materials produced at seven centers and a more cursory glance at some products from a few others revealed mixed quality of research — both among and within centers. Some research produced was of very high social science quality, while other work could have been substantially improved and expanded.

The National Center on Education and Employment, a recently closed center, produced some high-quality work.[51] For example, its study of youth training in the United States, Britain, and Australia is a sophisticated statistical analysis of several national longitudinal surveys of young men. Researchers discovered, for example, that youths in the United States initially received less training upon entry into the labor force than in the other two countries but that they catch up with their foreign counterparts over time. However, better-educated American youths were much more likely to receive additional training than less well educated youths, although the latter might have benefited the most from additional education (Tan et al. 1991).

Similarly, the National Center on Education and Employment carefully and thoughtfully composed a series of works on the changing nature of the American economy and its influence on the skills that will be needed by future workers. Some of the projects were extensive, critical reviews of the literature on schools and jobs, while others were technical analyses of the relationship between education and the economy (Natriello 1987; Altonji 1990). One strength of the center lay in its ability to attract distinguished and accomplished economists and persuade them to turn their attention and analytical skills to the issues of schooling and the economy.[52]

The Center for Research on Effective Schooling for Disadvantaged Students at Johns Hopkins University also conducted some important and innovative research. Particularly impressive was the Success for All program, an effort in early education interventions to help at-risk children. The Success for All program worked closely with all students in their first years in school and was able to help most students enrolled in some of the more disadvantaged areas of inner cities. Their research showed that a much higher percentage of students enrolled in a Success for All program was able to read than students in control schools.[53] Interestingly, researchers found that intensive tutoring of first-grade students may have prepared them to read more effectively than had they been enrolled in a Head Start program.[54]

Some centers have carried out important analyses of federal, state, and local education policies. For example, the Rutgers University Center sponsored and assembled a timely and useful collection of essays on systemic reform. The essays explored the theoretical and practical aspects of a coherent reform strategy and presented the differing views of education policy analysts. Education policymakers in Washington, DC, frequently used this particular volume, which served as a thoughtful but complex introduction to the notion of systemic reform (Fuhrman 1993). In general, the Rutgers University Center policy studies were of higher quality than most comparable policy work at regional educational laboratories.

These are only a few examples intended to demonstrate that many existing centers conduct first-rate social science research on education. Therefore, critics claiming that the quality of research produced by these centers was uniformly low and that the results were unsound and unreliable would do well to look more closely at the work of some centers.

Although some centers and projects within centers carried out important and scientifically sound research, others had room for improvement. Often centers that did first-rate work in one or more areas did not perform at an equally high level in other areas. For example, the National Center on Student Learning at the University of Pittsburgh was certainly one of the stronger research centers funded by OERI. Its work on acquisition and learning in mathematics was highly regarded and well received by outside reviewers of their grant applications in 1985 and 1990 and continuation grant applications in 1987 and 1992. Yet several of the same reviewers questioned the quality and utility of this center's work on aspects of social studies such as history. Indeed, its publications and its 1987 continuing grant application revealed the simplistic and descriptive nature of some of the social studies research in contrast to its mathematical work.

While some center-based research was statistically sophisticated, observers raised questions about its methodological rigor. The Center for Research on Evaluation, Standards, and Student Testing at UCLA undertook very important and thoughtful work on duplex designs, which permitted the use of more complex testing samples while still yielding valid student-level scoring. As large-scale educational assessment grows in this country, the development and use of duplex sampling will permit a broader and more useful employment of test score results (Bock 1989).

On the other hand, size of sample and type of statistical techniques limited some of the work done at the centers. For example, the studies from the Center for the Study of Writing and Literacy at Berkeley often were based upon analyzing a single individual or investigating only a few students (Sperling and Freedman 1987; Dyson 1991; Sperling 1991). Moreover, the analytical techniques used in many studies tended to report activities or use simple descriptive statistics rather than employing sophisticated statistical procedures — in part, of course, due to limits imposed by their small sample sizes (Higgins, Flower, and Petraglia 1991; Dyson 1987). While it is sometimes useful to analyze an individual or a small group of individuals closely, such studies by themselves do not necessarily represent trends in diverse populations or settings.[55]

Another problem with some studies conducted at the centers is dependence upon convenience rather than representative samples. The UCLA Center, which has produced some of the more rigorous studies, used a questionnaire completed by eighty-five elementary and secondary school teachers who attended a teacher leadership institute to analyze the effects of teachers' actions in classrooms. While the author admitted that this investigation may not be representative because of the small sample size, she did not consider any potential bias that may have been introduced as a result of considering only individuals who attended a teacher leadership conference and volunteered to fill out the questionnaire (Herman 1990).[56]

Similarly, it was unclear whether new ideas or products were tested on a representative group of teachers or only a self-selected subset of those who volunteered to participate in this particular activity. For instance, the Pittsburgh Center disseminated and evaluated its Math[3] Program to thirty-seven additional teachers. Unfortunately, rather than being able to assign the Math[3] Program randomly to teachers, it had to rely upon those who volunteered to participate in this rather intensive two-year effort. Consequently, findings from this evaluation were limited by the fact that the results were based upon the special subset of teachers who chose to join this project.

One might also question the particular research design of some studies. A study of teacher attitudes about various teacher evaluation systems, for example, analyzed teachers in Florida and Wisconsin. The strategy for comparing teachers, however, could have been improved. Florida teachers were selected from the Miami and Tampa areas and the Wisconsin teachers from Madison and Green Bay — the latter seemingly different communities from those in Florida. Moreover, the Florida sample included both novice and experienced teachers, but the Wisconsin sample included only experienced teachers (an unfortunate development because the Tampa subsample indicated that teacher experience yielded significant and complex effects on the ratings). Given the complexity of the issues addressed in this study, the small sample of only forty-eight teachers severely restricted the controls and the statistical analyses that could be performed. The Rutgers Center could have considerably strengthened this interesting and important study if more attention had been paid to the initial research design (Peterson and Comeaux 1990).

Even some of the more analytically rigorous projects have important methodological issues warranting further attention. The Success for All program at the Johns Hopkins Center was certainly one of the more carefully designed and statistically rigorous efforts among the centers. The researchers at the Johns Hopkins Center examined the ability of their Success for All program to help young students in some of the more disadvantaged urban neighborhoods. One nice feature of their work was the decision to select similar schools in the same type of neighborhoods as statistical controls. Moreover, in order to deal with possible problems introduced in the schools due to different rates of pupil placement in special education programs, they matched students from the separate schools on the basis of their spring standardized test scores in kindergarten.

However, two potentially important statistical problems have yet to be fully resolved. First, one criterion for school participation in the study included agreement to participate by administration and teachers via secret ballot. Since the control schools did not require such a commitment, it may be possible that participating schools had a somewhat more dedicated administration and teaching staff than control schools. Second, it is difficult to determine whether the matching of students from one school with those in another on the basis of a kindergarten standardized test score actually provided an adequate control for possible differences. To be sure, since students in the program schools and those in the control institutions came from disadvantaged neighborhoods, the potential range of differences was somewhat minimized. Yet, as suggested by several of the outside reviewers and the OR staff, the matching criteria may not have been sufficient by themselves to ensure that no errors were introduced into the study.[57]

Sometimes the studies provided insufficient details for the reader to assess and interpret the findings. An analysis of history textbooks, for example, did not clearly indicate the number or characteristics of students tested. Although simple correlations were provided in the essay, the lack of information about the size of the sample obscured the strengths of those associations. Moreover, the fact that this study was conducted in a Catholic school — an important contextual factor potentially affecting the results — was revealed only in conversation with the authors (Britt, Georgi, and Perfetti 1992).

Overall, the quality of research and development at the OERI-funded centers was uneven. As we have seen, some of the work exemplified excellent social science analysis while some left considerable room for conceptual and methodological improvement. While no effort was made to arrive at a precise distribution of the product quality produced by the seven centers in this study, it did appear that the work was generally of a higher quality than comparable efforts at the five OERI-funded regional educational laboratories also investigated (although the research or development work of a particular lab such as Far West was as good or better than that produced by most of the centers).[58]

Center Review Process

As mentioned earlier, at various periods in NIE's history, the existing centers were simply renewed without competing for continued funding. In 1985, the centers were required to recompete, and a number of them lost funding to outside competitors. Analysts investigating the process of the center competitions in 1985 and 1990 concluded that they were based on a fair and efficient peer review system (Finn 1986; Garduque and Berliner 1986; Moorman and Carroll 1985; Sroufe 1991). Evidence I reviewed during this study indicated nothing to the contrary.[59] Indeed, it appears that in recent years the Office of Research has been so anxious to avoid any appearance of favoritism or bias that the center receiving the highest peer review ranking has always received the grant — even when, as occurred in the case of two closely ranked center proposals, the recommendations of the OR staff members most directly involved in the review process had to be ignored.[60]

As reflected in the 1990 guidelines for funding competition, OERI gradually established a pattern of emphasizing dissemination over research.[61] While applicants were encouraged to provide detailed research designs and were rewarded by reviewers for doing so, it appeared that a detailed design was not always advantageous. In the funding competition for one particular center, records indicate that the center that did not detail its research plan for the entire five-year period may have benefited in comparison with the center that did. Moreover, many center competitions provided an excellent, detailed reviewer critique of the research, although the reviewer's scores did not fully reflect those comments. In other words, sometimes scores assigned to the "technical soundness" section varied less than one would expect on the basis of written comments.

One major difference between successful center research proposals and successful field-initiated research proposals may be that the latter are usually required to provide a much more detailed research design than the former. Center research project proposals were often brief summary descriptions rather than detailed research plans. Some reviewers of center proposals complained of the difficulty of evaluating the scientific validity and feasibility of projects because of inadequate information about the specific research designs. Center project proposals often emphasized the strategy or goals of the research effort rather than a detailed plan for carrying it out. Field-initiated research proposals, on the other hand, usually were expected to provide short, critical reviews of the literature as well as detailed research plans. Moreover, because center research projects were submitted as a package rather than as individual components, funding covered some individual research projects that would not have been acceptable by themselves.[62]

Another frequently mentioned criticism of the center review process was that outside panels consisted of both researchers and practitioners. Although no observers commented that the practitioners should be entirely excluded from the assessment of center proposals, some observers did contend that researchers should first evaluate the technical quality of the proposals since many practitioners may not have sufficient social science training to properly judge research design and methodology. Only after this initial review should practitioners and policymakers play a role in the final selection. While this proposed two-tier selection process was certainly defensible and perhaps even the best way to proceed, the mixed review panel of researchers and practitioners did not appear to play a major role in the funding outcomes of the seven centers studied. Indeed, relatively few differences existed between the researcher and practitioner scores on successful center funding applications.[63] Perhaps this relative lack of difference was due to the fact that such little weight was given to "technical soundness" that possible variations in the overall score on the basis of "technical soundness" were minimized.

The extent and quality of reviewer comments for both the initial center proposals and their continuation applications varied greatly. Some reviewers provided thoughtful and constructive assessments, while others did not appear to have devoted much time or energy to this activity. Since OERI did not pay reviewers even a modest honorarium for their efforts, it was not surprising that many reviews were so limited.

Although some reviewers of proposals and continuing applications did an excellent job overall, many (if not most) were rather deficient in discussing in any detail questions about the methodology, budgets, or the staffing of the research proposals. This was due in part to the fact that many proposals provided little detailed information about research designs for the individual projects. As a result, center monitors and the centers themselves were denied the opportunity to examine potentially important, constructive information regarding research projects.

Finally, each center was required to establish its own evaluation process. Many centers distinguished between an overall advisory board and a separate process for evaluating center products (such as technical papers and publications). The Berkeley Center, for example, effectively used its national advisory board to discuss broader research and dissemination issues, but its national board did not attempt to assess the statistical and technical aspects of each research project. The Johns Hopkins Center developed a general review process for its publications but did not subject them to an in-depth assessment of scientific validity. Instead, it asked scholars to present their forthcoming work at a weekly seminar for critical feedback about their methodology and interpretations. Unfortunately, not all of the authors were able to submit their work for scrutiny at one of these sessions — especially those who worked as subcontractors at another university. Thus, while a few centers had very active and useful outside advisory and evaluation groups to help with research priorities and quality control, many did not appear to use such mechanisms as effectively.

Center Monitoring

Interaction with and monitoring of centers by OR varied widely. Each center was assigned an OR monitor and a backup. Each monitor reported to one of four division leaders in OR: the Learning and Instruction Division (Anne Sweet), the Schools and School Professionals Division (Hunter Moorman), the Higher Education and Adult Learning Division (Clifford Adelman), or the Education and Society Division (Ivor Pritchard). In addition, the director of center management and operations (Ned Chalker) had a small staff for assistance. Both the division heads and the director of center management and operations reported to the director of the office of research (Joseph Conaty).[64] At the time this study was conducted, this arrangement was informal. The lines of authority and division of responsibilities between the division heads and the director of center management and operations were not always clear. In practice, however, all parties seemed able to work together quite harmoniously.

One problem in the current monitoring system involved the variance in monitor response or resolution of a particular situation. The division heads and the director of center management and operations attempted to coordinate the activities of the center monitors, leaving, however, practical room for differences. The problems in variance were compounded by the fact that some center monitors had only short-term appointments in OERI. Thus, the need to recruit and train new monitors was an ongoing pressure.[65] Under NIE, a special handbook was developed to assist in the training of monitors (Gruskin 1975). Similarly, Sally Kilgore, a former OR director, and other OR staff members developed a handbook in 1988 that several of the monitors found helpful

(Ashburn et al. 1988). Unfortunately, that handbook gradually became dated and obsolete so that by 1992 nothing comparable for new or continuing center monitors remained.[66]

The disagreement among division heads and monitors regarding the importance and nature of a monitor's position accounted for the diversity of practices among them. Some division heads and center monitors, for example, saw their relationship with the centers as a very active one requiring considerable time and effort. Others viewed the centers as another set of grantees that neither needed nor deserved intense scrutiny and involvement. Moreover, there appeared to be some differences among the recent assistant secretaries of education on both the level of involvement among center monitors and the types of activities they should perform. For example, while some staff members have seen themselves as liaisons to the centers, Diane Ravitch, the former assistant secretary of OERI, preferred that they function as monitors of centers.

Center monitors also varied considerably in terms of training and orientation. While a few center monitors had only some college education, others had earned a Ph.D. or Ed.D. degree. Some had extensive personal experience in conducting or supervising research, while others had little previous exposure to it. Similarly, while the training and experiences of some monitors fit nicely with the subject matter of their center, others worked in areas far removed from their previous expertise or interests. A few center monitors were so deeply involved and knowledgeable about the content of their centers' activities that they even co-authored work with the personnel of that institution.[67] But some centers complained that the OR center monitors were not familiar with their work or knowledgeable enough about academic research to be of much assistance.

Monitors also varied in the amount of consideration and discussion they lent to the research design and methodology employed in the center's research projects. Some monitors devoted relatively little time or effort to researching these issues, while others were deeply involved in discourse regarding them. For example, the monitor for the Johns Hopkins Center raised questions about the issue of matched sampling for the Success for All program and tried unsuccessfully to persuade the researchers to display more concern about this issue. Similarly, the monitor for the Berkeley Center questioned various aspects of the research design and strategy for that institution's projects.

One major problem center monitors faced was the frequent lack of sufficient travel funds to visit their centers or to bring in the experts required to evaluate the research produced by their centers.[68] Under NIE in the 1970s, center monitors sometimes were able to assemble teams of experts to accompany them on visits to their centers. As OERI becomes more concerned about improving the centers' quality of research as well as assisting them with other activities, Congress would do well to provide more funding for travel and consultants.

Finally, some monitors paid close attention to the budget from a programmatic perspective, but others did not. Those interested in a close review of budget information, especially from a comparative perspective, were handicapped by the fact that the results from the computerized Project Management Information System did not provide the necessary information for analysis. Moreover, although the PMIS office sometimes sent OERI the appropriate research activities information from the project input forms necessary for a more in-depth budget analysis, the appropriate monitors did not receive such information.[69] In general, the impression was given that the analysis of individual project research budgets and staffs received little attention from center monitors and outside reviewers.

In 1987, the Office of Research undertook a third-year review of the centers. Control and direction of those reviews were placed in the hands of individual monitors; thus, the quality of those efforts varied considerably from center to center. Overall, the center reviews examined in this study dealt only marginally with the quality of research and development produced by the centers.

The 1992 third-year review for seventeen of the centers was much more rigorous and systematic than those of previous years. The review asked outside reviewers and center monitors to comment specifically upon the quality of the work produced by the centers during their first two years; the results of this review were scrutinized by both OR and the Office of the Assistant Secretary.[70]

One source of uncertainty among OR staff members centered on how much legal authority center monitors had to make changes in the grants. Some said that since funds were grants rather than contracts OR could not insist on major changes or deletions of entire projects — although center monitors often persuaded the centers that changes and a redirection of funding were warranted and prudent. Other observers believed that monitors retained the legal authority to terminate any specific project deemed inadequate — although usually this authority would be exercised in the context of redirecting grant monies to other projects within the same center. In any case, it appeared that until 1992 OR had not terminated the funding for a specific project within a center and consequently decreased the overall funding level for that center.

The Department of Education grant regulations stated that "the Secretary may make a continuation award for a budget period after the first budget period of an approved multi-year project if: . . . Continuation of the project is in the best interest of the Federal Government" (U.S. Department of Education 1992). In other words, if OR decided, for example, that one of the center projects was inadequate from a research perspective or unnecessary from a government perspective, it reserved the right to terminate that project and reassign the money to other activities within the center or transfer the funds to other centers.[71]

In the 1970s, NIE occasionally did remove funds from a particular center project or projects and then reallocate the funds to another project. But in more recent years OR did not follow that same practice — perhaps in part because some monitors and OERI leaders were unaware that they could follow this procedure. In the third-year review of the centers, however, one specific center project was defunded and the monies used for other center expenditures.[72] The defunding of specific center projects deemed unworthy and unsalvageable by center monitors and reviewers should be pursued as a last resort and on a limited basis because it sends a clear message that OR is willing to fund only those projects of demonstrable quality and "in the best interest of the Federal Government."

Another major problem in the relationship between the centers and OR stemmed from the lack of effort on the part of monitors to incorporate and use findings from center-based research within OERI. Basically, few individuals within OR were able to conduct serious original research or synthesize existing studies. Moreover, the lack of OR specialists made it difficult for the office to interact intellectually with staff members at many of the centers.

The lack of research personnel and activity within OR seriously weakened that group's ability to monitor and interact substantively with the centers. In later years, this situation worsened, as personnel were shifted from OR to other divisions within OERI. The number of full-time equivalent (FTE) employees in OR dropped from sixty-eight in FY87 to fifty-eight in FY91 — a 15 percent decrease. As a result, the ability of OR staff to carry out original analyses or synthesize research findings from the centers decreased as the number of centers funded by OERI increased.

Diane Ravitch, the former assistant secretary, agreed that the OR had been understaffed, and she authorized the addition of four more researchers to the staff in late 1992. She envisioned the new staff members as part of a separate unit within OR that would specialize in synthesizing existing research and undertaking original investigations. However, Ravitch's tenure in office was terminated by the change in administrations, and her proposed expansion of OR was placed on hold and later reversed.

CHAPTER 2

Analysis of the Quality of Research and Development at the OERI Regional Educational Laboratories

The previous chapter presented a history and assessment of the Office of Educational Research and Improvement's research and development centers, a major area of research expenditure for the agency. Now we turn to an investigation of the type and quality of research and development produced by the second type of OERI-funded institution, the regional educational laboratories, which were created just two years after the R&D centers were established. From FY66 to FY98, OERI invested approximately $1.59 billion (in constant 1996 dollars) in these labs — about 30 percent more than the amount allocated to the R&D centers from 1964 through 1998.[1] As with the R&D centers, no one has systematically investigated the characteristics and quality of the research and development produced at the labs.

This analysis explores the nature and quality of research and development produced by the labs since 1985. Compared to the earlier study of research and development at the R&D centers, this undertaking is more complicated because the mission of the labs has not always focused as directly or explicitly on research and development. Therefore, this analysis will pay considerable attention to the varying constitutions of research and development activities at these institutions and will assess the quality of their work. Again, we will need to examine the changing overall trends in lab budgets and the relative amounts expended on research and development. Since this analysis does not address the labs' effect on schools or their role in providing technical assistance to states and local communities, it is not a comprehensive investigation of the overall functioning of the labs. Rather, this inquiry focuses on an assessment of the quality of research and development produced at the labs.

The study begins with an analysis of the labs' creation in 1966 and their subsequent development. Because the labs underwent many major changes in focus and direction, this chapter will examine their historical background in considerable depth. Following this history is an analysis of the quality of research and development work at five of the labs in 1992 and 1993. Finally, we will consider the relationship between the labs and the OERI staff in an effort to suggest methods to improve lab research quality.

I. Historical Development of the Labs

The previous chapter described the federal government's growing role in supporting educational research in the late 1950s and early 1960s and the frustration over the piecemeal and fragmentary nature of that initial research. The R&D centers were established in 1964 as part of a concerted effort to develop sustained and cumulative educational research, and the centers were authorized under Title IV of the Elementary and Secondary Education Act of 1965.

The Gardner Task Force

In 1964, President Lyndon Johnson established a number of task forces to consider what actions the federal government should take in various areas. The task force on education, headed by John Gardner, played a key role in the establishment and operation of the educational laboratories. Whereas the Gardner Task Force virtually ignored the role of the newly created R&D centers, it made the creation of the educational laboratories a centerpiece of its recommendations for bold new ways to improve learning. Moreover, in its relatively extensive discussion of the laboratories, the task force set forth a particular vision of those institutions that provides some of the most detailed information about the original intent of the lab founders.[2]

The Gardner Task Force, in language almost identical to some of the current rhetoric of reform, called for "a massive burst of innovation." Since it saw educational development as ever changing, it called for "a system designed for continuous renewal, a system in which reappraisal and innovation are built in. That is why references to research and development, to innovation and experiment, appear in every chapter of this report" (Gardner 1964, 33).

This task force on education believed that a dozen (perhaps even two or three dozen) newly created laboratories could overcome the lack of adequate dissemination and adoption of new educational ideas and practices (Gardner 1964, 34). It explicitly stated that these labs should not be "small-scale efforts, operating out of a corner of a department of education, rooted in the interests of a few faculty members, and having little connection with the daily practice of education in the community."

Instead, it saw them as "more closely akin to the great national laboratories of the Atomic Energy Commission and [sharing] many of their features" (34). Although they should pay considerable attention to basic research, "the central focus of the laboratories will be on the development and dissemination of educational innovations" (35).

Given their emphasis on developing educational innovations and disseminating them to the local schools, members of the Gardner Task Force valued the testing and refining of materials. Therefore, they recommended that each lab have one or more experimental schools under its jurisdiction. "Taken collectively, these experimental schools might constitute a nationwide network to test the feasibility of new methods" (Gardner 1964, 36). They advocated that labs establish links "with numerous schools (or school systems) for the sake of teacher training and the field testing of new programs" (35). Unlike the situation in the early 1990s, when only three of the ten labs were affiliated with a university, the Gardner Task Force argued that all labs should have a university connection.[3]

Although the existing R&D centers and the proposed labs might overlap to some degree, they were seen as different but complementary entities. "The Laboratories described here go beyond the centers created by the Office in certain respects, chiefly the following: (a) considerably greater emphasis on development and upon the dissemination of innovation, (b) the use of experimental schools and extensive pilot programs in the regular schools and (c) provision for teaching training as an integral part of the program" (Gardner 1964, 37).

Creation of the Labs

The ideas of the Gardner Task Force regarding educational laboratories played a very important role in the development and passage of Title IV of the Elementary and Secondary Education Act of 1965. Title IV authorized the establishment of a network of large-scale labs, but it did not require them to encompass experimental schools or teacher training as an integral part of their activities. Moreover, while universities could apply for the funds to create these labs, so could nonprofit groups unaffiliated with universities (Kearney 1967).[4]

Those involved disagreed considerably regarding the size of labs and the celerity of lab creation. The Gardner Task Force envisioned well-funded, large-scale institutions. Some lab proponents also argued for gradual phases so that labs would have ample time to discover the institutional arrangements best suited for them.

Contrary to this advice, and partly in hope that Congress would quickly increase funding, a large number of labs were quickly created and placed in various regions of the country. In January 1966, ten labs were funded, and by the end of that year twenty were under contract. Nineteen were designed to serve the states, and one, the Center for Urban Education, was intended to assist major urban areas. The Gardner Task Force divided the regions in such a way that some states were split between two or more labs; on average, there were fewer than three states per lab (Mason 1988, 2:8). In FY66, Congress allocated $42 million (in constant 1996 dollars) to the labs, and this amount doubled during the next year. The total subsidy in constant dollars for the labs peaked in 1970, and by the mid-1990s it had dropped to about one-half the amount of three decades earlier.

Compared to the expectations of the Gardner Task Force, the labs have been rather modest in size. The initial lab funding rose from an annual average of $2.2 million (in constant 1996 dollars) in FY66 to an annual average of $6.7 million in FY70—a level at which it remained or even slightly increased despite dramatic reductions in the total number of labs in the early 1970s. The average annual funding for labs declined in the second half of the 1970s and 1980s so that in FY97 the average annual lab budget in constant dollars was only $5 million.

There was considerable debate over the national versus regional orientation of the labs. The Gardner Task Force had emphasized the national nature of the labs, but many staff members at the U.S. Office of Education stressed their regional functions—in part because they believed that all congresspersons wanted a lab in their own regions. Francis Keppel, an early proponent of national rather than regional labs, shifted his position. When someone challenged Keppel about his support of regional labs, he justified his new position: "Title IV labs are going to be a porkbarrel. Every Congressman is going to want one in his region" (Dershimer 1976, 86). Moreover, since the designation of "national" labs raised fears about excessive federal control, it seemed more prudent to call them "regional" labs.[5] This tension between the national and regional focus of the labs was not satisfactorily or conclusively settled, and it remains an important unresolved issue today.

Responses to the Labs

The initial responses to the labs were mixed. In an influential and frequently cited analysis of the R&D centers and labs in the late 1960s, Francis Chase, dean of the School of Education at the University of Chicago and a close ally of Gardner, enthusiastically endorsed the concept and management of labs (although he also provided constructive suggestions on how to improve their operation).[6] He regarded the activities of the R&D centers and labs as complementary and cited several instances of close cooperation between them (Chase 1968, 9–12).[7] He particularly stressed the joint role of the centers and labs in systematically developing educational products and disseminating them to schools (26–27).

Chase advised the laboratories to focus on a few large, long-term projects rather than spreading their efforts and resources too broadly.[8] Moreover, while he acknowledged the regional nature of the labs, he viewed them primarily as national institutions that would provide systematically developed and field-tested products well beyond their local areas (Chase 1968, 36–37).[9] He also recognized that serious development efforts would be expensive and time consuming (51–52).[10]

While Chase wholeheartedly endorsed the concept and activities of the labs, other analysts were less sanguine about their achievements and direction. The U.S. House Special Subcommittee on Education, which was investigating the Office of Education, expressed strong reservations about the actual operations of the labs. For example, the subcommittee found considerable confusion about their mission — even among some labs' staff. Similarly, the subcommittee often found no clear distinction between the R&D centers and the labs. Moreover, the members voiced grave concern about the large proportion of high salaries among lab personnel. However, both the subcommittee and Chase did agree that the erratic and uncertain funding of the labs made long-term planning extremely difficult (U.S. House 1967a, 224–29, 240).

Just as it appeared that the situation of the labs in the late 1960s finally might be stabilizing and improving, serious congressional opposition arose regarding an expansion of their funding. Some of this opposition proceeded from the rise of certain legislators to key positions or alterations in their responsibilities, but much of it issued from competition for funds, which were scarce due to the escalation of the Vietnam War.[11]

The creation of twenty relatively small labs in the mid-1960s had been predicated upon the expectation for greatly expanded federal funding. While the White House did propose a 50 percent increase in lab funding for FY69, Congress provided only a 4 percent increment. As a result, USOE terminated five of the labs and signaled the end of the planned rapid expansion (Dershimer 1976, 98–101). Although there was a modest increase in lab funding in FY70, a 14 percent decrease the following year led to the closing of another four labs. The even larger declines in funding of the newly created National Institute of Education meant continued reductions in federal support for laboratories, and by 1975 only eight labs remained.[12]

At the same time that the overall lab budget declined in the early

1970s, Congress reviewed and revised the manner in which the labs and the R&D centers were funded. The Gardner Task Force and the report by Francis Chase had argued for large-scale labs with stable funding. But Congress and other federal agencies attacked the Bureau of Research within USOE for failing to provide immediately usable products. This attack led to a fundamental redefinition of the research and development process. No longer content to let individual researchers or institutions pursue their own agendas, the Bureau of Research stressed "mission-oriented" research — a concept borrowed from the Defense Department. Labs and R&D centers now were expected to compete directly for specific research projects rather than receiving their federal funds outright. This "program purchase" approach initiated by the Bureau of Research continued when the labs and R&D centers were transferred to the NIE, which was created in June 1972 (Sieber 1974, 478–502; Sproull, Weiner, and Wolf 1978).

The labs and R&D centers strenuously objected to the program purchase policy because it fragmented their activities and emphasized short-term planning. They had banded together for informational purposes in 1969 at the insistence of the federal government and eventually created the Council for Educational Development and Research. While initially CEDaR did not focus on lobbying, it moved to Washington, DC, in 1974 and argued for the Ford administration and Congress to reverse the program purchase policy.[13]

The NCER and the Campbell Panel

The National Council on Education Research and NIE commissioned ten consultants to do a quick three-month review of the funding policies of NIE. Most of the consultants on the "Campbell panel" were prominent educators, and many had considerable previous experience with research and evaluation activities. While the consultants raised important questions about the effectiveness of the present lab system, they observed that "for us the only question about the basic concept of the laboratories is how to make it work well, not whether the laboratories should exist. The need for established, long-term, R&D institutions still impress [*sic*] us" (Campbell et al. 1975, 24).

Since the consultants examined the labs and R&D centers amid substantial decreases in NIE funding, they were concerned that a proper balance of research activities be maintained. Therefore, the Campbell panel recommended in its report that "no more than about a third of NIE's programs funds be allocated to work at the resulting special institutions [labs and R&D centers]" (Campbell et al. 1975, 72).

Sam Sieber, one of the ten consultants, added an appendix that detailed his views on the requirements of a national educational R&D system. He addressed a topic not widely discussed in the body of the report—the importance of "excellence or quality control" (Campbell et al. 1975, 90).[14] Sieber briefly noted some factors that had led to the neglect of concern about quality: "the vagueness of evaluative criteria, the lack of consensus on procedures, and the failure of a major sponsor — NIE—to develop any agency-wide mechanism for assessing quality." Continuing, he recommended that "perhaps what is vitally needed is a national task force or commission on the quality of educational R&D" (90). Unfortunately, his plea for examining the quality of the work produced by NIE, and later OERI, has been ignored almost entirely.

Not everyone agreed with all of the Campbell panel recommendations, particularly those suggestions that affected the labs. Richard Rossmiller, chairman of CEDaR, and Robert Scanlon, a member of the board of trustees of CEDaR, appeared at the House hearings on NIE reauthorization and questioned the wisdom of the proposed, seemingly exclusive, national orientation of the labs (U.S. House 1975b, 109).[15] Rossmiller and Scanlon did not object altogether to a national orientation for the labs but only to an exclusive one at the expense of their regional ties: "In other words, the labs and centers are 'national' in terms of their scope of work. But they should also maintain strong ties to their region and state" (110).

Another objection lay in the governance of the labs. Rossmiller and Scanlon disagreed with the Campbell panel's suggestion that NIE take a larger role in setting the priorities of the labs as well as in monitoring them more closely (U.S. House 1975b, 110). But they did agree with several other recommendations, such as continued support of NIE in general and of the labs and centers in particular. They also called for a rigorous evaluation of all NIE products, including those developed by the labs and centers.

> The questions, "How well does it work?" and "what difference does it make?" are frequently raised about the outcomes of research and development. The laboratories and centers take the position that quality control in product development is the single most important variable in their work. However, government pressure to disseminate products, coupled with the expense of ensuring quality control, often works against us. We believe that NIE has the responsibility for developing, in conjunction with educational practitioners and the research and development specialists, effective quality-control procedures. (116)

The National Council on Educational Research, the policy group that advises NIE, "reviewed the consultants' report and is in general agreement with both their analysis and conclusions." It agreed that NIE "should take responsibility for the general institutional health of educational research and development and that substantial Institute resources should be directed toward a group of research and development institutions working directly with NIE on a long-term, large-scale basis" (NCER 1976, 1). The council called for the establishment of two to four national laboratories selected from the existing R&D centers and labs (U.S. House 1975b, 111). Moreover, as the "new system is gradually phased in, NIE should continue to reserve a substantial (but declining) proportion of its budget for supporting, developing, and strengthening existing laboratories and centers capable of high quality research" (NCER 1976, 1). In an appendix to its document, the council detailed its vision of the new national labs and the old regional labs. The regional labs, the council suggested, should continue to provide assistance and services to practitioners in their local areas while also conducting R&D programs of national significance (NCER 1976, appendix C). Thus, the council opted for a middle course between the labs' almost exclusive national orientation, recommended by the Campbell panel, and the maintenance of the existing labs' regional focus desired by others.

Five key members of the Senate Committee on Labor and Public Welfare strongly objected to the efforts of NIE and NCER to create the proposed new national labs while gradually reducing the number or funding of the existing regional labs (Randolph et al. 1977).[16] In response, Harold Hodgkinson, NIE director, quickly reassured the committee that NIE would not dramatically revise the lab system or phase out existing labs as long as they fulfilled their stated missions: "The question, then, is not whether we will support labs and centers, but how we will insure that a lab and center program and the institutions in it are as strong as possible." Hodgkinson reiterated that federal responsibility for the labs and centers should include a "rigorous assessment of these institutions . . . and, if necessary, [a] phase out of special relationships with those which can't pass muster after considerable support from NIE" (1977b, 2).[17]

While NIE director Hodgkinson readily acquiesced to the congressional pressures, the National Council on Educational Research was more hesitant. It withdrew its original proposal to create a few national labs and reduce the number of regional labs, but it chastised Hodgkinson for agreeing to a "special institutional relationship" with the labs before the quality of each of their institutions had been established. Indeed, an NCER committee convened to review these issues believed "that the Institute is not paying sufficient attention to considerations of quality and relevance which the Committee believes to be at least equal in importance to considerations of stability and political comity" (Corbally 1977, 6). The NCER committee defined *quality* in a broad, comparative sense (a definition that might be worth resurrecting even today):

> A principal test of quality and merit, however, must be a comparison with other potential awardees. This is true of all Federal agencies engaged in fields where absolute tests are not available. It is not clear that this emphasis on quality, merits and comparative judgment is being adequately emphasized in the NIE review process. Too often, when considering labs and centers in relation to other R&D organizations, the Institute finds itself in the posture of having to prove that a lab or center is incompetent or mediocre in order to shift funding from previously-established patterns. (6–7)

Panel for the Review of Laboratory and Center Operations

While the Campbell report of 1975 reiterated the Gardner Task Force's vision of large-scale national labs, directives from Congress led to a rather different view of the labs. First, Congress legislatively mandated the continued existence of the labs and R&D centers. Second, it called for the creation of a new panel to review and assess the existing labs and R&D centers and to make recommendations for their long-term development. As we shall see, this important panel rejected the Gardner Task Force's national vision and advocated regional labs. The panel's position coincided with the growing sentiment of certain NIE segments that the existing labs were neither producing high-quality products nor responding adequately to suggestions from the NIE lab monitors.

Under congressional pressure for the more immediate influence of research and development upon schools and for more dissemination, the new NIE director, Patricia Graham, tried to involve more educational practitioners in NIE activities. During earlier negotiations between NIE and CEDaR, Congress had mandated a panel to review the labs and R&D centers. Graham selected a sizable contingent of practitioners for the fifteen individuals on this panel.[18] The large number of practitioners on the new panel departed from the composition of the Campbell group and probably contributed to the redirection of the labs' mission. Since the Panel for the Review of Laboratory and Center Operations actively remained in operation for two years, the group considerably influenced the perception and treatment of labs.

The Panel for the Review of Laboratory and Center Operations rejected the initial vision of the labs as large-scale national research and development institutions, as proposed by the Gardner Task Force and reiterated by the Francis Chase and the Campbell panel. Rather, it recommended more regionally controlled and oriented labs (Panel for the Review of Laboratory and Center Operations 1979, 8). While the panel accepted research and development as legitimate lab activities, it stressed the regional nature of these activities. Moreover, the panel emphasized both the role of labs in providing technical assistance to the regions and the importance of dissemination. Thus, the national orientation of labs fell by the wayside, and thereafter neither NIE or OERI upheld this view as an ideal model for the labs.

The Labs' Role in Curriculum Development

The labs withstood another major change in the late 1970s due to NIE's growing hostility toward supporting large-scale curriculum development. The federal government had become increasingly involved in supporting curriculum development after the Russians launched Sputnik in 1957.[19] For example, the National Science Foundation spent $180 million from 1957 to 1975 to support curriculum projects (Saylor 1982). In 1964, the Gardner Task Force had explicitly recommended that the labs "develop and disseminate ideas and programs" (Gardner 1964, 34). As a result, many of the R&D centers and labs in the late 1960s and early 1970s developed and distributed curriculum packages. For instance, the University of Wisconsin R&D Center created the Individually Guided Education (IGE) project, and CEMREL, the St. Louis based lab, developed the Comprehensive School Mathematics Program (Saylor 1982, 66).[20]

As the federal agencies entered the area of curriculum development, however, they increasingly faced critics who argued that this was an inappropriate role for the national government. Particular criticism was directed at the NSF-funded upper elementary school social studies course, "Man: A Course of Study" (MACOS), which was accused of subverting American traditional values and beliefs (Schaffarzick 1979).[21] Moreover, some publishers attacked the courses developed by the R&D centers and the labs for duplicating and undercutting their efforts. As a result, the National Council on Educational Research appointed a task force to examine and guide NIE's curriculum development activities.

The NIE Curriculum Development Task Force examined the issue in considerable detail and proposed four policy alternatives ranging from abandonment of NIE curriculum development activities to continued freedom for R&D centers and labs to undertake full-scale curriculum development. NIE director Hodgkinson announced in early 1977:

> NIE's primary contribution to the improvement of instructional programs and materials is to sponsor (1) the conduct, synthesis, and dissemination of relevant research, (2) efforts to strengthen, facilitate, and coordinate others' work in improving instructional programs and materials, and (3) the prototypic development of new instructional programs and materials. Among these, research activities represent the Institute's highest priority, followed by efforts to strengthen, facilitate, or coordinate others' work, and then prototypic development. Finally, full-scale development may be considered by NIE, but only for certain limited purposes and only when none of the primary activities will suffice (Hodgkinson 1977a, 109).[22]

NIE's limited support of curriculum development activities as well as the mandate from Congress to remove itself from this area had a profound effect on many of the R&D centers and labs. As the R&D centers terminated development, most of them simply turned their attention to other areas of research. For the labs, however, the congressional decision to discontinue NIE-funded, full-scale curriculum development meant that many of their extensive research and evaluation efforts would now be abandoned altogether. Coupled with the labs' growing focus on regional issues and the provision of technical assistance, many labs gradually lost the high-quality personnel working on curriculum development who were an indispensable component of the Gardner Task Force's original vision for staffing of the labs.

Partisan Effects on the Labs

The labs encountered another major and at first seemingly cataclysmic event in the presidential election of 1980. Although previous partisan changes did not directly influence lab management, the 1980 election advanced individuals who disagreed with some basic assumptions of those who had staffed NIE during the Nixon, Ford, and Carter administrations. Just when NIE and CEDaR were beginning to reach a mutual accommodation in the late 1970s on how to view and manage the labs, Edward Curran, the first Reagan appointee to head NIE, sought to abolish the agency entirely. Moreover, Curran and his successor, Robert Sweet, dismissed many of the NIE employees and replaced them with individuals who were skeptical of the existing educational establishment. While Curran and Sweet did not succeed in eliminating NIE, due in part to the strong intervention of the secretary of education, Terrel Bell, their efforts disrupted many of the working relationships that had begun to crystallize earlier — including the emerging partnership between CEDaR and NIE.[23]

Substantial reductions in the budget, as part of the overall effort to reduce federal domestic spending, compounded the difficulties at NIE. Its budget was reduced from \$82 million in FY80 to \$53.2 million in FY82 — a 35 percent decrease. If the lab and center funding had stayed constant, as previously negotiated in their five-year contracts, little money would have remained for other projects in FY82. The Omnibus Reconciliation Act of 1981 stipulated that NIE could proportionately adjust downward all of its grants and contracts to finance the decrease, but CEDaR successfully lobbied to protect most of the lab and center funding. The Continuing Resolution Appropriation specified that lab and center funding could be cut by no more than 10 percent for FY82. Although NIE did reduce lab and center funding by the full 10 percent, the magnitude of the overall budget reduction meant that it had to cut other programs even more severely.

There had been periodic complaints that while the labs and centers continued to receive a disproportionate share of NIE funds they did not have to face any open competition to maintain their funding. Therefore, the Omnibus Reconciliation Act of 1981 also stated that labs and centers "shall upon completion of existing contracts, receive future funding in accordance with government-wide competitive bidding procedures and in accordance with principles of peer review involving scholars and State and local educators to ensure the quality and relevance of the work proposed" (U.S. House 1981, 729).

Curran and his successor, Sweet, wanted to terminate the existing lab and center contracts immediately in 1982, arguing that by that time NIE would have completed its initial three-year agreements with these institutions. But the labs and centers objected, insisting that their entire five-year contracts or grants with NIE be funded. Eventually, CEDaR persuaded the Senate Appropriations Committee to require NIE to fund these institutions through 1984 (Zodhiates 1988, 85–90).

Competition for the Labs and Centers

Manual Justiz, who succeeded Sweet as the director of NIE, initiated a highly public and open competition for the labs and centers. This process included an extensive examination of the purposes and functions of the laboratories, which culminated in a set of recommendations by the NIE Laboratory Study Group. The Laboratory Study Group listed a variety of tasks for these institutions but noted that "laboratory responsibility would be relatively less in the area of research and relatively greater in development and other transformations of research to directly useful products and processes" (NIE Laboratory Study Group 1983, 3). The study group also considered five other specialized functions for the labs but concluded that the existing "general purpose" laboratory model, with its multiple constituencies and purposes, was optimal (10). The study group accepted the regional nature of the labs but called for closer coordination between NIE's national priorities and the labs' activities. It suggested a 50 percent increase in overall funding for NIE with a proportionate boost for the labs. "As additional funds are made available to NIE," the group recommended "that NIE provide some resources for competitive opportunities for the laboratories, consistent with their basic purposes" (4). Unlike the 1975 Campbell panel, which worried about too much extraneous outside funding for the labs, the study group "recognized the importance of laboratories seeking other funding sources to expand the impact of their core NIE support" (4). It also called for more effective monitoring of the labs and urged a clearer distinction in functions between the labs and centers. Finally, it emphasized the need for closer cooperation between the labs and centers and stated that "NIE and the labs should interactively develop plans for addressing national priorities" (8).[24]

Many of those involved were skeptical that the 1985 competition for labs and centers would be impartial and open. However, almost everyone agreed that NIE managed to conduct a fair and effective peer review process.[25] The request for proposals (RFP) for the laboratories identified five tasks for these institutions: (1) develop effective governance, management, planning, and evaluation systems for the laboratory; (2) work with and through existing organizations to improve schools and classrooms; (3) work with state-level decision makers on school improvement issues; (4) work to create research- and development-based resources for school improvement; and (5) work in collaboration with centers and other laboratories on regional and national educational problems (NIE 1984, 18–25).

The 1985 request for proposals maintained many general trends in the treatment of labs in the late 1970s and early 1980s, including their regional orientation and control. The RFP stressed that labs must continue to provide technical services for their regional clients. But it also shifted the emphasis in several ways. In the past, labs had pursued a wide variety of tasks in furthering general educational improvement. Now NIE instructed them to *"focus on school and classroom improvement."* Moreover, it expected labs to *"feature dissemination and assis-*

tance strategies" (emphasis original). Finally, the RFP not only encouraged labs to collaborate with other labs and centers but required them to
set aside a small but fixed proportion of their funds for this effort (NIE
1984, 10, 11, 16).

Although NIE continued to designate research and development
as lab activities, now it stressed short-term investigations, applied research and development, and the dissemination of research-based information to schools. Compared to the original vision of the labs in the
1960s and early 1970s, however, research and development activities
were deemphasized in the 1985 competition. Only 20 to 35 percent of a
lab's work program was assigned *"to create research and development
based resources for school improvement"* (NIE 1984, 13–14, 25, emphasis original).

The entire concept of development had been substantially revised
since the early 1970s. Whereas many labs had originally developed
large-scale, field-tested curriculums, the guidelines now called for more
modest products "such as research-based training designs, directories,
guides or other practical materials that support the improvement process
in their region" (NIE 1984, 25). While NIE had been prepared earlier to
at least entertain the idea of some ambitious curriculum proposals, now
the institute explicitly and unequivocally stated that "laboratories may
not use NIE funds to engage in long-term curriculum development efforts" (14).[26]

By the end of the 1985 competition, nine labs were in operation—
six former and three new ones.[27] Labs were apportioned regionally
with no overlap in jurisdiction. The Office of Educational Research
and Improvement was reorganized so that the labs were placed within
the Programs for the Improvement of Practice, while the centers were
overseen by the Office of Research. Moreover, a staff team at PIP oversaw the entire lab program, and an individual staff person monitored
each lab.

The Cross Lab Review Panel

Chester Finn, the assistant secretary for OERI, launched an extensive
external review of the labs in the summer of 1987. Christopher Cross,
the former ranking minority staff member on the House Subcommittee
on Select Education, headed up the outside review panel. Teams of
external reviewers and an OERI lab monitor visited each of these institutions for two and a half days, evaluated their progress, and proposed
three- to five-year plans (using standardized evaluation criteria developed for this review).

The Cross Lab Review Panel concluded that PIP's external review process was thorough and competent, but it observed that "the panel received relatively little information about the quality or impact of lab products" (Cross et al. 1987, 3). It recommended a study focused on the quality and significance of the work. It questioned the overall clarity and vision of the labs' mission and noted "that the labs are very strongly oriented to their regions." While the panel members praised the regionality of the labs, they also believed that "there are some legitimate roles outside the region which labs might become involved with" (7). They noted the labs' continued shift away from research as a result of the 1985 competition and voiced concern about the availability of practitioner-oriented research (6).

The panel did not attempt to make any judgments on the overall quality of the labs but did comment that since each of the external review teams looked at only one lab it lacked the opportunity to make comparisons. As a result, "the panel believes there is a tendency for reviews of this type to produce positive results. . . . This does not mean the results from this review are to be disbelieved, but the tendency for positive findings to result from such a process should be kept in mind" (Cross et al. 1987, 2).

While the Cross Laboratory Review Panel hesitated to make any conclusions about the labs' overall quality, Assistant Secretary Finn did not. After reviewing carefully the reports of the external review panels and the lab monitors and the response of the labs, Finn expressed strong doubts about the work of the labs. Based upon this extensive two-year review, he concluded in an internal OERI memo that he did not "see any evidence that the taxpayers' substantial investment in labs these past two years has yielded any RESULTS of any sort" (Finn 1987).

Assistant Secretary Finn frequently complained about the lack of flexibility in OERI research funding—due mainly to the congressional stipulation that the labs and centers receive the bulk of funds, leaving almost nothing for field-initiated research projects. While he had some criticisms of the centers, he reserved his strongest attacks for the labs. At a congressional oversight hearing on the functioning of OERI, he testified:

The laboratories, in particular, have not been a very remunerative investment *per se*. This is not to say that they do nothing useful—they and their energetic Washington lobbyists are quite capable of finding hundreds of laboratory customers who will claim satisfaction with services provided by the laboratories. But I am saying that, given their present activities and configurations, and given the

current fiscal constraints on the government, the laboratories represent a profligate use of OERI funds in relation to the benefit they
generate.

This is so for several reasons. I have already mentioned that laboratory impact is amorphous and difficult to assess, and that these institutions simply cannot provide services to more than a few districts in
our immense education system. But congressional protection of the
laboratories and, to be blunt, the insatiable appetite of the laboratories for federal funds, have shielded them from any real competition
from other forms of dissemination and technical assistance. As a
result, they have become entrenched institutions whose primary goal
seems to be self-perpetuation. (U.S. House 1988a, 171)

The growing skepticism and overt public hostility to the labs within
OERI dissipated to a large degree when Cross replaced Finn as the
assistant secretary in 1989. Having worked with the labs as chairman of
the Laboratory Review Panel and having been employed previously by
the House Subcommittee on Select Education, Cross anticipated continued funding for the labs and sought modest improvements in their activities, particularly by expanding the labs' and centers' dissemination
work. Cross did not envision radical changes in either the direction or
the management of the labs.[28]

At the time of the 1990 request for proposals, the National Academy of Sciences was undertaking a broad review of OERI and the
legislative reauthorization of OERI was pending. Therefore, the RFP
called only for minor changes, anticipating greater alterations to the
laboratory programs as a result of the academy study and the reauthorization legislation. OERI introduced a number of small but significant
changes for the 1990 RFP, such as reducing the disparities in regional
funding, focusing the mission of the labs on "at-risk" students, serving
small rural schools, emphasizing early childhood education, and allowing for greater flexibility in the delivery of services. Whereas the 1985
RFP stated that the amount of money spent on applied research should
be approximately one-half of that spent on assistance, the 1990 RFP
permitted labs greater freedom in determining the appropriate mixture
of expenditures on these tasks.[29]

Despite efforts to increase the amount of competition, only eleven
labs in the ten regions submitted eligible proposals. (One other application was ruled ineligible because it was received after the deadline.)
OERI refunded eight of the existing nine labs (but not the one from the
Southeastern Region, which lost to the single competitor) and created a
new lab for the Pacific area. Interestingly, since the panels judged two of

the nine noncontested lab proposals very weak and problematic, OERI requested a third review for those two proposals.

II. Assessment of the Laboratories in 1992–93

As with the analysis of the R&D centers, due to time constraints I could study only a sample of the labs. The detailed 1992–93 examination assessed five of the ten labs in existence at the time:

1. Regional Laboratory for Educational Improvement of the Northeast and Islands (primary site at Andover, Massachusetts), cited as NE/I or the Northeast Lab.
2. Southwest Educational Development Laboratory (primary site at Austin, Texas), cited as SEDL or the Southwest Lab.
3. Mid-continent Regional Educational Laboratory (primary site at Aurora, Colorado), cited as McREL or the Mid-continent Lab.
4. Northwest Regional Laboratory (primary site at Portland, Oregon), cited as NWREL or the Northwest Lab.
5. Far West Laboratory for Educational Research and Development (primary site at San Francisco, California), cited as FWL or the Far West Lab.

The five labs investigated in this study were suggested by the staff of the Educational Networks Division (END) of the Programs for the Improvement of Practice. The labs selected were intended to exemplify the current range and variety of research and development activities, but they did not necessarily represent the five labs not studied.[30] The greater diversity of labs, compared to R&D centers, increased the difficulty of generalizing with regard to the system from any particular sample. On the other hand, by studying five of the ten labs versus five of the twenty-three centers, a much greater proportion of the institutions was covered.

This analysis focuses on the labs' quality of research and development. Since the labs engaged in a wider variety of activities than the centers did, the appropriate facets for inclusion in this investigation were sometimes unclear. One guiding principle did remain clear: to examine in detail all task 3 activities that encompassed the labs' applied research and development efforts.[31] I also considered other research-related work such as lab efforts to analyze a region's needs or evaluate their own work as well as similar undertakings in their unique initiatives (e.g., early childhood projects or rural education activities). Moreover, the analysis included any other materials or activities identified as research related by the staff of the labs. Because this study emphasized the research-related activities and capabilities of the labs in the broadest sense, I also investigated relevant lab work funded outside of OERI and suggested by the staff of the labs. Thus, the analysis included some of the Mid-continent Lab's developmental work, even though OERI no longer financed it.

As with the analysis of the centers, all five labs' 1985–93 deliverables available from the staff at END were examined, including the published and unpublished research-related materials. Since END no longer maintained the past deliverables of two of the five labs, it was necessary to reassemble those items from the labs. Due to a shortage of space, OERI occasionally discarded some old deliverables when institutional liaisons changed, causing difficulty in reassembling the materials for analysis.[32] The analysis also included lab budgets, 1985 and 1990 funding proposals, written comments of the proposal reviewers, communications from internal and external evaluators, and exchanges between monitors and their contractors. My visit to all five labs provided an excellent opportunity to tour the facilities and meet with the staff.[33] I interviewed each of the END institutional liaisons several times and found invaluable my frequent attendance and participation at the weekly PIP lab team meetings. Several lab directors provided helpful written comments about the draft report. Finally, all of the lab directors and I held two meetings to discuss this report, including a session on April 7, 1993, after the labs had ample opportunity to review a draft of this document.

Distribution of Research-Related Activities of Labs

The previous section revealed that labs in the 1960s and 1970s were expected to allocate a large proportion of their funds to applied research or development activities. With the gradual elimination of large-scale curriculum development projects in the late 1970s and early 1980s and the relative deemphasis of research-related activities in the 1985 and 1990 competitions, the role of applied research and development in the labs has diminished. Indeed, some knowledgeable individuals initially wondered whether an analysis of the labs was not a wasted effort, since they perceived that labs presently conducted little research-related or development activities.

Yet even a cursory glance at the budgets of the labs suggested that considerable funds still were being expended on just task 3—the conduct of applied research and development. In FY92, the ten labs spent approximately $7.8 million (current dollars) of OERI funds on applied research and development alone, while the R&D centers spent only an estimated $14 million on all OERI-funded research activities. Moreover, more than one-fifth (22.2 percent) of the lab budgets were allocated to task 3. Aside from indirect costs and fees, task 3 made up 28.5 percent of OERI funds allocated to the labs. Only task 2, providing assistance to the regions, received more funding (32.9 percent of the total budget). Thus, while the amount and percentage of OERI funds for labs' applied research and development declined over time, their research and development remained a major expenditure for OERI.[34]

The percentage of the total budget money expended on task 3 varied greatly among the labs for FY92 — ranging from 12.2 percent at the Pacific Lab to 33.0 percent at the Northwest Lab. Overall, the five labs investigated spent an average of 22.4 percent of their total budgets on task 3 activities, while the other five devoted an average of 22.0 percent of their total budgets on these activities.[35]

It was difficult to compare the direct and indirect costs of the labs and centers because the institutions did not categorize and subdivide their budgets identically. Nevertheless, I determined that the indirect costs of the five centers studied were 27.6 percent, while the indirect costs and fees for the ten labs were 22.1 percent. The inexact figures deter reliance on the specific differences, but it may be that the labs spent slightly less than the centers on indirect costs and fees. OERI's comparative lab and center expenditures on indirect costs and fees for services and products warrant further investigation.

Finally, we turn to the labs' ability to obtain additional outside funding for their institutions. In recent years, OERI has encouraged the labs to seek such funding to supplement their budgets. This campaign appears to have succeeded, since only one-half of the lab funding came from the regular OERI lab budget. But labs differed greatly in their ability to garner outside funding. Two received only about one-fourth of their monies from the OERI lab budget, while three received 90 percent or more from that source. Of the five labs investigated in this study, an average of only 39.7 percent of their funds came from OERI lab money compared to an average of 73.6 percent of the funds for the other five labs.[36]

The OERI staff disagreed on the desirability of encouraging labs to seek more non-OERI funding. In the late 1960s and early 1970s, OERI sometimes discouraged labs from seeking outside funding, which might have diverted their attention and energies from the needs of NIE. During the 1980s, however, the emphasis shifted toward encouraging outside funding, especially as some believed that the federal government might terminate support of the labs altogether. Given the evolving attitudes toward outside funding by NIE and OERI, perhaps it is time for this agency to consider this issue once again.

Many of the positive and negative aspects of non-OERI funding for labs fall under the consideration of federal versus regional priorities. Regional governing boards were already setting much of the lab orientation and direction, thus reducing potential conflicts. If more lab funds and activities were focused on national priorities under the guidance of OERI, then labs' acceptance of large amounts of non-OERI funds could pose a problem for the allocation of lab staff and resources. On the other hand, additional outside funding might allow the labs to make more efficient and effective use of OERI monies through the cost sharing of projects and the use of federal education funds to build upon work initially sponsored by others. Therefore, it is unlikely that any simple formula will produce an ideal overall portfolio of lab funding. Most importantly, OERI should always strive to make sure that federal interests in lab activities are protected, even as these institutions simultaneously respond to the needs of their other funders.

Research Topics of Labs

The previous section revealed that a considerable portion of lab funds were spent on task 3 — applied research and development. Another perspective on overall lab expenditures is provided by looking at the distribution of lab activities as these were recorded on OERI's project input forms (or PMIS forms) for FY92.[37] These forms divided activities into seven categories: policy studies, evaluation, basic research, applied research, development, statistics, and dissemination. Unfortunately, compared to similar data provided by the centers, overall the labs apparently did not return this information to OERI as carefully and accurately. Nevertheless, the PMIS returns provide a rough idea of their self-reported activities.

Although the quality of data from the PMIS forms left much to be desired in terms of categorization and accuracy, the overall contours of the five labs' descriptions of their activities were instructive.[38] According to their PMIS forms, these five labs devoted considerable amounts of money and energy to dissemination, including approximately 32.6 percent of their total OERI funds. Unfortunately, PMIS did not provide more detailed information about the nature of that dissemination, but in the case of the labs dissemination appeared to consist mainly of directly providing clients with information and technical assistance.[39]

Information from PMIS on the distribution of activities (excluding dissemination already discussed) revealed that labs devoted very little effort to basic research (3.1 percent), evaluation (10.2 percent), or statistics (1.2 percent). While the PMIS forms showed that only 12.7 percent of lab efforts were devoted to policy studies, that figure may underestimate this activity because some policy analyses were placed under the applied research category as well.

The two major lab activities according to the PMIS forms were applied research (27.7 percent) and development (45.1 percent). Together they accounted for almost three-fourths of lab research-and-development-related activities. Compared to similar data for the centers, the labs proportionately allocated more funds to development, while the centers focused more on applied research, evaluation, basic research, and statistics. The labs and centers spent almost equal proportions on policy studies (though the labs' proportion is higher when the policy studies categorized under applied research are included).[40]

One problem with the use of PMIS categories to compare lab activities and funding allocations is that respondents often employed them for rather different purposes. For example, while sometimes *applied research* at the labs referred to efforts to conduct original research on some specific problem, at other times it referred to activities performed to synthesize existing research or write policy papers based upon existing research. Indeed, much of labs' applied research was actually the synthesis or use of existing applied or basic research rather than the support of original research.

The previous chapter discussed the strengths and weaknesses of R&D centers' heavy reliance upon case studies for their applied research investigations. While individual case studies provided an effective way to initially explore or later scrutinize some problem, researchers could draw only limited conclusions from their findings since they were not representative of the population as a whole. Moreover, unless individual case studies were placed in a contextual or comparative framework, they were not conducive to meaningful research or policy inferences.[41]

The labs frequently relied on case studies as a means of conducting their applied research. Often the result was studying a particular institution or process that was relatively isolated from their other research or development endeavors and thereby limited in its usefulness and generalizability. For example, the Northwest Lab analyzed the grading practices of fifteen teachers within a particular high school and properly acknowledged the limitations of generalizing the findings from this single case study (Stiggins, Griswold, and Frisbie 1990).

Occasionally labs made efforts to embed case studies in a larger research effort. In the 1980s, for example, the Northeast Lab was a primary sponsor of studies that sought to understand and improve urban high schools. It commissioned a telephone survey of 178 urban high schools that had introduced some significant educational innovation. It also sponsored five in-depth, qualitative case studies of innovative urban high schools or junior high schools (in Boston, Cleveland, Los Angeles, New Jersey, and New York City). Based upon the results of the survey and the five case studies, the lab offered explanations for why and how innovations introduced into the public secondary schools in urban communities had succeeded or failed in helping to improve student learning outcomes.[42]

Similarly, the Southwest Lab sought to improve rural education by working with small, rural schools serving disadvantaged students in five states (Arkansas, Louisiana, New Mexico, Oklahoma, and Texas). While not all of these demonstration sites used identical achievement tests or employed the same set of contextual indicators, the Southwest Lab made an effort to compare the five case studies whenever possible.[43]

Much of the work categorized as applied research by the labs comprised syntheses of existing research or of written policy papers incorporating relevant research findings.[44] The topics for these papers ranged widely, from an understanding of language development and education to concern about schoolwide and classroom discipline (Conklin, Hunt, and Walkush 1990; Cotton 1990b). However, there was sometimes considerable duplication among the laboratories in their research syntheses and policy papers. For example, many labs, often as part of their task 6 activities, produced research summaries or policy papers about early childhood education. While some summaries and papers did have a particular regional slant or orientation, many might have been equally applicable and useful in another part of the country (Jewett 1991a; Lally and Mangione 1991; Hansen 1988; McREL 1990a).

Thus, OERI and the labs should reexamine how labs produce and distribute research syntheses and policy analyses. Sometimes the labs commissioned their own research or policy papers. At other times, they used the one-page summaries developed by CEDaR.[45] Occasionally, the labs used materials developed or funded by OERI directly.

Confusion abounded regarding the great duplication and waste of research syntheses and policy papers developed at OERI and the labs and centers. Besides funding the extensive work of the labs and centers, OERI sponsored several other research activities. The Office of Research had initiated an Education Research Guide Series, which provides a four-page summary of topics such as cooperative learning, performance assessment, and reading recovery. The National Center for Education Statistics provided publications such as *NAEPfacts* and the *Education Research Report*. In addition, NCES had also begun a two-page Issue

Brief Series. Finally, the Educational Resources Information Center sponsored sixteen ERIC clearinghouses, which develop voluminous short research and policy syntheses, bibliographies, digests, and books for parents, researchers, and practitioners. Therefore, before an individual lab or center commissioned a research synthesis or policy paper it might have been prudent to check whether a roughly comparable product already existed. Moreover, OERI should have coordinated its own publication activities.[46]

If, after consulting the existing stock of research syntheses and policy analyses, a lab or center detected the need for more work in an area (or if it deemed existing products inappropriate or inadequate) it might want to commission additional papers. In some situations, however, the lab or center might economically and effectively turn the work over to some other OERI-funded group, whose staff might be more experienced and knowledgeable in that area. In any case, the entire issue of producing and disseminating research syntheses and policy analyses needs to be thoroughly reconsidered.

While labs reported spending more than one-fourth of their budgets on development, they disagreed on the meaning of that term. Sometimes they used the category "development" to cover activities such as task 1—the establishment of effective governance, management, and planning systems.[47] In other instances, they used the term *development* to describe the creation of classroom materials and the training of teachers and professionals. Only rarely was *development* associated with the more classic and traditional definition—the repeated and systematic testing and improvement of some educational product or curriculum.

Given the common usage of the term *development,* it was not surprising that the labs employed the concept so broadly. Nor was it harmful as long as the exact definition was clear in every situation. Unfortunately, so much confusion and uncertainty surrounded the word that without an explanation it did not effectively communicate what was being done.

When the labs were created in the mid-1960s, the Gardner Task Force and others assumed that these institutions would play a major role in the development of educational curricula and materials. The Gardner Task Force envisioned development in the more traditional sense—the use of iterative and systematic testing to improve curricula or other educational products using large-scale field studies. Indeed, the task force insisted that each lab have its own experimental school as one element of systematically assessing and improving its products (Gardner 1964).

Many of the labs in the 1960s and early 1970s did employ this concept of development. For example, the Southwest Lab developed a short handbook, which described the development process for educational products. It broadly defined an educational product as able to "comprise instructional materials, hardware, or software; it can comprise a technique or a process; or it can comprise any combination of the above" (Randall et al. 1970, 4).

The Southwest Lab then described six stages of the developmental cycle: context analysis, conceptual design, product design, pilot test, field test, and marketing and diffusion. Educational products did not have to proceed linearly through the stages (products adapted from elsewhere usually were introduced in a stage other than the first). The lab's flexible product development model could vary from one product to the next. But throughout the entire process, the emphasis was on continuing evaluation and testing of the educational product. A product was pilot tested usually "under controlled conditions in selected schools which are in proximity to the Laboratory and . . . conducted by the originators of the test products" (Randall 1970, 25). Then the product was subjected to large-scale field testing "to determine the ultimate utility and viability of the system under test, and to facilitate marketing and diffusion of the system by measuring its effectiveness, cost, endurance, and potential and by ascertaining the effects upon the system of the many variables existing in a natural environment" (29).

The Southwest Lab was not alone in its interest in the systematic development of educational products. Most of the labs' developmental energies in the 1960s and 1970s were devoted to improving curricula. As discussed previously, NIE opposed large-scale curriculum development in the late 1970s and OERI explicitly prohibited it in the request for proposals for labs in 1985 and 1990. A few labs managed to continue some curriculum development, although at least one felt it prudent to create a separate, subsidiary corporation so as not to violate OERI's prohibition against large-scale curriculum development activities. Thus, the Mid-continent Lab used OERI funds to support the research phases of a major curriculum project and then completed the developmental phase of this activity with corporate monies (Marzano et al. 1988, 1992).

While a few large-scale curriculum development projects continued at the labs with non-OERI funding, most turned to smaller projects and used less systematic ways of assessing and improving their products. The Northwest Lab, for example, had developed its Onward to Excellence Program for over a decade but had never undertaken an extensive and rigorous large-scale field test of the project. Instead, the Onward to Excellence Program utilized the experiences of teachers and other professionals who had used the program to make adjustments and improvements.[48]

The RFP guidelines for the 1985 and 1990 lab competitions expressed the expectation that labs would undertake only short-term applied research or development projects (ones that could be completed within the five-year contract period). They placed no emphasis on developing large-scale, ongoing, cumulative projects and in fact implicitly seemed to discourage such efforts. Therefore, it was not surprising that many of the applied research or development projects were small and often unrelated investigations.

The regional focus of the applied research also limited some of the labs' ability or willingness to use OERI funds to investigate questions at sites outside their immediate geographic area. For example, the Northeast Lab obtained a sizable grant from the Apple Computer Corp. to study the impact of computers in the classroom. When the funding for this interesting and important project abruptly and unexpectedly ended, the Northeast Lab was unwilling to use OERI-funds to complete it because the classroom sites for the project were outside their region.[49] Others, such as the Far West Lab, did not feel quite as territorially bound by the confines of their regions and were more willing to operate on a national basis.[50]

Although the labs existing in 1992–93 were about one-third smaller in constant dollars than those in the early 1970s, the reduction in funding did not adequately explain the small size of most of their applied research and development projects. Aside from indirect costs and fees, administrative expenses, and dissemination expenditures, in FY92 the average amount of money directly available for applied research and development (task 3) was substantially greater for each of the labs than for most of the individual R&D centers. But overall the labs chose to spend less of their task 3 funds on original applied research and development than did most of the R&D centers. Moreover, even given the small amount of money that the labs devoted to original applied research and development, they generally followed the preference of many R&D centers and spread the limited funds among several small-scale, short-term projects.

Quality of the Applied Research and Development

Almost any discussion of the quality of applied research and development produced by the labs evokes strong feelings — often among those not familiar with much of the work at those institutions. Many academics and policymakers, particularly scornful of the labs' quality of research and development, view them as second-rate institutions compared to the R&D centers or the funding of individual researchers. Strong antipathy extended even to some OERI staff members and leaders (though not among most of the END workers who monitored the work of the labs). Moreover, many critics tend to issue a blanket condemnation of the research and development of the labs. This tendency is due in part to the widespread perception that congressional earmarking of funds for these institutions has come at the expense of field-initiated research.

Part of the skepticism over the quality of the labs' work may be a self-fulfilling prophecy. In the 1985 and 1990 lab competitions, OERI directives discouraged long-term applied research or development projects and emphasized immediate technical assistance to clients. Therefore, it should not be entirely surprising that many policymakers and academics now have difficulty finding original lab research or development projects worth praising.

Nevertheless, some of the labs have produced some first-rate applied research and development since 1985. Particularly impressive has been the work at the Far West Lab. Building upon its long tradition of excellent research, the Far West Lab produced some of the more innovative and interesting applied research and development in 1992–93—often funded with non-OERI monies.[51]

The Far West Lab specialized in fairly sophisticated and thoughtful policy analyses. Using funds from both OERI and the Utah State Office of Education, it evaluated the Utah Career Ladder System for elementary and secondary public school teachers. The state's forty superintendents and school board presidents were interviewed by telephone. Surveys were mailed to all principals in the state and to a random sample of fifteen hundred teachers.[52] The Far West Lab also analyzed the teacher salary distribution in ten districts and investigated the implementation of the Career Ladder System in twelve districts. Unfortunately, it did not collect any data on changes in student outcomes, but on the basis of interviews with principals and teachers it concluded that "the policy is powerfully and positively changing both the teaching profession and the ways schools are organized to teach students. Utah's Career Ladder System is a model that deserves national attention" (Amsler, Mitchell, Nelson, and Timar 1988, 2).

Similarly, the Far West Lab analyzed the effect of the introduction of a computerized, self-paced math program (the so-called Rubin program) in five elementary schools and one middle school. Using information from a five-year longitudinal study, the Far West Lab analyzed the standardized math achievement scores of those who had been in the program for varying lengths of time. The results of this study provided only a lukewarm endorsement of the Rubin program. "Primary students in the Rubin program did less well than their regular program counterparts during the first two years of implementation but . . . intermediate grade students did better. Growth rates were higher for students in the Rubin program for four years than students in the program for two years" (Burns 1988).

Finally, the Far West Lab sponsored one of the more sophisticated and in-depth policy reviews of the relationship between class size and student learning. Based upon an extensive and careful review of the existing secondary literature, it concluded that "reducing class size has a substantial and cumulative effect on student learning" but that "the costs of class size reductions are enormous" (Mitchell, Carson, and Badarak 1989, 67–68). Using data from a large number of studies of class size, it found a curvilinear relationship between class size and achievement and then tried to develop a theoretical model to explain the pattern (68).

None of the other four labs in this investigation attained the overall quantity or quality of applied research and development as the Far West Lab. It devoted more of its OERI funds to task 3 than did any other lab except the Northwest (and Northwest spent a larger proportion of its task 3 monies on dissemination rather than applied research or development). Moreover, with some notable exceptions, most of the applied research produced at the other four labs was not as conceptually or methodologically rigorous or sophisticated as that prepared by the Far West Lab.

Yet several applied research or development projects at the other four labs were praiseworthy. For example, the Northeast Regional Lab, using funds from the Apple Corp., produced a useful assessment of the computer-based Apple Learning Series: Early Language (ALS-EL) in elementary classrooms (Harvey, Kell, and Drexler 1990). The Southwest Regional Lab produced an important six-year longitudinal study of language and reading achievement in bilingual classrooms (Mace-Matluck, Hoover, and Calfee 1989). The Mid-continent Lab generated valuable development work in vocabulary instruction and curriculum frameworks (Marzano and Marzano 1988; Marzano et al. 1988, 1992; Marzano 1992). And the Northwest Lab conducted a longitudinal analysis of Washington state's Early Childhood and Assistance Program (Child, Family, and Community Program 1991).

But various work supported by the labs also had serious conceptual and statistical limitations. Some applied research appeared to be preliminary and highly descriptive (Schwab, Hart-Landsberg, and Wikelund 1991). Major projects sometimes lacked clear research designs. The Northeast Lab launched an intensive collaborative action research effort in three sites but did not have an adequate research design for that large-scale and long-term undertaking.[53]

The statistical analyses of some studies were flawed and misleading. For example, Thomas Owen and Carolyn Cohen investigated the attitudes and opinions of entry-level workers in four states: Hawaii, Idaho, Oregon, and Washington. Each of the states appeared to have used a different strategy for sampling companies and workers. The overall completion rate was extremely low (20 percent for the workers and 29 percent for the companies), and the completion rates for the four states varied considerably. Yet the investigators simply combined the results from the four states without adjusting the data for the unequal return rates. Despite all of these shortcomings, they claimed that the "data might also be used as a benchmark from which to measure change in future years" (Owens and Cohen 1991).

Similarly, McREL sent questionnaires to local public school superintendents in the seven states it served. The response rate, averaging only 40 percent, varied among the states (ranging from 27 percent for Nebraska superintendents to 53 percent for Wyoming superintendents). Despite considerable variation in response rates, the analysts simply grouped all returns to get an overall regional profile. This grouping resulted in delusory assertions—for example, the state of Nebraska, which had 27 percent of the region's superintendents, was alleged to contribute only 19 percent of the returned questionnaires. If an individual state's response had no variation, then indiscriminate totaling would not have affected results. But often superintendents in one state gave clearly and sizably different answers from other superintendents in their state. As a result, the detailed tables in the McREL *Policy Notes,* which indicated whether answers from a particular state's superintendents had a statistically significant difference from the regional mean, might have been inaccurate if we had recalculated the regional means based upon the questionnaires stratified by the rate of return. In any case, given the low and unequal response rate to the questionnaires, the analysts should have addressed these problems more adequately (McREL 1990).

Although labs prioritized the evaluation of programs (including their own), they often did not design these assessments adequately. The Northwest Lab, for example, could have improved its study of the impact of its interesting and important Onward to Excellence (OTE) Program. The analysts did not explain why they chose certain OTE programs in the impact study and excluded others.[54] Moreover, by studying only ten of the more successful OTE programs in-depth, they could not ascertain why some succeeded and some failed. They would have done well to look also at some schools that did not join the OTE program in order to discover whether any improvements in the OTE schools partly resulted from more general changes affecting all schools during those years. Finally, rather than using a definition of *success* based only on whether the program achieved one of its goals, the definition might have been expanded and made more standardized. Otherwise, the analysts might have defined OTE programs that set low goals as equally or even more "successful" than programs that had set higher goals.[55]

Typical shortcomings of many lab demonstration and evaluation projects were the lack of standardized measures that made comparisons meaningful and the failure to include appropriate controls in their research designs. For example, the Southwest Lab investigated small and economically disadvantaged rural schools in five states over several years. Each of the five demonstration schools, all which had indicated an interest in improving their student achievement scores, were visited each month by a SEDL staff member responsible for facilitating change in that institution. Changes in education indicators over time were used to assess the improvements. Unfortunately, since the five sites did not use overall standardized measures of educational success, I found it impossible to make any systematic comparisons among the five schools. Since it appeared that the schools that chose to participate were not necessarily typical of others in that region, it was difficult to know how much to generalize from these findings. Moreover, since the study contained no control schools, I could not establish which factors were instrumental in making the improvements in student achievements. Thus, the SEDL project basically remained a limited but interesting demonstration effort at five diverse sites; unfortunately, its work did not provide the type of information that would be useful in ascertaining more generally or conclusively the key factors in improving rural education (Jolly, Hord, and Vaughan 1990).

Much of the labs' research-related work consisted of summarizing and synthesizing existing materials for policy papers. Some policy briefs were quite well done and useful. The Northeast Lab, for example, wrote a nice series of briefing papers on teacher quality, pension portability, and teacher incentives (Newton 1987; Title 1990, 1989). The Midcontinent Lab also produced some useful policy papers on subjects such as early childhood education (McREL 1990).

But some briefing or policy papers were simply a loose catalog of research giving inadequate attention either to the quality of the work cited or the diversity of materials in the field. Kenneth Hansen's policy paper on early childhood education, for instance, did not effectively cite or use existing research literature on this subject (1988). Similarly, Kathleen Cotton's glowing and uncritical discussion of the benefits of early childhood education ignored the studies that questioned the efficacy of programs such as Head Start (1990a). Janet Jewett's review of research states that "Studies recommend limiting elementary class sizes to 15 in public schools and stress small group size for preschool children" (1991b, 10). In fact, most of the studies of class size in elementary schools presented a much more complex picture — including a publication from OERI three years earlier (Tomlinson 1988).[56]

Overall, the quality of research, evaluation, and development produced by the labs varied greatly — even more so than among the R&D centers. Contrary to the statements of some policymakers, some of the work of the labs was of high quality and usefulness. Most materials from the Far West Lab, for example, were as well done conceptually and statistically as the products from most R&D centers. Yet serious weaknesses lay at the core of much research conducted by the other labs. While some staff members in all labs appreciated and could produce high-quality research, not all of them had a strong commitment to the type of rigor and expensive methodology necessary for improving the quality of materials produced under task 3.[57]

The American taxpayers have spent more than $1.59 billion (in constant 1996 dollars) on the labs since 1966. A sizable proportion of this money was designated for research and development. Of the funds dedicated to research and development, much has been ill-spent — especially during the past fifteen to twenty years when applied research and development appears to have decreased in both quantity and quality. The original and useful vision of the lab founders has not been fulfilled since many labs have become mainly technical assistance providers for their regional clients. Given the labs' limited production and the uneven quality of original applied research and development, OERI's continued, substantial investment in this area needs to be reconsidered thoroughly and carefully.

Of course, more recent years have seen an influx of lab expenditures for activities other than applied research or development, the quality and efficiency of which this analysis does not address. Therefore, the disappointing quality of applied research and development produced by the labs does not necessarily reflect on their overall work.

Lab Review Process

As already explained, the labs faced competition for the first time in 1985 and 1990. Although lab employees had felt concern about the process, by all accounts the competition was fair and noncontroversial. Despite concerted efforts by OERI to stimulate competition for the lab contracts, most incumbents were unopposed in either 1985 or 1990.

The competition for 1990 specified that OERI would award separate grants to each of the ten regions designated (the nine previous regions plus the addition of the Pacific Basic Region). The reviewers employed seven criteria in making the awards: regional needs (10 points), relationships in the region (20 points), institutional capability (15 points), plan of operation (25 points), key personnel (20 points), evaluation plan (5 points), and adequacy of resources (5 points).

Unlike the criteria for the R&D centers, relatively little emphasis was placed on the mission statement for the labs.[58] The OERI placed more emphasis on the importance of ties to the region and collaboration with other organizations.

The discussion of research and development activities in the competition manual listed a large number of acceptable deliverables, including newsletters, policy papers, concept papers, research reports, resource guides, handbooks, bibliographies, occasional bulletins, instructional materials, technical papers, synthesis papers, manuals, conference proceedings, and research instruments (OERI 1990, 52). But the reviewers' scoring sheets placed almost no emphasis on the importance of a specific research design for the proposed projects. Under the plan of operation, the quality of the project design functioned as one of ten subcategories but received little attention during the competition.

The five 1985 and 1990 applications studied strikingly lacked specificity for many proposed research or development projects. Most applications omitted important project information such as what types of instruments would be used to measure student outcomes or what size of samples would be drawn. Perhaps this lack of detail reflected in part the OERI lab guidelines, which required only short-term research and development projects and not a detailed research design. But this lack of specific details exhibited in activity proposals was also a more general characteristic of the applicants' response to the other questions.

Since most of these labs faced no real competition, many reviewers chose not to make elaborate comments regarding the nature or quality of the proposed research and development activities. In the case of two regions, however, the proposals were deemed so weak that the labs needed to resubmit their revised applications twice before they were judged minimally acceptable.

Thus, while the lab competitions were fair and well handled, little attention was paid to the nature or quality of the proposed research and development activities in 1985 and 1990. A few reviewers did question the lack of specificity in the plans, but most accepted the original or revised lab submissions without much protest. While the OERI staff tried to improve the overall quality of the lab proposals, in several instances it was difficult to overcome the lack of a carefully specified research design or of a detailed development plan.

In both the 1985 and 1990 lab competitions, applicants were required to develop their own self-evaluation plans. For example, the Regional Educational Laboratory request for proposals in 1990 described task 5 as a lab conducting an evaluation of its own activities. Labs were expected to do both formative and summative evaluations. Among the four questions raised in the formative evaluation section, one explicitly addressed the issue of the adequacy of the research design: "Do applied research projects have appropriate designs that are carefully implemented?" (OERI 1990, 29). The issue of research quality received further reinforcement and clarification in the proposal's statement that "the contractor shall develop and implement a plan to assure high quality of its deliverables and R&D products and publications" (31).

Unfortunately, the lab self-evaluations and quality assurance had very mixed results. The Far West Lab generally did a good job of quality assurance and developed a critical and useful system of reviewing its activities. Each individual program or project evaluated its own products and activities, but the director of planning and evaluation reviewed their evaluation plans and reports as well as provided technical assistance. A sample of the lab's publications was sent out for external review (Hood 1990). While the Far West Lab might have made some improvements in its impact analysis, on the whole it seemed to cope successfully with the requirement to monitor and assess the quality of its products and services.

At some other labs, however, the self-evaluation activities were less successful. The labs devoted much of their evaluation activities to an analysis of client satisfaction—a legitimate concern and one of the four formative evaluation questions asked in the 1990 lab RFP. But they paid much less attention to a critical assessment of the quality of the applied research or development projects. Moreover, some labs failed to submit their research synthesis or policy papers to the scrutiny of other experts in the field. As a result, while OERI had intended the lab self-evaluation activities to play an important role in maintaining the quality of services and deliverables produced by the labs, in practice the results were often disappointing.

Lab Monitoring

The Programs for the Improvement of Practice, under the direction of Eve Bither in 1992 and 1993, was one of the major offices within the Office of Educational Research and Improvement and had the responsibility for overseeing the activities of the labs. The Educational Networks Division, then under the direction of David Mack, was one of the three divisions within PIP and administered the Regional Educational Laboratory Program.

Six programs, including the labs, were administered within END. The Laboratory Team, then under the direction of Charles Stalford, directly oversaw the labs.[59] Each lab was assigned a separate institutional liaison responsible for overseeing the activities of his or her lab and coordinating those activities with other members of the Laboratory Team.[60] While the institutional liaisons had many other responsibilities within PIP, their work with the labs was their primary responsibility.

Chapter 1 revealed some confusion among the center monitors with regard to the exact nature of their jobs and the rules and regulations that governed the R&D centers. A partial explanation for the confusion among the nearly two dozen center monitors was their subdivision within the Office of Research into four divisions, which had different philosophies about the role of a center monitor. Moreover, the monitors rarely met as a group to discuss common problems and the right interpretation of the rules and regulations governing their grantees. At that time, the OR did not have a handbook for monitors, which might have helped to standardize their responses and practices.

The activities and interpretations of the institutional liaisons' regulations were more coordinated, despite the fact that the individual labs exhibited considerably more diversity among themselves than did the R&D centers. A major reason for the coordination among the institutional liaisons was that all members of the Laboratory Team met for several hours each week to discuss policies and practices. These frequent meetings gave the liaisons an opportunity to obtain advice and discuss their interpretations of the rules and regulations governing the labs. Moreover, END had recently developed an institutional liaison handbook, which was useful for instructing new members of the Laboratory Team and for helping to standardize practices and interpretations (Educational Networks Division 1992).[61]

Like the center monitors, the lab institutional liaisons had considerably diverse backgrounds and experiences. Given the greater range of various activities performed by each of the labs than by each of the R&D centers, the individual liaisons experienced greater difficulty in effectively monitoring their entities than did the center monitors. The Laboratory Team recognized this problem and recommended "a team approach to monitoring the quality and usefulness of the program activity of the laboratories" (Educational Networks Division 1992).

The institutional liaisons varied considerably in their ability to evaluate lab research and development activities. A few were well prepared to assess the research design and statistical procedures used by their labs, but most did not have the training and research experience necessary for that task.[62] Many institutional liaisons had sought assistance from other OERI employees in evaluating some of the research and development work performed as part of the lab's task 3 assignment. In the past, an evaluation unit within END had assisted lab liaisons. Unfortunately, the elimination of this unit caused lab liaisons more difficulty in obtaining assistance in evaluating their labs' research work.

In theory, the R&D centers and labs were administered quite differently, since funding of the former issued from grants or cooperative agreements and funding of the latter came from contracts. Presumably, government contracts could be more closely monitored by the OERI staff than either grants or cooperative agreements, but in practice the reverse appears to have been true. Probably the major explanation for this seeming discrepancy lay in OERI's increasing relinquishment of the labs' governance and direction to their regional boards. As a result, even though OERI has contracts with the labs, many institutional liaisons felt uncertain or ambivalent about their authority over these institutions. Most liaisons appeared to feel less able to direct and guide the activities of their institutions than did their center monitor counterparts.

Most center monitors were able to visit their institutions only once a year, but the lab liaisons were expected to conduct biannual site visits. In addition, the lab directors and some of their employees were more likely to meet with representatives from OERI in Washington than were the center directors and their staffs. The more prevalent physical contact between the labs and OERI staff helped some of the institutional liaisons to become more knowledgeable about certain aspects of their contractors than were their colleagues who monitored the centers.

The lab liaisons examined the budgets submitted by their contractors but did not seem to pay much attention to substantive budget allocations. Both the labs and their institutional liaisons generally ignored the PMIS forms, which provided guidance on spending. While almost all labs did complete the PMIS forms as required by contract, some did so in such a casual and eclectic manner as to render the results suspect for analytic or comparative purposes. Many labs did not sufficiently detail their budgets to permit an analysis of expenditures by individual project. Some of the institutional liaisons did not seem to pay much attention to the information from PMIS in analyzing how their labs were functioning.

Chapter 1 noted the reluctance of center monitors to terminate the funds of individual research projects deemed unworthy and unsalvageable (and to redistribute the funds to projects within the same center or another R&D center). The labs held this same aversion. Institutional liaisons appeared very reluctant to arrest the funding of individual projects within their labs. One reason could have stemmed from the inherent difficulties involved in evaluating the quality of the diverse services provided by these institutions. Most lab directors were not seriously concerned that OERI would stop funding any of their individual projects.

Perhaps the most surprising discovery of this study was the lack of a detailed third-year review of the labs in 1992. The OERI had completed a thorough and careful third-year review of the labs in 1987, including the use of outside teams of experts, which visited those institutions. These reviews had uncovered important weaknesses in some labs and provided OERI with useful information for planning for the 1990 competitions. Indeed, compared to the third-year R&D center reviews for 1987, the 1987 lab reviews were much more systematic and rigorous.[63]

As was revealed in the previous chapter, the Office of Research conducted a thorough and detailed third-year review of the R&D centers in 1992. Part of the impetus for the review of the centers came from OR and part came from Diane Ravitch, the former assistant secretary of OERI, who was anxious to investigate and improve the quality of research being done by the R&D centers. A simultaneous undertaking of a comparable third-year review of the labs would have made sense, especially since several of the labs funded in 1990 did not receive high marks from the original reviewers.

Several explanations lay behind the decision to not subject the labs to a third-year review in 1992. The Office of Grants and Contracts (OGC) of the U.S. Department of Education did not encourage a third-year review because it interpreted the existing contract as a five-year package that could not be renegotiated.[64] Some of the leaders in PIP wondered whether a third-year review might be too expensive if teams of outside reviewers were used as in 1987. Moreover, PIP appeared to have little concern that the quality of the labs' products and services were seriously deficient and in need of closer scrutiny. Perhaps the growing sense that the labs were being guided and monitored more by themselves than by the institutional liaisons militated against the desire for a systematic third-year review of these institutions.[65] Finally, with the energy of the Office of the Assistant Secretary focused on the third-year review of the R&D centers, few paid attention to PIP's decision against a third-year review of the labs.

Whatever the reasons for the decision not to conduct a thorough third-year review, that decision was unfortunate. The uneven quantity and quality of research and development work revealed in this investigation of five labs suggested that a more careful and thorough review of all activities of the ten labs would have proved useful. Moreover, since the National Academy of Sciences' analysis of OERI did not consider in any detail the functioning of the R&D centers or the labs, an OERI-sponsored third-year lab review might have been timely both for the improvement of lab functioning and for lab preparation for the 1995 recompetition.

Given the explicit requirement that the labs conduct self-evaluations of the quality of their service deliverables, the institutional liaisons should have paid closer attention to these efforts. If the labs fully and satisfactorily implemented self-evaluations, much of the quality assurance work of the institutional liaisons would have been done for them. Then the institutional liaisons could have relied more on the labs' own evaluation systems and only periodically checked for effective functioning to guarantee the quality of their work.

Some analysts emphasized further improvement in the quality of lab self-evaluations. Indeed, a few knowledgeable and thoughtful employees of PIP have questioned the focus on the role of the institutional liaisons for enhancing quality of the research and development products; rather, they would rely on use of total quality management (TQM) at the labs to improve and ensure the quality of their research and development work.[66]

Everyone involved in evaluation of lab research and development work agreed that the responsibility for developing and employing appropriate mechanisms for ensuring quality ultimately began with the labs. It was less evident that many, if not most, of the labs would have developed and used a system based upon the TQM principles, especially without active and ongoing prodding by the OERI institutional liaisons. As discussed earlier, the Far West Lab developed and administered an effective self-monitoring system for ensuring the high quality of its products. But most of the other labs investigated in this study did not. Labs had few tangible incentives to devote more of their scarce resources to upgrading their quality of research and development — particularly when improvements usually entailed high additional costs and OERI and their other clients continued to accept the lower-cost and lower-quality R&D products without too much question. For TQM to work effectively, OERI management first must accept the need for such changes and improvements and then be willing to invest the necessary resources for creating and supporting such a culture.[67] Therefore, while OERI should have worked with the labs to improve their self-evaluation systems, the institutional liaisons still would have needed to monitor the quality of the research and development produced by the labs.

Overall, the Laboratory Team in OERI gave the impression that it was composed of some very capable individuals who pursued their responsibilities earnestly and diligently. Moreover, the organization and functioning of the Laboratory Team as a group were exemplary. Yet the ambiguities of the lab-OERI relationship were sufficiently great to prevent the institutional liaisons from exercising the type of leadership and active monitoring needed, given the uneven quality of research and development produced by the labs.

CHAPTER 3

Congressional Oversight of Federal Research and Development Centers and Regional Educational Laboratories

The first two chapters traced the origins and development of the R&D centers and the regional educational laboratories. They examined in considerable detail the quality of the work produced by those institutions in the late 1980s and early 1990s, and they considered some of the factors that fostered or hindered the quality of the work at the centers and labs.

What role did Congress play in overseeing centers and labs from the 1960s to the early 1990s? Congress not only created and funded the centers and labs, but it frequently prescribed their structure and mode of operation. Indeed, persistent congressional intervention on behalf of the centers and labs significantly reduced the ability of the National Institute of Education and its successor, the Office of Educational Research and Improvement, to develop flexible and scientifically sound research and development programs. Moreover, the interplay between center and lab lobbyists and Congress raises questions regarding the role that outside pressure groups play in setting and carrying out educational research and development.

I. Congress and the Centers and Laboratories in the 1960s

As discussed in chapter 1, the U.S. Office of Education established four research and development centers in 1964 under the authority of the Cooperative Research Act of 1954. In an effort to overcome the fragmentation inherent in individual research efforts, the USOE mandated that the R&D centers be large, national institutions, each designed to focus on a specific educational issue.[1]

Large-scale research and development institutions received a further boost when President Lyndon Johnson created an educational task force headed by John Gardner. The Gardner Task Force report did not focus on the R&D centers but emphasized the need for "the establishment of large-scale National Educational Laboratories which would develop and disseminate ideas and programs for improving educational practices throughout the country" (Gardner 1964, 33). The task force report envisioned national educational laboratories functioning in a similar vein to the Atomic Energy Commission and stressed the importance of testing and developing materials and providing teacher training. The report recommended the establishment of one or more experimental schools for each lab, distinguishing them from centers by means of the labs' greater emphasis on development, dissemination, and teacher training.[2]

The centers and labs attracted the attention of Congress through the Elementary and Secondary Education Act of 1965. President Johnson laid out the administration's proposal for ESEA in a message sent to Congress on January 12, 1965. The act dispensed federal aid to publicly funded elementary and secondary schools that served children of low-income families. However, the proposal also provided aid to libraries, helped with the creation of supplementary educational centers and services, and provided assistance to state educational agencies. These latter provisions were intended in part to provide indirect assistance to children in private schools.[3] President Johnson's message to Congress also called for the creation of regional educational laboratories (*Congressional Quarterly* 1966, 1376). Citing National Science Foundation advances in the teaching of the sciences, the president portrayed the regional educational laboratories as a means of providing comparable assistance in other disciplines (ibid.).

Immediately following President Johnson's message to Congress, Congressman Carl D. Perkins (D-KY), chairman of the General Education Subcommittee, introduced the administration's draft of ESEA (H.R. 2362) in the House, while Senator Wayne Morse (D-OR), chairman of the Labor and Public Welfare Education Subcommittee, introduced the bill (S. 370) in the Senate. Extensive but expedient hearings were held in both the House and Senate. Overcoming long-standing opposition to general federal aid for education, the focused, less expansive ESEA bill was enacted in both houses by votes of 263 to 153 and 73 to 18, respectively.[4]

Legislative discussions regarding ESEA focused primarily on the extent and nature of federal funding for private students and fears about increasing federal control of public schools. Relatively little attention was given to Title IV, which authorized the regional educational laboratories. Indeed, most hearing participants either ignored Title IV or alluded to it only perfunctorily in their testimonies, although administration witnesses did mention the relatively small amount of money spent on educational research. Anthony Celebrezze, the secretary of health, education, and welfare, testified that "of the $15.3 billion spent for research and development under Federal funds, $23 million of that is spent by the Office of Education" (U.S. House 1965b, 71). In his section by section analysis of the administration's bill, Francis Keppel, commissioner of education in HEW, reiterated President Johnson's call to expand research, researcher training, and dissemination. Commissioner Keppel also emphasized the importance of the regional educational laboratories and requested $45 million in FY66 for Title IV–specifying that half would be reserved for the construction and support of ten to fifteen regional educational laboratories (99–102).

While most members of Congress and the invited witnesses either praised or ignored the provisions of Title IV, a few Republican representatives and senators did raise objections. Although the minority views in the ESEA House committee report did not oppose federal involvement in research in general, they did question the particular proposals set forth in this bill (U.S. House 1965a, 77). Some senators also objected to the intrusion of federal influence on curriculum matters through Title IV. And a few members in the Senate committee report also lamented the failure to restrict the maximum amount of money provided to an individual researcher (U.S. Senate 1965, 84).

After the passage of the Elementary and Secondary Education Act in 1965 (P.L. 89–10), congressional attention shifted away from the research provisions of that bill. When ESEA was revised and expanded in 1966, the role of the centers and laboratories received relatively little attention in either legislation or debates (*Congressional Quarterly* 1967, 286–97; *Cong. Rec.* 1966, pt. 19, 25328–89, 25527–89).

As discussed in previous chapters, considerable confusion and debate ensued within the USOE on the type and number of centers or laboratories it should create. Although there was a general consensus on the nature of the centers, there was less agreement on the responsibilities of the laboratories. While the Gardner Task Force and recent ESEA legislation envisioned and provided for large-scale national laboratories, USOE staff drifted gradually and erratically toward regional and somewhat more service-oriented institutions. Moreover, the Gardner/ESEA emphasis on a few large, well-financed laboratories gave way to the desire for many regional laboratories scattered throughout the United States. By September 1966, the number of facilities totaled thirty: ten R&D centers and twenty laboratories (Dershimer 1976). The appropriations for FY67 (in current dollars) for the centers was $8.1 million and for the laboratories $19.2 million, and an additional $12.4 million was slated for the construction of centers or laboratories (U.S. House 1967b, 204).

During the 1950s and early 1960s, Congress had exercised little over-sight of federal research operations. This partially reflects its general low involvement in federal agency oversight activities during those years.[5] This lack of oversight also reflects the particular experiences of the House Committee on Education and Labor from which Graham Barden (D-NC), the conservative Democratic chair of that committee during the 1950s, delegated few powers and responsibilities to the subcommittees.[6]

However, the scope and power of the individual subcommittees expanded considerably with the elevation of Adam Clayton Powell Jr. (D-NY) to the chairmanship of the House Committee on Education and Labor in 1960. When Carl D. Perkins replaced Powell as chair of that committee in 1966, the responsibility of the subcommittees to undertake oversight activities was maintained and even expanded (Reeves 1993). For example, Edith Green (D-OR), chair of the Special Subcommittee on Education, conducted an unusually thorough investigation of USOE in 1966. Extensive hearings focusing on different aspects of USOE were held in Washington and seven other cities. In the course of this investiga-tion, the Special Subcommittee on Education analyzed the operations of the Bureau of Research, the agency responsible for administrating the newly established centers and laboratories. In its hearings and final report, the subcommittee raised questions about the development and management of the centers and laboratories (U.S. House 1967b).

The centers received little attention or criticism from the Special Subcommittee on Education. While some questions were raised about the differences between the missions of the centers and laboratories, the members of the subcommittee were generally sympathetic to the orienta-tion and proposed activities of the centers. Since the centers had been created only recently, the Special Subcommittee on Education did not comment on the quality of the work produced by them (U.S. House 1967b, 224).

The Special Subcommittee on Education, and Chairwoman Green in particular, were much less sympathetic, if not outright hostile, toward the laboratories. Much of their animosity stemmed from the subcommit-tee and chairwoman's view of the laboratories as engaged in unnecessary and unfair funding competition with the existing regional educational offices or the state educational departments. Green was particularly critical of the laboratory directors' relatively high salaries since these lucrative packages diminished the ability of the federal and state govern-ments to attract or retain the most qualified individuals for their own educational posts (U.S. House 1967b, 229; 1966, 232–36, 640–43, 948–52, 1031). Members of the Special Subcommittee on Education also questioned the extent of overlap in functions among the laboratories, centers, federal regional educational offices, and state departments of education (U.S. House 1967b, 228–29; 1966, 644–45, 949, 978–79, 1025–29, 1031–34, 1039–40, 1050–51, 1217, 1242–43, 1265, 1272, 1277–79, 1287, 1369). They displayed frustration at the lack of clarity or consistency of the laboratories' mission.[7]

Members of the Special Committee on Education were surprised to discover that some of the directors of the laboratories viewed themselves as completely independent of the USOE (U.S. House 1966, 637). Chairwoman Green challenged the earlier decision to allow the laboratories to function almost independently of USOE (642).[8] The subcommittee recommended in its report that "reporting requirements of the Bureau for laboratories should be reevaluated in terms of the missions and responsibilities to be defined" (U.S. House 1967b, 240). In addition, several members of the Special Subcommittee on Education were both surprised and outraged at the creation of twenty laboratories (U.S. House 1966, 1030).[9]

Congress did not act immediately on the recommendations of the Special Subcommittee on Education, but the questions raised about educational research in general, and the laboratories in particular, continued to trouble some members. Indeed, Green and some of her colleagues on the Special Subcommittee on Education resurrected those concerns when the controversies over the National Institute of Education arose in the early 1970s (Dershimer 1976, 96).

Despite the strong criticism of the nature and number of laboratories by the Special Subcommittee on Education, the Bureau of Research in USOE did not revise its plans. Harold Howe, commissioner of education, continued to defend the twenty laboratories (U.S. House 1967c, 90). Rather than reducing the number of laboratories, the Bureau of Research initially requested an increase in the budget for laboratories and centers from $29.6 million to $86 million for FY68. The Department of Health, Education, and Welfare and the Bureau of the Budget reduced that figure to a more modest $36.1 million (139–41, 544–55). Daniel Flood (D-PA), the new chair of the House Appropriations Committee, was not especially hostile to educational research or the laboratories but was unwilling to expend his own political capital on their behalf as his predecessor had done (Dershimer 1976, 96). In the end, Congress appropriated $34.6 million for the laboratories and centers for FY68 (U.S. House 1968, 700–702).

In response to continued congressional questions about the relevancy of much of the educational research, together with growing concerns among the original proponents of national laboratories, the Bureau of Research attempted to shift the focus of the laboratories toward the systematic development of educational products rather than the provision of services to regional clients. The Bureau of Research also persuaded the Johnson administration to request a substantial 50 percent increase in research funds for FY69 (Dershimer 1976, 86–103).

The timing of the request for increased funds was unfortunately inopportune. Mandated to reduce the federal budget by $6 billion, the House and Senate slashed the education budget dramatically, and the administration's request for increased educational research funding was not immune to this fiscal "belt tightening" (*Congressional Quarterly* 1968, 593–603). During extensive House and Senate floor debates on the cuts, most attention was given to efforts to restore funds to service programs such as Title I of ESEA; almost no discussion addressed the effects of the proposed reduction in the research budget (*Cong. Rec.* 1968, pt. 14, 18876–941, 18559–99; pt. 20, 25797–808, 25910–79). The appropriations for centers and laboratories for FY69 were nearly identical to those of the previous year.

Although it avoided direct criticism of the number of laboratories during congressional FY69 budget debates, the Bureau of Research now acknowledged that its hopes for a major expansion of the educational research budget would not be realized. Therefore, the bureau decided to reduce the total number of laboratories in order to provide adequate funding for those that remained. It reduced the number of laboratories by five in 1969 and by another four the following year (Dershimer 1976, 98–103). Thus, by the end of the 1960s anticipated increases in support for the centers and laboratories had not materialized. The reason was not that Congress found these institutions particularly unsatisfactory but because the overall level of funding for all domestic programs suffered — especially as the costs of the Vietnam War escalated. As a result of these changes, the high hopes and expectations that some envisioned for the centers and laboratories in the mid-1960s all but vanished in practice.

II. Congress and the Centers and Laboratories in the 1970s

Dissatisfaction with the USOE research program increased by the end of the 1960s and led to the reorganization of federal educational research. After Nixon's election to office, he established a working group to reconsider federal educational policy. Daniel Moynihan and his assistant, Chester "Checker" Finn, were asked to review the existing educational R&D programs in USOE, and they concluded that the state of educational research was weak and inadequate. During the election campaign, Nixon had called for the establishment of a National Institute for the Educational Future. After the election, Moynihan had little difficulty in persuading the new administration to sponsor such an institution (Dershimer 1976, 119–30; Sproull, Weiner, and Wolf 1978, 11–35).[10] In his March 3, 1970, message on educational reform, Nixon proposed the establishment of a National Institute of Education (34).

Despite the presidential call for a National Institute of Education, the proposal did not become a top domestic priority for the Nixon administration — in part because its chief White House advocate and architect, Moynihan, soon returned to Harvard University. But plans for the creation of NIE continued within the educational bureaucracy. Although USOE devoted the rest of 1970 to developing preliminary plans for NIE, serious legislation to establish that agency was not introduced in both chambers of Congress until January 1971.

The NIE Bill in the House and Senate

The proposal for NIE met with little enthusiasm in the Ninety-second Congress. Eleven months passed before the Congress even held hearings on the legislation. The Senate included the proposal as part of its Education Amendments of 1971 but did not devote much attention to it in hearings or the final legislation. In the House, the bill was assigned to the Select Subcommittee on Education of the Committee on Education and Labor. Under the energetic and able leadership of John Brademas (D-IN), the subcommittee held eight hearings on NIE between February and June 1971. These provided the most extensive congressional discussion of educational research and development during the entire decade (Brademas 1987, 27–48).

The House Select Subcommittee on Education was not a representative or unbiased forum for the discussion of the operation and utility of educational research. Its members were considerably more liberal than their congressional colleagues. Indeed, both the Democrats and Republicans on that subcommittee were more liberal than their counterparts in each party.[11] Moreover, while the House was more evenly split on the advisability of establishing NIE, the members of this subcommittee voted fourteen to three in its favor. Interestingly, even among some members of this subcommittee, interest in NIE was limited. Few members (39 percent) attended more than one of the eight hearings, and a sizable proportion did not show up for any of them (38 percent). Only the chairman, Brademas, attended all of the hearings.[12]

The Select Subcommittee on Education listened to twenty-two witnesses and received written testimony from another eighteen. Only one of the witnesses, the superintendent of public instruction from Illinois, opposed the establishment of NIE. The other experts, though often raising serious questions about the quantity, quality, or usefulness of existing educational research, all endorsed the creation of NIE. None of the major national educational organizations and scholarly associations testified at those hearings, and there appears to have been little public interest in the proceedings (Sproull, Weiner, and Wolf 1978, 60–71; Timpane 1988). Moreover, several of the representatives as well as some of the witness acknowledged that educational research had little public or congressional support (U.S. House 1971b, 158).

Most hearing participants agreed that the federal government had spent too little money on educational research in comparison with similar expenditures on defense, business, and health. While the administration hinted that programs worth approximately $115 million would be transferred immediately to NIE, most witnesses thought that at least twice that amount would be necessary.[13] Elliot Richardson, secretary of the Department of Health, Education, and Welfare, expected that NIE's budget in FY77 would fall between $310 and $420 million (U.S. House 1971b, 103). Some prominent and knowledgeable analysts, including Hendrick Gideonese and Roger Levien, even argued that by 1980 NIE should have a budget of a billion dollars (329–30).

Present at the hearings was an undercurrent of fear that educational research and specifically NIE would not receive necessary funding increases. Indeed, there was concern that the lack of adequate resources would doom the entire educational research operation (U.S. House 1971b, 37). Witnesses disagreed considerably among themselves regarding the current state of educational research. Some thought that little good research was available for immediate dissemination. Daniel Moynihan, for example, worried less about the dissemination of research findings into the classroom than about the lack of high-quality educational research produced (24). Because of these concerns, Moynihan and the Nixon administration left the dissemination of research findings to the USOE rather than thrusting it upon NIE.

Others maintained that ample educational research already existed but that the findings had not been adequately distributed to classroom teachers (U.S. House 1971b, 40). Throughout the hearings, representatives frequently pointed to the inadequate dissemination system and questioned whether it should indeed be left to USOE as the administration had proposed. Brademas again stated, "One of the reasons, I think, that educational research has had trouble winning support in Congress, is an apprehension on our part that research is done and then sits on a shelf and never gets out into the communities that are the users" (30).

Given the emphasis on the R&D centers and the laboratories in the mid-1960s, it is surprising that they were the object of so little discussion during the hearings. The Select Subcommittee on Education relied heavily on Roger Levien's report, "National Institute of Education: Preliminary Plan for the Proposed Plan," which only briefly addressed the role of the centers and laboratories. In his scheme, Levien did envision the continuation of these institutions (U.S. House 1971b, 588–89). But rather than the centers and labs continuing to depend almost entirely upon federal funds, Levien suggested that they become gradually self-supporting and receive only limited institutional support from NIE. Levien hoped that in the long run most of the center and laboratory funds would be won in direct competition with other research organizations (589).

One of the few witnesses who discussed the role of the R&D centers and laboratories during the NIE hearings, James Gallagher (director of the Frank Porter Graham Child Development Center at the University of North Carolina), concurred with Levien's recommendation:

There was a time where the major argument for educational laboratories was that we needed these major institutions to carry out these big projects. And we did. I think the time is pretty well past for just institutional support. I think what needs to be done is to put the laboratories and R&D centers under a program support basis. If they can develop in those laboratories or R&D centers major programs that are worthy of support, let's support them. But let's not support them merely as institutions (U.S. House 1971b, 41).[14]

Thus, the eight congressional hearings on the establishment of NIE reinforced the idea that the R&D centers and laboratories were no longer expected to play a crucial role in educational research and development as originally envisioned. Federal funding of the centers and laboratories was to be more dependent upon their programmatic usefulness to NIE than upon a policy stipulating institutional support for the R&D centers and laboratories.

In both the Senate and the House, the bill to create NIE was added to the larger Higher Education Act of 1971. The NIE portion of the bill sailed uneventfully through the Senate, but the legislation encountered some difficulties in the House. In discussions on NIE on the House floor, H. R. Gross (D-IA), chair of the House Committee on Post Office and Civil Service, challenged the entire NIE portion of the bill because it dealt with matters of personnel practices — something previously allocated exclusively to Gross's committee. Therefore, Brademas was compelled to reintroduce his NIE bill (minus the offending sections) from the House floor as an amendment to the Higher Education Act.

The Higher Education Act of 1971 was both long and complex; thus, the debate on NIE provisions was necessarily brief. It was, however, more contested than discussions at the earlier hearings. While several members of Congress rose to support the establishment of NIE, two objected. William Scherle (R-IA), a member of the Appropriations Committee, opposed NIE because he believed the agency was wasteful and unnecessary (*Cong. Rec.* 1971, pt. 30, 39274). Edith Green (D-OR), an earlier critic of USOE and the representative shepherding the Higher Education Act through the House, also opposed the creation of NIE. She pointed out that its establishment would be unimportant and that the monies proposed for this institution might be better spent elsewhere (39275).

Since the Nixon administration had recommended the founding of NIE and the proposal received nearly unanimous bipartisan support from the House Select Subcommittee on Education, one might expect that the amendment offered by Brademas would have sailed through the full House without much opposition. But when the question was called on the amendment in the House it barely survived by a shaky 52 to 50 vote. Congressman Ashbrook (R-OH), an opponent of the amendment, demanded a roll-call vote. The amendment to establish NIE was sustained by a more comfortable margin of 210 to 153 (*Cong. Rec.* 1971, pt. 30, 39277).

Because the roll call vote on the establishment of NIE was one of the few occasions when almost all House members went on record for or against the agency,[15] I examined this particular vote in great detail, computerizing and statistically analyzing biographical information about the 435 members of the Ninety-second Congress.[16]

The major statistical procedure I employed is known as multiple regression analysis. Support for or opposition to the creation of NIE on November 4, 1971, was the dependent variable to be explained by the characteristics of the legislator or his or her constituents.[17] Eight independent variables were used to account for the differences in support for NIE: the Americans for Democratic Action (ADA) index of liberal voting behavior in the House in 1971, party affiliation, whether the representative was from the South, the gender of the representative, whether the representative was Catholic, whether the representative was ever a teacher, educator, or served on a local school committee, the age of the representative, and whether the representative was a member of the House Education and Labor Committee. Altogether, information on all of these variables was available for 365 representatives (data were missing on one or more of these variables for 22 of the members).

Overall, 57.8 percent of the representatives taking a public position on this amendment supported the establishment of NIE. The multiple regression analysis using these eight independent variables succeeded rather well in predicting whether a representative supported the creation of NIE. The adjusted R^2 was .3807 — a respectable figure for explaining roll call analysis.

Liberals usually tend to be more supportive of new or expanded federal programs than conservatives. Therefore, it is not surprising that the single best predictor of support for NIE was the index of voting support for Americans for Democratic Action in 1971. Representatives who scored highly on the ADA index were much more likely than others to support the establishment of NIE.

Party affiliation was the second most effective predictor of NIE support. Ordinarily, one might expect Democrats to be more supportive of new federal educational programs than Republicans. In this case, however, the Nixon administration had pushed for the establishment of NIE while many Democrats complained that the Republican emphasis on educational research was intended merely to distract them from the administration's opposition to further federal aid for education. Thus, 54.5 percent of the Democrats supported the NIE legislation while 62.8 percent of the Republicans endorsed it. Even after I controlled for the effects of other independent variables, Republicans were still more likely to have supported the creation of NIE.

There also were large regional differences in support for NIE. Representatives from the southern states were likely to be opposed to the creation of NIE, while those from the New England, Middle Atlantic, East North Central, and Pacific states were much more supportive.[18] After being controlled for the effects of the other variables, statistics indicated that representatives from the South remained unusually hostile to the legislation. This factor was the third most effective indicator of how a representative voted on NIE.

Only ten female representatives served in the Ninety-second Congress. Nevertheless, gender was the fourth most effective predictor of support for NIE. The roll call vote showed that 58.2 percent of the male representatives, compared to only 44.4 percent of the female, favored the creation of NIE.

Since federal support for education usually favored public over parochial private schools, one might expect that Catholic representatives, who comprised more than one-fifth of the House, might be more opposed to another federal education initiative than their Protestant or Jewish counterparts. Interestingly, 64.0 percent of the Catholic representatives supported NIE, compared to only 54.2 percent of the Protestant ones. After the effects of the other variables were controlled for, however, Catholic representatives were less likely to support NIE. This factor, however, was not a strong predictor of the vote outcome.

From the career biographies of the representatives, it was possible to identify a sizable number of individuals who had been teachers or educators or had served on local school committees. As these persons had been previously associated with education, one might have expected them to be particularly supportive of additional federal funding for educational research. In fact, those who had been teachers, educators, or members of local school committees were somewhat more supportive of NIE (62.3 versus 56.9 percent). But after the effects of the other variables were controlled for, these educators were actually less likely to endorse the creation of NIE — although the overall variable was a weak predictor.

Raised in an environment in which the federal government was less active in education than presently, older representatives are sometimes less supportive of new federal initiatives than younger ones. After controlling for the effects of the other factors, I discovered that older representatives were slightly less enthusiastic about NIE than younger ones, but again this was not an important overall predictor of voter behavior.

Finally, membership in the House Education and Labor Committee might have been expected to increase the willingness of a member to support NIE — especially since the legislation received the almost unanimous backing of the House Select Subcommittee on Education. Indeed, 75.0 percent of the members of the House Education and Labor Committee supported the NIE amendment, whereas only 56.1 percent of their noncommittee colleagues endorsed it. Even when the effects of the other variables were controlled for, membership on the House Education and Labor Committee was still predictive of support for NIE but was the weakest predictor of any of the eight independent variables in this analysis.[19]

NIE's Rocky Start

Although the House and Senate had approved the creation of NIE in August and November of 1971, respectively, differences over other aspects of the Higher Education Act stalled the final passage of the legislation until June 1972. On August 1, 1972, NIE was officially created. Responsibility for the R&D centers and laboratories, as well as oversight of most other USOE research activities, was transferred immediately to NIE. Altogether, former programs worth approximately $110 million were moved to NIE in August 1972. In October, both the Senate and House appropriated $110 million for NIE for FY73.

Although many had high hopes for NIE, the agency was devastated by the unwillingness of the appropriations committees, especially in the Senate, to provide adequate funds. For FY74, the administration requested $162 million for NIE but received only $142 million from the House Appropriations Committee and $75 million from the Senate Appropriations Committee. The conference committee's recommendation of $75 million for FY74 prevailed, and NIE was forced to cut back even many existing programs it had inherited. NIE's request for $25 million in supplementary funds for FY74 was summarily dismissed by both the House and Senate appropriations committees.

NIE funding fared no better the following year. The administration requested $130 million from the House Appropriations Subcommittee for FY75 but received a recommendation of only $100 million from the House Appropriations Committee. The full House reduced that already low recommendation to $80 million. The Senate Appropriations Subcommittee recommended $65 million, but the full Senate Appropriations Committee voted zero funds for the agency. After the conference committee reached agreement, Congress appropriated only $70 million for NIE for FY75. Thus, rather than doubling or tripling the initial funding, as many of the organization's advocates originally anticipated, Congress slashed NIE's budget by more than one-third.

The debacle of NIE's early appropriations has been carefully analyzed and amply documented by Lee Sproull and his colleagues and need not be repeated in great detail here (Sproull, Weiner, and Wolf 1978, 72–105). However, certain elements are worth emphasizing since they provide additional insights into the congressional oversight of NIE in general and of the centers and laboratories in particular.

The fiscal well-being of federal agencies during congressional appropriations is sometimes adversely affected by the larger political context in which the agencies are placed. The NIE budget suffered in part because many Democrats were furious that the Nixon administration had proposed sizable cutbacks in most health and education programs but recommended a large increase for NIE in FY74. For example, Sen. Warren Magnuson (D-WA), one of the most ardent and powerful foes of increased NIE funding, attacked the administration's domestic budget proposals (*Cong. Rec.* 1973, pt. 25, 32965).[20]

In addition, NIE suffered because it never became a major domestic priority of the Nixon administration. At the same time, some Republican senators and representatives who had supported the creation of NIE mainly as an administration initiative had second thoughts about the advisability of voting to expand yet another federal educational program. In addition, the unfolding Watergate scandal severely eroded the administration's influence with Congress and distracted the White House's attention from its own domestic initiatives.

Both the Senate and House continued to question the value of educational research, expressing the opinion that the monies could be better spent providing direct support for teachers and students in classrooms.[21] Moreover, many had the perception that educational research grants and contracts were not closely monitored in either NIE or Congress. In sponsoring her successful amendment in the House to reduce FY75 funding for NIE by 20 percent, Congresswoman Green complained that thousands of education grants and contracts had never been completed and many of those that had been finished were never read or used (*Cong. Rec.* 1974, pt. 16, 21677).[22] Others charged that NIE in particular wasted money on extravagant and unnecessary expenditures. Congressman Gross, citing a General Accounting Office (GAO) report, denounced the NIE administration (21675).

Throughout Senate and House appropriations deliberations, NIE was criticized for lacking a coherent and focused research plan.[23] Opponents also voiced the complaint that rather than providing a new and more systematic approach to educational research and development NIE simply continued (or even duplicated) the lackluster work previously done by USOE. As Green charged, "NIE is not one single bit different from the Office of Education except in name" (*Cong. Rec.* 1974, pt. 16, 21677). Perhaps the harshest and most unfair remarks were reserved for Thomas Glennan, the first NIE director. Senator Magnuson berated the incompetence of Glennan while defending the decision of the Senate Appropriations Committee to reduce NIE's funding.[24]

Congressional oversight of educational research in general and the R&D centers and regional laboratories in particular was uneven and erratic in the first half of the 1970s. During one of the House floor debates over NIE funding, several representatives criticized the lack of serious congressional oversight of educational grants and contracts (*Cong. Rec.* 1974, pt. 16, 21676). Albert Quie (R-MN) confirmed that the House Education and Labor Committee had failed to adequately oversee educational programs and Clarence Brown (R-OH) stated that the Government Operations Committee did not oversee educational grants and contracts either (21679).

On a few occasions, the Senate or House appropriations subcommittees considered at greater length particular aspects of educational research policy. For example, the Senate Subcommittee on Appropriations for FY71 and FY72 received testimony from several center and laboratory supporters who wanted Congress to significantly expand the funding for those institutions. These exchanges provide some insights into the portrayal of centers and laboratories before Congress in the early 1970s and are worthy of consideration in more detail.

CEDaR's Lobbying for Center and Laboratory Funding

Funds for the centers and laboratories remained relatively constant in the late 1960s and early 1970s, resulting in the shutdown of several of these institutions in order to provide more funds for those that continued operations. Interestingly, even though the Nixon administration recommended substantial increased monies for educational research, it did not request a substantial funding increase for the centers or laboratories in FY71 or FY72. Consequently, supporters of these institutions mobilized themselves to attempt to persuade Congress to increase funding. For example, in 1970 a representative of the American Education and Research Association (AERA) appeared for the first time before the Senate Subcommittee on Appropriations to request more funding for the centers and laboratories.[25] The following year, James Becker, chair of the newly created Conference for Educational Development and Research, also petitioned for increased funding (U.S. Senate 1971, 123–30).[26] Created in December 1970 to coordinate the activities of the centers and laboratories and to represent their interests, CEDaR was a relatively insignificant and ineffective organization at the time of this petition. When it moved its operation to Washington, DC, in January 1974, the organization, under the continued leadership of Joseph Schneider, quickly became the most effective lobbying group on behalf of educational research and development — in large part because it learned to work effectively with certain key members of Congress. At the same time, NIE failed to impress many legislators and experienced no success in obtaining increased funding.[27]

Proponents of increased funding for the centers and laboratories argued that more monies were needed to develop research products and ideas for use in classrooms (U.S. Senate 1971, 102). While senators and representatives listened patiently and sympathetically to pleas for additional funding for the centers and laboratories, they took no action to increase support for these institutions. Moreover, as congressional attention shifted to the creation and funding of NIE for FY74 and FY75, discussions of the role of the centers and the laboratories faded into the background.

Overall, congressional discussions on educational research and development in the first half of the 1970s were limited and sometimes inaccurate. While the NIE authorization hearings had been quite extensive and informative, most of the center and laboratory oversight hearings were limited in scope and analysis. As Sproull and his colleagues pointed out in their 1978 book, some of the statements made by leading members of Congress, such as Senator Magnuson and Congresswoman Green, indicated considerable confusion and misunderstanding about NIE and educational research (Sproull, Weiner, and Wolf 1978, 72–105). Occasionally members of the Senate Appropriations Committee, such as Mike Mansfield (D-MT) and Magnuson, tried to coerce NIE to fund controversial endeavors such as the Mountain Plains Project.[28] Congressional attempts to earmark NIE funds for specific programs increased in the second half of the 1970s.

Permanent long-term funding of the centers and laboratories was not an initial NIE goal. As demonstrated in the previous two chapters, it attempted in its early stages to implement the "program purchase" policy first proposed by Charles Frye of the USOE staff (NIE 1975, 7). Under the program purchase approach, centers and laboratories were to bid on individual research and development projects rather than expecting a guaranteed amount of funding. The NIE first reviewed the existing center and laboratory contracts and then made a determination on which should receive continuation funding through FY75. Due to the proposed limited increase in NIE's small budget for FY76, the agency planned to shift to the more competitive program purchase plan, expecting overall center and laboratory funding to receive dramatic cuts (13).

During the appropriations hearings, Congress did not devote much time and energy to discussing the proposed reduction in funding for the centers and laboratories; nor did it carefully analyze the wisdom of earmarking funds for these institutions. Rather, Senator Magnuson continued to attack NIE for failing for six months to appoint a new director (U.S. Senate 1975a, 4–27). On the House Appropriations Subcommittee, Congressman Obey (D-WI), questioned NIE's decision to reduce funding for the centers and laboratories (72–75). Robert Michel (R-IL), however, warned of the dangers of earmarking any funds for the centers and laboratories since it would create too much rigidity in the operation of NIE (100).

Once CEDaR realized that its continued funding might be threatened by NIE's hostility to many current centers and laboratories, it decided to protect its clients by persuading Congress to earmark funds for them. In January 1975, CEDaR director Joseph Schneider drafted a detailed action plan designed to protect the centers and laboratories:

A strength of the plan is its flexibility. Thus it's built to respond accordingly. For example, if CEDaR fails to secure a commitment from the administration, then we'll work with the authorizing committees to have language in their bill instruct NIE to fund programmatic r&d. If the House committee fails to do this, then we'll pull out all stops to accomplish it in the Senate committee. If we strike out in both committees, we'll still have the two appropriation committees to work. And if it appears we are failing there, then the CEDaR staff will sharply increase its efforts to secure funding for its members from the other government agencies. (Breedlove 1996, 200)

After the hearings, CEDaR, working together with center and laboratory staff, managed to persuade members of the House and Senate appropriations committees to thwart the planned reduction in institutional funding. Both the House and Senate reports and the language in appropriation bills directed NIE to provide up to $30 million for the centers and laboratories; NIE then promptly complied by allocating $26 million for the centers and laboratories for FY76 (U.S. House 1976a, 950).

As CEDaR became more involved in political activities in Washington, DC, it emphasized the informational nature of its efforts in order to protect itself from charges of lobbying. As Schneider put it:

CEDaR is running a real risk in being identified as a "lobbying" effort. I think it would be a mistake for us to glibly assume that we can appear political without running two real risks: one, a government agency might consider us troublesome; if so, by raising questions about the expenditure of overhead funds for CEDaR support, the agency could threaten our substance. Second, an IRS or government audit of our activities might jeopardize our continued existence. The way around this problem, I believe, is to make our communication efforts as legitimate as possible. And this is done simply by preparing print documents that have an "informational" slant of interest to an educational audience. Our defense, then, can be that although we share these documents with members of Congress, they are actually intended for an audience of individuals concerned with educational research and development. Also, our oral presentations before Congress and other groups can be explained as being necessary to support the printed documents. (Breedlove 1996, 198)

Although critics of CEDaR continued to point to its political lobbying, the organization managed to avoid challenges to its nonprofit status
from the Internal Revenue Service (IRS) or some other government
agency.

Its success in appealing directly to Congress for center and laboratory funding prompted CEDaR to use this approach repeatedly — even
though the process necessitated the portrayal of NIE as an incompetent
agency and thereby undermined its overall support on Capital Hill.
Thomas Carroll, former chief of program planning and policy at NIE,
later viewed this initial battle with CEDaR as a watershed event:

> This battle with CEDaR marked a watershed for NIE. The laborato-
> ries and centers, which were NIE contractors and grantees, had be-
> come major competitors with NIE for federal research funds. NIE
> and CEDaR were locked in an annual cycle of conflict over appro-
> priations. In this cycle CEDaR used the same strategy every year.
> First, it portrayed NIE, or its director, as inept or a threat to the
> programs of the laboratories and centers. Second, it went to the
> Appropriations Committees with a message that if Congress did not
> protect the laboratory and center budget, the federal government
> would lose a significant investment in educational research and devel-
> opment. Congress would then "earmark" or set aside approximately
> $30 million a year for the laboratories and centers. (1988, 45)

NIE's Reauthorization of 1975

The NIE was scheduled for reauthorization in 1975. In preparation for
this process, NIE commissioned a three-month study by a panel of ten
experts on the centers and laboratories. The panel, headed by Roald
Campbell, rejected "the earlier U.S. Office of Education notion of supporting independent institutions which set their own agenda, or the
current NIE concept of purchasing discrete products from an undifferen-
tiated set of institutions" (Campbell et al. 1975, 27). Instead, it called for
a long-term, stable relationship with a much smaller but better-funded
set of national (not regional) laboratories and centers.

The Campbell report also offered interesting and candid observations about the increasing role of Congress and CEDaR in micro-
managing NIE. It identified CEDaR as the single most influential and
active political voice in Congress on behalf of the centers and laboratories.[29] The panel also criticized recent efforts of some members of Congress to control NIE activities. The Campbell report called for more
flexible NIE funding and observed that "as confidence in the agency

diminished, report language has begun to give direction to NIE, culminating in the present deliberations over the 1976 budget, where close to one half the budget was earmarked by the House, as the price of granting the modest $80 million budget requested." Moreover, the panel noted that "some individual Members give strong hints about their interest in seeing certain projects continued, independent of their potential for research" (Campbell et al. 1975, 36, 37). The panel also found that NIE was being blamed by some in Congress for intrusion by CEDaR and expected the agency to come to terms with these lobbyists.[30]

According to Campbell and his associates, Congress's constant criticisms of NIE and congressional unwillingness to provide adequate funding made the agency less willing to fight for its own interests in the face of concerted political opposition. As the report states, "this history of criticism and pressure on the budget by Congress had a severe impact on the agency and has led to reducing the political risks taken at every possible point" (Campbell et al. 1975, 37).

During the House and Senate NIE reauthorization hearings in 1975, witnesses revisited major issues with regard to the centers and laboratories. The Senate Subcommittee on Education held only one day of hearings on NIE with only Senators Claiborne Pell (D-RI) and Jacob Javits (R-NY) in attendance (U.S. Senate 1975b). The House Subcommittee on Education, on the other hand, held six days of hearings and heard from a sizable number of witnesses and representatives (U.S. House 1976b).

Overall, the administration's bill for the reauthorization of NIE introduced only a few changes. Accepting the recommendations of NIE, the legislation established five priority areas for the agency (U.S. House 1976b, 1). While most witnesses at the hearings endorsed the five priorities in principle, some questioned the wisdom of enacting them into the legislation since it might prevent NIE from responding quickly to new, promising areas of research and development. The administration, however, chose to designate priorities in the legislation so that Congress would become a full partner in the future direction of NIE (1310).

John Corbally, chair of NIE's National Council on Educational Research, and Claiborne Pell, chair of the Senate Subcommittee on Education, exchanged interesting and revealing remarks on who should direct the activities of NIE. When Corbally complained about the high percentage of NIE funds earmarked by Congress, Pell quickly responded, "I think basically the Congress is supposed to set the policy and your job is to implement it as effectively as possible and give your advice to the Secretary and to the Director as to how he should implement that policy." When Corbally continued to disagree, Pell referred him to the legislation, which he claimed stated that "the intent of Congress is to set policy guidelines whether broad or narrow." A few moments later, after consulting the existing NIE legislation, Pell apologized: "Dr. Corbally, you were right in that the law says that the Council which you chair shall establish general policies for and review the conduct of the Institute. You were correct in that. I may have over-expressed my thoughts" (U.S. Senate 1975b, 1148, 1150). Thus, even the chair of the Senate subcommittee overseeing NIE had not realized the extent of independence and autonomy lawfully accorded the agency.

The hearings contained considerable debate over the role of the centers and laboratories. Most of the witnesses envisioned an important role for them but often recommended large, nationally oriented institutions (U.S. House 1976b, 110). Richard Rossmiller, chair of CEDaR, wholeheartedly endorsed the continuation of the centers and laboratories. He agreed that management of them could be improved but took strong exception to the recommendations of the Campbell report, which called for fewer, nationally oriented institutions placed under the direct guidance of NIE (110). However, some individuals, such as Thomas Glennan, the former director of NIE, questioned continued, guaranteed funding for current centers and laboratories (78).

In the same vein, several witnesses endorsed the program purchase approach, which provided some base funding for the centers and laboratories but expected them to compete with other research organizations for the funding of specific projects. James Gallagher, director of the Frank Porter Graham Child Development Center at the University of North Carolina, testified, "But one should not automatically give these institutions program money just because they are there as research and development centers. If they are quality organizations they should be able to compete well for funds, once this basic support money is available to them to insure the stability and continuance of the organization itself" (U.S. House 1976b, 79). Roger Levien, who had been instrumental in the initial design of NIE, stated, "There should not be a large portion of the R&D budget set aside just for labs and centers, but only a smaller part as base support money; the other parts should come from the programs" (79).

Congressional earmarking of funds for the centers and laboratories evoked considerable disagreement. A few individuals defended the practice, which they saw as necessary to protect the existing federal investments in the centers and laboratories. Rossmiller, chair of CEDaR, acknowledged some improvements in the relationships between NIE and the centers and laboratories but wanted Congress to continue protecting these institutions legislatively (U.S. House 1976b, 115). Most other witnesses, however, deplored the idea of congressional earmarking and wanted NIE to retain more flexibility in carrying out its agenda (90–91).

Senator Pell also expressed concern about the quality of the evaluations of federal educational programs. Citing a constituent complaint, he attacked the government for relying heavily on in-house evaluations or using only reviewers who proved to be uncritical of the programs they assessed. While Virginia Trotter, the assistant secretary for education, countered these accusations, Pell was unsatisfied and wrote into the 1975 legislation a requirement that a permanent outside panel of experts monitor the work of the centers and laboratories (U.S. Senate 1975b, 1142–47).

The administration requested only an annual appropriation of $80 million for NIE for the next three years. Almost all of the witnesses indicated that this figure was too modest and urged Congress to appropriate a larger amount. The final bill signed into law on October 12, 1976, authorized $100 million for FY77, $200 million for FY78, and $200 million for FY79 (NIE 1977, 2).

The Senate bill included a 25 percent earmark of NIE funds for the centers and laboratories and strongly endorsed the operation of these institutions (U.S. Senate 1976, 107). Ignoring the recommendations of the Campbell panel and accepting the arguments put forth by CEDaR, the Senate called for a regional orientation for laboratories and recommended the creation of additional ones to service other regions (ibid.).

The Senate report required that a panel review proposals submitted to NIE for funding, oversee center and laboratory activities, and submit an annual report to NIE and Congress. The report further obliged the NIE director to provide the overseeing panel with its own staff and to put in writing any agency disagreements with the panel (U.S. Senate 1976, 108).

The House version of the bill did not earmark funds for the centers and laboratories, nor did it call for the establishment of a panel to monitor center and laboratory activities. Nevertheless, the House report endorsed these institutions and stressed the need for a regional distribution of the laboratories (U.S. House 1976c, 79).

The conference committee eliminated the 25 percent earmark and agreed that NIE was to retain control of the quality of products of the centers and the laboratories; it also reaffirmed congressional support for these institutions. The committee provided for the establishment of a Panel for the Review of Laboratory and Center Operation to examine the center and laboratory long-range plans. The panel mandate was limited to January 1, 1979, when its final report was due (NIE 1977, 3–6).

During the Senate discussion of the conference report, Jacob Javits expressed support for the elimination of the earmarking: "I am pleased that the ill-advised set-aside of funds within NIE has been dropped by the conferees" (*Cong. Rec.* 1976, 122, pt. 26, 33447). In House discussions, Carl Perkins, the chair of the conference committee, continued to express his doubts about NIE and hoped that it would work together with teachers and local administrators (33640).

NIE may have reached the nadir of its existence by the mid-1970s. Although it was reauthorized in 1975, congressional skepticism about the value and effectiveness of the agency remained. Reauthorization hearings revealed that Congress had little confidence in NIE's past leadership and questioned the usefulness of the research and development produced to date. Research funding for FY75, FY76, and FY77 remained stuck at around $70 million—well short of the recommendations made at NIE's inception (and only about one-half of its funding for FY73). While the final reauthorization legislation did not include set-aside funding language for the centers and laboratories, it was clear that Congress intended to preserve these institutions even if this required seriously reducing NIE's ability to reallocate its limited resources. Moreover, the appropriations committees continued to earmark funds for the centers and laboratories even though the authorizing committees rejected this approach.

NIE's Improved Situation

The second half of the 1970s witnessed several significant improvements in NIE's situation: (1) new and effective NIE directors; (2) reorganization and the development of stable, long-term planning; (3) receipt of modest congressional praise for the agency; (4) increased funding; and (5) improved relationships with the centers and laboratories. Although some tensions continued between NIE and Congress and some additional questions about the role of the centers and laboratories were raised, on the whole NIE began to make a modest but visible recovery from the large-scale devastations of the early and mid-1970s.

Overall, Congress had been unimpressed with the leadership of NIE during the early 1970s. Thomas Glennan Jr., director of NIE from November 1972 to November 1974, antagonized several key members of Congress and never fully regained the confidence of either the House or the Senate. Glennan's replacement, Harold Hodgkinson, assumed the directorship of NIE in June 1975 and fared much better than his predecessor. He reestablished positive lines of communication with Congress and won the support of some key members. President Gerald Ford's 1976 defeat led to Hodgkinson's forced retirement, but he was succeeded by another energetic and skillful director, Patricia Graham. Although Graham had spent most of her career in academia, she proved to be a resourceful and talented NIE director who won the respect and support of key congressional leaders. Unfortunately for NIE, she returned to her post at the Harvard School of Education after two years of service but was replaced by her capable deputy, Michael Timpane (who remained acting director of NIE through the reauthorization of the agency in 1980).[31] Although NIE suffered from a relatively rapid turnover in directors during the second half of the 1970s, the high caliber of that leadership was more effective in its dealings with Congress.

The agency experienced at least four reorganizations between August 1972 and November 1974. Sproul and his colleagues noted that "special powers are associated with the idea of reorganization. NIE top management repeatedly employed it to solve major problems even though there was no evidence that it helped in previous difficulties" (Sproull, Weiner, and Wolf 1978, 160). The numerous reorganizations produced serious, unintended consequences for the agency: "Instead of reassuring outside observers, the repeated reorganizations created the impression of instability and lack of direction" (161). As the agency stabilized and set down roots in the mid-1970s, it found less need for periodic reorganization.

Upon Graham's arrival in the spring of 1977, however, NIE was suffering from a public image of a disorganized federal agency lacking rigorous standards. Therefore, she undertook a major reorganization that simplified the administrative structure and related the agency more directly to the five major themes mandated by Congress. She created a new structure for research and development programs: (1) a program for educational policy and organization; (2) a program for teaching and learning; and (3) a program for dissemination and the improvement of practice (NIE 1978). Although the question remains as to whether the time and energy devoted to the reorganization was worth the result, some outsiders applauded the new centralized focus of NIE and a few praised the increased attention to basic research attributed partially to the reorganization. There is little direct evidence that members of Congress and their staffs were particularly enthralled by the reorganization effort, which they viewed mainly as an internal NIE affair. But perhaps the ability and willingness of Graham to make such a decisive change contributed in some degree to her favorable image among policymakers on Capitol Hill.[32]

Congress probably was more impressed by the quality of two congressionally mandated studies on "Title I" and "Safe Schools," completed in 1977, in which the conferees on H.R. 15, the Education

Amendments of 1978 (P.L. 95–561), acknowledged the contribution of NIE (U.S. House 1980b, 43). The success of these studies led to additional mandated policy assignments on school finance, adult education, and community education, helping to make NIE more useful to its congressional oversight committees.

The first increase in funding for NIE since its founding was an important index of Congress's changing view of the agency. Appropriations for NIE rose dramatically from $70.4 million in FY77 to $90.1 million in FY78—a sizable 28.0 percent increase (followed by a more modest 3.9 percent increase the following year and a 2.6 percent decrease for FY80 as the Carter administration and Congress tried to reduce overall federal expenditures) (U.S. House 1980b, 53). At the same time, however, the increase must be viewed from a broader political perspective. The appropriations for FY80 were still 36.1 percent less than NIE had received for FY73. Moreover, given the high rate of inflation during the 1970s, NIE's funding in real dollars for FY80 remained 27.9 percent less than even in FY74 (the disastrous year when its budget was cut by 47.0 percent). Thus, while Congress did reverse its long-standing antipathy toward NIE in the second half of the 1970s, its increased appropriations did not return the agency to the funding level of the early 1970s.

The 1980 reauthorization legislation contained one promising indication of the potential for increased financial support for NIE: the nearly successful effort to set aside a certain percentage of federal education dollars for research. Several educational organizations exerted a concerted and coordinated effort to legislatively mandate that NIE receive a small proportion of federal funds (U.S. House 1980b, 52). In a historic shift in funding policy, the Senate endorsed a set-aside of .75 percent for NIE funding for FY81 and up to 1.5 percent for FY85. The House, however, disagreed. Nevertheless, the conference committee did authorize $125 million for FY81 and $215 million by FY85—a substantial increase in support for NIE, testimony of the growing confidence Congress vested in that agency (U.S. House 1980a, 204).

During the second half of the 1970s, thanks in large part to the new and effective activism on the part of CEDaR, Congress became more prescriptive and protective of the labs and centers. While the Senate's explicit earmarking of funds for the centers and labs was omitted from NIE's reauthorization in 1976, the legislation clearly indicated that NIE should protect and nurture these institutions. At the prodding of CEDaR, Congress stated that the labs should remain regional entities and mandated the creation of a panel to review their status and activities (Breedlove 1996, 153–218).

Bowing to the growing political pressure from CEDaR, NIE began to negotiate directly with that organization in 1976 on matters relating to the labs and centers. Although federal funding agencies rarely enter into formal agreements with lobbying groups, NIE signed memorandums of agreement between itself and CEDaR in April and October 1976. The October memorandum detailed FY78 funding for the labs and centers contingent upon the amount of monies received from Congress.[33] It also committed NIE to guidelines for soliciting three-to-five-year plans from the labs and centers as well as details regarding the panel founded to review lab and center operations.[34] These highly unusual memorandums of agreement signaled that NIE, under strong pressure from a few members of Congress, had implicitly abdicated some of its power and authority to CEDaR.

The National Council on Education Research, NIE's appointed policy board, tried to fit NIE's increasingly limited options on lab and center policy within the larger strategy of supporting high-quality research and development institutions. The NCER viewed support for the labs and centers as an important, but not exclusive, component of an effort to encourage research institutions and agencies to contribute to NCER's programmatic objectives. These objectives were enunciated in its recently amended Resolution 18, which explained council policy on educational research institutions (Riles 1973).

Dissatisfied with this broader approach, CEDaR was concerned that it might be used to fund other institutions and supplant the work of the current labs and centers. As feared, NIE drew upon the recommendations of NCER and mailed a policy paper, "Solicitation for 3–5 Year Plans from the Labs and Centers," as a general announcement to interested parties. CEDaR persuaded five prominent senators concerned with protecting current labs and centers to draft a strong letter repudiating NIE's overall strategy toward educational research institutions (Randolph et al. 1977, 2).[35]

Harold Hodgkinson, laboring under heavy political pressure from influential members both of Congress and CEDaR, did all he could to accommodate the labs and centers. In an interesting and unusual memo, he admonished the NIE staff not to display any hostility toward the labs and centers.[36] Again responding to intense political pressure, NIE withdrew its original solicitation for three-to-five-year plans from the centers and labs. On March 25, 1977, it issued a new set of instructions for the official solicitation of long-range plans from the labs and centers. These new guidelines proved more acceptable to the concerned members of Congress and to CEDaR and helped to pave the way for an amicable relationship with the labs and centers.

Not everyone was pleased with the direction and nature of the growing accommodation between NIE and the labs and centers. John Corbally, chair of NCER, responded to the five senators who had drafted the original letter to NIE, stating that the council disagreed with the opinions set forth in their letter and reminding them that Congress had created NCER to set the policies of NIE. Moreover, Corbally criticized the NIE staff for rewriting the three-to-five-year solicitation plans in response to outside pressures. Nevertheless, given the fait accompli of the arrangement between NIE and the labs and centers, NCER reluctantly endorsed Hodgkinson's actions but warned that NIE should not enter into any long-term, special relationships with the labs and centers without adequate attention to the quality of work they produced (Corbally 1977). In a surprisingly candid and harsh public criticism of NIE, the NCER committee reviewing the lab and center activities challenged Hodgkinson's premature assurances to the labs and centers of their special status. Moreover, "in its dealings with the labs and centers, the Committee feels that the Institute is not paying sufficient attention to considerations of quality and relevance, which the Committee believes to be at least equal in importance to considerations of institutional stability and political comity" (ibid., 6).

The council was frustrated by the increasing political pressures from Congress and CEDaR to protect the labs and centers regardless of the quality of work they produced. They also resented the lack of consideration and equal treatment accorded to alternative sources of educational research and development in the awarding of a large proportion of NIE grants and contracts. In an angry discourse on proper federal procurement practices, the council's review committee reminded NIE and Congress:

> A principal test of quality and merit, however, must be a comparison with other potential awardees. This is true of all Federal agencies engaged in fields where absolute tests are not available. It is not clear that this emphasis on quality, merits and comparative judgment is being adequately emphasized in the NIE review process. Too often, when considering labs and centers in relation to other R&D organizations, the Institute finds itself in the posture of having to prove that a lab or center is incompetent or mediocre in order to shift funding from previously-established patterns. This extraordinary presumption runs counter to standard procurement standards and to the will of Congress as expressed in numerous statues governing NIE and other Federal agencies. It runs counter to the goal of

obtaining the best and most economical work for public funds. (Corbally 1977, 7)

The congressionally mandated Panel for the Review of Educational Laboratories and Center Operations was created in September 1977. Compared to most other NIE expert panels, this was composed of a larger proportion of teachers and educators than researchers. Moreover, the process by which panel members were selected ensured that the panel would be particularly sympathetic to the current labs and centers and to the broader concerns raised by CEDaR.

The new panel's first assignment was to review the long-range plans for the labs and centers and to provide recommendations to NIE for negotiating with selected institutions for a longer, more permanent tenure. Given its limited mandate of four months, the panel had to act quickly. Ignoring NCER's repeated pleas to consider the quality of lab and center work, the panel focused instead on the nature of the general, long-term plans submitted by each institution.[37] Despite the limited time frame in which it examined these institutions and its inability to consider questions of quality or even conduct site visits, the panel recommended that NIE enter into special, long-term relationships with fifteen of the seventeen labs and centers (Panel for the Review of Laboratory and Center Operations 1978, 1).

The panel continued its work for a year past its four-month mandate and used more opportunities to analyze operations of current labs and centers. It submitted its final report to Congress in January 1979 and strongly endorsed the concept of regional educational laboratories and research and development centers. Unlike some previous critics, the panel characterized these institutions as "a vigorous set of research and development institutions doing work of quality and significance for American education" (Panel for the Review of Laboratory and Center Operations 1979, iv). At the urging of CEDaR and the recent recommendations of Congress, the panel suggested that the labs shift their focus from national to regional tasks and the control of their activities from Washington to the local region (35).

The panel recommended that NIE establish long-term agreements with seven of the eight labs and seven of the nine centers and provide the remaining three with assistance designed to help them prepare for such a relationship (Panel for the Review of Laboratory and Center Operations 1979, 13). The panel endorsed the idea of five-year agreements with the centers and labs, recommending that the work of these institutions be rigorously reviewed in the third year. Those judged as proceeding successfully would be granted another five-year extension, while those deemed unsatisfactory would receive two years in which to correct any deficiencies (vi–vii). Thus, the panel endorsed in essence the indefinite continuation of fourteen of the seventeen current labs and centers while making provision for the periodic review of their performance.

Based on both the panel's report and its own deliberations, NIE issued its "Long-Term Special Institutional Agreements with the Seventeen Existing Laboratories and Centers" in January 1979. This document repeated and enacted most of the recommendations of the panel. Labs were to be regionally oriented and governed. Centers were to respond to national research and development needs as identified by the field and NIE. Funding for these institutions was set for five years, and the work of each lab and center would be rigorously reviewed at the end of the third year (NIE 1979, 6).

Thus, after considerable struggle and negotiation, NIE, CEDaR, and Congress had reached a relatively amicable understanding on the long-term prospects for the current labs and centers. Although not everyone at the NIE congressional reauthorization hearings in 1980 agreed with the new directions, remarkably little discussion or controversy about the labs and centers ensued.[38] Participants raised a few questions about the propriety of using NIE funds to finance lobbying efforts such as those undertaken by CEDaR.[39] Perhaps the only major attack on the labs and centers was the revelation of financial wrongdoings and questionable practices at CEMREL, one of the eight regional educational laboratories. These disclosures placed everyone involved in the embarrassing position of explaining why the panel and NIE had recommended a long-term agreement with this institution with no awareness of the problems that surfaced afterward.[40] Despite these isolated difficulties, the overall picture was one of relative tranquility and harmony between the Congress and NIE with regard to the labs and centers.

III. The Reagan Revolution and the Labs and Centers

Ronald Reagan's landslide election and the unexpected Republican capture of the Senate dramatically altered the Washington scene in 1980. The new administration moved quickly to curtail federal domestic spending, replace categorical federal programs with state block grants, and deregulate federal policies governing state and local behavior. While the Republicans were unable to achieve many of their specific objectives, their overall success in slowing federal expenditure increases forced the government to reconsider existing priorities.

The new Reagan administration felt little sympathy for the newly created Department of Education, widely regarded as President Carter's political reward to the National Education Association. The administration sought to consolidate most federal educational programs into a few block grants and halt federal spending increases for schooling. Though ultimately thwarted in much of its education agenda, the Reagan administration did manage to contain educational appropriations during its first term. Congressional appropriations for the Department of Education rose from $13.9 billion in FY80 to $15.3 billion in FY84, a 10.1 percent increase. But in real dollars federal expenditures during that period dropped by 14.4 percent (Verstegen 1990).

Budget Cuts in NIE

The scramble to secure scarce dollars intensified during the early Reagan years, and NIE fared poorly in comparison with almost all other programs in the Department of Education. Even those members of Congress who supported NIE were unwilling to fight for research and development funds at the expense of service programs. For example, during the negotiations over the proposed budget cuts in Congress, NIE proponent Sen. Robert Stafford (R-VT) indicated that he was prepared to eliminate small, nonessential agencies like NIE if service programs like Title I could be spared (Zodhiates 1988, 41). As a result of such attitudes, while overall the Department of Education allocations fell by 11 percent in real dollars between FY81 and FY88, NIE lost 70 percent of its funding during that same period. Special Programs was the only unit in the Department of Education that lost more than NIE (Verstegen and Clark 1988).

Some programs in the Department of Education experienced only modest overall budget reductions, but the NIE research budget was hit immediately and continued to decrease during the course of the Reagan administration. Funds were reduced by 14.9 percent from FY80 to FY81 and slashed another 18.6 percent the following year. After a modest improvement of 4.1 percent in FY83, the agency received another 13.3 percent cut in FY84. Overall, NIE lost 37.5 percent of its funding from FY80 to FY84 (50.6 percent in real dollars), a devastating reduction for an agency that had only just begun to recover from the precipitous funding declines of the early 1970s.

The Omnibus Reconciliation Act of 1981, the legislation mandating budget cuts, usually offered federal agencies flexibility in carrying out their reductions, and NIE was allowed to reduce its budgets proportionately. In an additional effort to provide the most efficient and effective services with diminished funds, Congress stipulated that labs and centers "upon completion of existing contracts, receive funding in accordance with government-wide competitive bidding procedures and in accordance with principles of peer review involving scholars and State and local educators to ensure the quality and relevance of the work proposed" (U.S. House 1981, 729).

Faced with the huge reduction in funding, NIE proposed to cut lab and center funding proportionately. But CEDaR again managed to thwart the agency, lobbying successfully for the Continuing Resolution Appropriation, which mandated that lab and center funding be cut by no more than 10 percent. The net result of CEDaR's lobbying was a near halt in the early 1980s in NIE funding for most activities other than the labs and centers.

The Government Accounting Office (GAO) examined the extent and nature of the budget cuts in NIE and documented the devastation of federally sponsored education research resulting from the combination of overall budget cuts and congressional protection of the labs and centers. The number of NIE awards to grant applicants plummeted from 476 in FY80 to 122 in FY84 but increased slightly to 168 in 1985, comprising a 64.7 percent decrease in awards from FY80 to FY85 (U.S. GAO 1987, 21).

Not all program areas within NIE were equally affected by the budget cuts. From FY80 to FY85, labs and centers remained relatively stable but awards of teaching and learning grants dropped from 185 in FY80 to 85 in FY85. Unsolicited proposals (e.g., field-initiated individual grants) collapsed from 58 awards in FY80 to none in FY84 and FY85. Similarly, awards for educational policy and organization dropped from 93 to 15.[41]

During periods of severe budget cuts, local administrators are often given considerable leeway in reallocating available funds, since they best understand overall priorities and resources of their agencies. But congressional mandates protecting the labs and centers as well as continued support for legislatively mandated programs such as the Educational Resources Information Centers and the National Assessment of Educational Progress severely eroded NIE's flexibility. While approximately 55 percent of NIE's FY80 research obligations were mandated, that figure had risen to 79 percent by FY84 (U.S. GAO 1987, 76).

At the same time that Congress cut NIE's budget and mandated more of NIE's activities, the agency itself tried to respond to critics by devoting greater attention to dissemination. The percentage of awards for dissemination rose from 22 percent in FY80 to 43 percent in FY85 (excluding lab or center work). Dissemination activities during those years rose from 29 to 41 percent at the labs and from 12 percent in FY80 to 21 percent in FY84 at the centers (U.S. GAO 1987, 25–27). Thus, the amount of NIE-funded research and development may have reached an all-time low during the first half of the 1980s.

Political Turmoil at NIE

Budgetary cuts were not the only challenge NIE and Congress faced during the early 1980s. The election of President Reagan and a Republican Senate brought new leaders to the Department of Education and NIE who disagreed with both past agency policies and one another. Many implicit assumptions about education and NIE's role in educational research and development, unchallenged during the 1970s, were now discussed and contested. The resulting political and ideological turmoil created the impression that NIE was becoming even more politicized than it had been, contributing to growing hostility toward the agency even among many of its former congressional and educational supporters.

The Reagan administration, hostile to the newly established Department of Education, tried unsuccessfully to abolish it. As secretary for the department, however, they chose Terrel Bell, a moderate Republican who had served as commissioner of education under the Nixon administration. Bell, a member of NCER (NIE's policy board) in the 1970s, was sympathetic to a federal role in educational research and development and played a key role in saving that agency from elimination during the early 1980s' budget cuts.[42] He also provided NIE with a brief respite from mounting internal political and ideological battles by designating Milton Goldberg, an effective and likable career NIE employee, as its acting director.[43]

Edward Curran, former headmaster of the National Cathedral School (a prestigious private school for girls in Washington, DC), assumed the directorship of NIE in October 1981. Active during the 1980 presidential campaign, Curran had strong White House connections. Curran, appointed over the objections of Secretary Bell, tried to reorient NIE toward a more conservative agenda. He and his allies regarded NIE as a narrow, ideological bastion of social science that had politicized research by using the agency to further a liberal agenda emphasizing educational equity at the expense of excellence. Not recognizing their own political motives, Curran and his assistant, Lawrence Uzzell, viewed themselves as trying to correct the mistakes of the past. Moreover, while they provided leadership for NIE during the early 1980s, they endeavored to abolish the agency as well as the whole Department of Education.

Isolating himself from most of the educational community as well as from the existing NIE staff, Curran refused to reappoint most excepted service employees whose terms were expiring, seeking instead to replace them with Reagan loyalists who did not share the social science bias of their predecessors. The agency had always experienced rapid staff turn-overs, but the situation became even worse during the early Reagan years. Due to the dramatic budget cuts, the total number of NIE professionals dropped considerably during these years. The total number of excepted service employees declined from 91 in FY79 to 39 in FY86 (a 57.1 percent decrease); the total number of civil service employees dropped from 191 in FY80 to 161 in FY86 (a 15.7 percent decrease). Of the 91 NIE excepted service professionals in May 1979, only six remained in the agency in 1986 (6.6 percent of the original staff); of the 191 NIE civil service professionals serving in September 1980, only 47 were at their posts in 1986 (24.6 percent of the original staff) (U.S. GAO 1987, 81–83). Thus, during the period of severe budgetary reductions, the professional staff of NIE was cut by nearly half; only about one-fourth of the professional staff in FY86 had been with NIE prior to Curran's appointment.

Curran as well his successor, Robert Sweet Jr., repeatedly clashed with the educational establishment, Congress, and Secretary Bell. Indeed, these directors were accused of politicizing NIE by changing research topics to reflect a right-wing agenda, ignoring the peer review system, firing NIE professionals, hiring unqualified employees previously active in Republican politics, and ignoring congressional mandates. A useful summary of Curran's views on education and research can be found in his unauthorized May 1982 letter to President Reagan calling for the abolition of NIE. Curran presented four major reasons for abolishing his own agency:

> (1) Research on education would continue without Federal funding through thousands of university departments, private foundations, scholarly journals, and other institutions which flourished before NIE was born. . . .
>
> (2) NIE is based on the premise that education is a science, whose progress depends on systematic "research and development." As a professional educator, I know that this premise is false.
>
> Education does not begin to have the conceptual rigor and compelling explanatory power of a genuine science. Its most fundamental questions are inescapably value-laden, and I would assert that federal agencies should not be in the business of formulating values. . . .
>
> (3) This agency wastes money. . . . Obviously, I intend to use my authority as Director to eliminate wasteful projects wherever I can.

At present, however, more than half of NIEs budget lies outside my direct control and in the hands of seventeen "labs and centers" located in various sections of the country. These institutions are curious hybrids of public and private sectors which in many ways combine the worst of both worlds: they are shielded not only from free-market competition, but also from accountability to elected officials. Their lobbying has succeeded to the point where Congress treats them like so many dams and bridges — public-works projects which receive favored treatment as long as they provide employment back home. . . .

(4) All government agencies are subject to political pressures, but the pressures on NIE seem to work overwhelmingly in only one direction: toward the left.

Under President Carter, NIE produced and marketed a television series explicitly designed to change children's values about traditional sex roles. NIE's studies on desegregation have historically been heavily tilted toward the pro-busing and pro-reverse discrimination camp, both in the choice of scholars to subsidize and in the conclusions those scholars have reached. (quoted in Zodhiates 1988, 101–4)

Prophetically, Curran closed his letter to President Reagan with an implicit indication that he might be fired soon.[44]

Secretary Bell, long in search of an excuse to eliminate Curran, fired him for insubordination since the letter to President Reagan had not been cleared through the Department of Education. Robert Sweet Jr., the deputy director of NIE and another conservative, was appointed acting director. Although Sweet endorsed the continued existence of NIE, he continued many of Curran's practices and incurred the wrath of special interest educational groups, the media, and some prominent members of Congress. Only when Manuel Justiz, an assistant professor of education from New Mexico and a Cuban immigrant active in Republican politics, was appointed director by Secretary Bell in August 1982 did the NIE begin to recover from its chronic ideological and political battles with former supporters of NIE.[45]

Educational lobbyists were dismayed by the policies of Curran and Sweet. While recognizing that attacks on NIE would also weaken the ability of that agency to protect its budget during ongoing funding cuts in Washington, former supporters of NIE felt they had no choice in attacking the agency because it had abandoned agendas and research practices that they considered essential. Neither side hesitated to appeal to Congress and the media; thus, the shortcomings of NIE were well publicized.

Its political and ideological battles became so intense that even many former supporters of the agency openly questioned its future. Chester Finn, a key participant in NIE's development, commented that the recent changes in that agency under Curran and Sweet "have persuaded me that the problems of N.I.E. that I already thought were serious are serious, endemic, and incurable" (quoted in White 1982, 13). Similarly, Sheldon White, a professor of psychology at Harvard University stated, "The more I've seen of Washington, the more skeptical I've become that really dedicated researchers could work year after year and protect themselves in that bureaucracy. I didn't believe that N.I.E. could work 10 years ago, and I don't believe it could work now" (1982).

Continued battles over NIE negatively impacted attempts to procure funding. Faced with the necessity to reduce federal expenditures in general, Congress was less than sympathetic to protecting the budgets of agencies in disarray. As a staff member of the Senate Appropriations Committee put it, "the feeling was 'Let's let N.I.E. put its house in order and then we'll take another look next year' " (Toch 1983a).

With lab and center funding protected by the appropriations committees, Curran used the congressional mandate for lab and center funding competitions as part of his justification for terminating the existing five-year lab and center contracts one year early.[46] In March 1982, Curran proposed that an open competition for labs and centers be held at the beginning of FY84. Both AERA and CEDaR opposed closing those institutions prematurely as a violation of the existing contracts and threatened to take NIE to court (Heard and Toch 1982).

Curran testified before the Senate Subcommittee on Appropriations that the Office of the General Counsel of the Department of Education had ruled that an early closing of these institutions was legal. Challenged to produce the internal legal document, Curran provided both that memo and an accompanying text from Daniel Oliver, the department's general counsel (U.S. Senate 1983b, 558). On the other hand, Joseph Schneider, director of CEDaR, dismissed the general counsel's ruling as "ridiculous" because it was based on language in the Omnibus Reconciliation Act, a nonbinding report. Moreover, Schneider argued that NIE had sufficient funds to continue supporting the existing labs and centers (Heard 1982b).

Congress found the arguments of CEDaR as well as those of the labs and centers more persuasive than those of NIE and the department's general counsel. Sen. Harrison Schmitt (R-NM) successfully inserted language that required the fifth-year funding of the lab and center contracts into the urgent supplemental appropriations report (Heard 1982a).

Congress also began to play a more active role in scrutinizing nominees for the NIE directorship. Manuel Justiz, nominated by Secretary Bell, enjoyed strong support from Republican senators such as Schmitt but was openly opposed by other conservatives, who would have preferred the appointment of acting director Sweet. During the rather hostile committee hearings on Justiz's nomination, Sen. Gordon Humphrey (R-NH) opened his remarks by stating that he "had hoped for the appointment of Robert Sweet, but I am not President" (U.S. Senate 1983b, 76). Although he was in agreement with almost all of Justiz's answers, Senator Humphrey took occasion to lecture the nominee on educational politics and to insist that NIE continue to employ Robert Sweet.[47]

Thus, oversight and direction of NIE reached a new level at which individual members of Congress could order the director of the agency to keep certain individuals in office so as to carry out a personal political agenda. Despite some expectation that Sweet would resign and return to New Hampshire, he successfully maneuvered an appointment as the executive director of the National Council on Education Research, the NIE advisory policy board. Using that position and the open support of the new conservative members of NCER, Sweet tried unsuccessfully to control NIE. With Sweet at the helm, NCER expanded its budget considerably, hired an independent staff, moved to separate quarters across the street from NIE, and issued numerous resolutions that limited the ability of the agency to function without NCER approval. The tense, unworkable state of affairs caused Congress to contemplate withholding all funds from NCER (Zodhiates 1988, 106–64). For example, Congressman David Obey (D-WI), a key supporter of the labs and centers, threatened to cut off all funds from NCER (U.S. House 1983, 1091–92). Finally, Congress and Secretary Bell removed Sweet from the NCER directorship. He transferred to the White House staff where he served as an education policy adviser.

Sweet's transfer failed to lessen tensions between the council and Justiz. One NIE observer initially predicted that Justiz "doesn't have a chance. He'll be eaten alive" (quoted in White 1982, 13). But thanks to his considerable political skills and staunch support from moderates Justiz was gradually able to consolidate his power within NIE (Zodhiates 1988, 139–64).

The 1985 Lab and Center Competition

As Justiz fought off attacks from the Right, he also moved ahead with plans for lab and center competitions. Given the political turmoil surrounding the labs and centers, few expected that NIE would be able to run a fair and timely competition — especially since it was continually being watched and attacked by CEDaR and other special interest groups. However, NIE managed to hold extensive hearings on the competition and commissioned an excellent set of papers for that purpose. Justiz publicly announced that the competition for the new labs and centers would be completed by September 1983.

However, Sen. Mark Hatfield (R-OR), representing a state in which both a lab and center were located, managed to insert language into the appropriations report that postponed the competition for another year. Ostensibly, the delay provided additional time to plan the competition; an aide to Hatfield also explained that the delay was devised to postpone the competition until after the upcoming presidential election, thus avoiding politicization of the awards (Toch 1983b). Other observers suggested that CEDaR had simply wanted to delay the competition in order to kill it. An unnamed, frustrated official at NIE stated,

> Every time we respond to Hatfield, such as agreeing to withhold the announcement of sponsors of the labs and centers until after the election, he gives us a new reason for delaying the competition. CEDaR is trying to get Hatfield to buy it time and to ultimately kill the competition. . . . CEDaR originally supported the competition, and publicly it still does. Frankly, I don't think they thought we could pull it off; their hope was that we would fall on our faces and have to delay it. (16).

Forced by CEDaR and Congress to postpone the lab and center competition until 1984, NIE redoubled its preparations for that event. It held extensive hearings on the competition, created several advisory groups, and commissioned numerous papers on the labs and centers (e.g., see NIE Laboratory Study Group 1983). Rather than applauding the expanded preparations that NIE sought, as predicted, the next year CEDaR attacked NIE for delaying the process and making it too complex (Schneider 1984). CEDaR went on to castigate NIE for broadly consulting the public and questioning some basic assumptions behind the current system of labs and centers (ibid.).

Justiz was outraged by CEDaR's charges. Most directors of federal agencies are reluctant to publicly express anger or hostility toward important lobbyists even when they strongly disagree with them. In an uncharacteristically harsh and scathing letter, Justiz denounced CEDaR's tactics:

> As I am sure you would expect, I am very disappointed in CEDaR's response. Our requests for your analysis of NIE's laboratory and

center plans were genuine and were made in the hope of benefitting from your members' experience. Those requests began nearly six months ago and throughout that period, despite our repeated appeals for your input, you always have had an excuse or said simply that you were working on it and would have your report to us soon. . . .

Joe, your gift for rewriting and interpreting history is unrivaled in the research community, and your letter is a hallmark of your ability. As an example, the "Long-term Special Institutional Agreements" policy statements discussed in your letter was supplemented in 1983 by additional statements of understanding that clearly define the terms and provisions of existing lab and center awards and the upcoming competition. Although all lab and center directors signed these statements of understanding, you make no mention of them in your review of events.

I must respond to one other point, in the hope that you will make a good-faith effort to represent the issue fairly. I appreciate the frustration you feel when you say "Enough is enough." This has been a very long process. But the length of the process is attributable in large part to a delay in the competition for one full fiscal year—a delay which CEDaR has taken the credit for obtaining from Congress. (Schneider 1984)[48]

For the first time in nearly two decades, the labs and centers faced open competition for funding. Despite the difficulties and setbacks that preceded it, the competition was conducted fairly and expeditiously. As detailed in chapters 1 and 2, NIE retained the general structure of the labs and centers. For example, the regional nature of the labs was preserved together with the orientation toward technical assistance. Under continued and explicit pressure from Congress, NIE established three new regional labs in the Midwest, Southeast, and Northeast. Given the political turmoil surrounding NIE in general and the labs and centers in particular, most observers were surprised and pleased by the overall manner in which the competition was conducted.[49]

Even as the lab and center competition was proceeding without incident, NIE suffered from other embarrassments. The midwestern regional laboratory, CEMREL, whose misuse of federal funds NIE previously had played down, was discontinued.[50] In addition, Justiz upset several members of Congress as well as representatives of educational groups when he ignored the rank-order recommendations of the peer review panel and awarded a new technology center to Harvard University (Euchner 1984a, 1984b). Some members of Congress, hostile even

to those lower-level Reagan appointees who questioned federal involvement in education, used the NIE appropriation hearings to denounce
them. For example, Sen. Lowell Weiker (R-CT) berated Lawrence
Uzzell for expressing the opinion that NIE and the Department of Education should be abolished (U.S. Senate 1985, 56). The agency's credibility was further damaged when an anonymous group of NIE employees,
disgruntled about hiring practices at the agency, accused Justiz of waste
and fraud, hastening his departure.[51] Thus, despite NIE's significant
strides in conducting a fair and open funding competition for the labs
and centers, it languished under several rather minor but nonetheless
distasteful controversies, which continued to damage its image among
policymakers and the public.

The 1985 Reorganization of OERI

Education secretary William Bennett replaced Bell in 1985 and moved
quickly to reorganize the Department of Education. The proposed plans
to merge NIE, the National Center for Education Statistics, and the
Library Programs into the Office of Educational Research and Improvement were widely opposed by most educational policymakers and researchers as unnecessary and as downgrading the importance of research
(Hertling 1985a). Officials such as John Jennings, majority staff counsel
of the House Subcommittee on Elementary, Secondary, and Vocational
Education, denounced the effort.[52]

After notifying Congress about the proposed reorganization, the
Department of Education proceeded with the planned merger of NIE,
NCES, and the Library Programs. The new plan called for the establishment of five programs within OERI (Information Services, Office of
Research, Center for Statistics, Programs for Improvement of Practice,
and Library Programs) and downgraded NCER to an advisory policy
group. Chester Finn Jr., a professor of education at Vanderbilt University active in educational policymaking in Washington, was named the
new assistant secretary of OERI (Hertling 1985b).[53]

CEDaR, fearing that the independence and autonomy of the labs
and centers might be compromised by the reorganization of OERI, tried
to halt the measure. To this end, it enlisted Rep. David Obey (D-WI), a
long-time ally, to threaten to amend the appropriations bill for FY86 to
prevent the reorganization (Hertling 1985c). While the amendment was
not added, it set the stage of OERI's reauthorization in 1986, when the
restructuring federal research effort was revisited.[54]

Although OERI was scheduled for reauthorization in 1985, Congress failed to act, automatically extending the agency's operation for

another year. The following year Congress reauthorized OERI and held a day-long hearing before the Subcommittee on Select Education. Because the Gramm-Rudman legislation required a balanced budget by 1991, Congress was now more focused on cutting programs than in previous years. Despite this pressure, the general tenor of the hearings was much calmer and more supportive of educational research than discussions of the early 1980s had been. Members of Congress, however, candidly admitted relatively little support for the funding of educational research and development activities during this period of budgetary retrenchment (U.S. House 1986, 3).

The 1985 reorganization of OERI was a subject of considerable interest during the hearing. Most members of Congress as well as most representatives of the major educational groups accepted the changes and saw in them some merit for educational research and development.[55] But a few education groups, especially CEDaR, were unhappy with the new OERI. Thomas Olson, executive director of the North Central Regional Educational Laboratory, feared that under the new organization labs and centers would lose their present relative autonomy and their independence from NIE (U.S. House 1986, 114).[56]

Most educational groups recognized the importance of changing the entrenched public and congressional perception that federal education research and development was so politicized that it deserved little support. Thus, despite initial misgivings about the OERI reorganization, these groups tried to overlook differences and work more closely with the new agency to develop a nonpartisan, objective research and development agenda. However, CEDaR was so concerned about protecting the current independence of the labs and centers that it continued to castigate OERI in order to convince Congress to protect its clients from any interference. Given CEDaR's orientation and goals, these tactics were understandable. But it is somewhat surprising that it managed to convince such important and large organizations as the National Education Association and the National PTA to join in such a campaign.

The outcome of the controversy over the OERI reorganization was mixed. On one hand, CEDaR and its allies did obtain a guarantee from Congress reaffirming the right of regional labs to continue setting their own research and development agendas.[57] But the rest of the educational research community gradually became uneasy with the seemingly narrow, self-serving lobbying of CEDaR on behalf of its client labs and centers and began to disassociate itself from that organization. Most newly funded centers, for example, declined to join CEDaR and created their own advocacy group affiliated with AERA (*Education Week* 1986). While three centers continued their affiliation with CEDaR, regional educational labs now comprised the bulk of its membership. Consequently, CEDaR's focus was concentrated more specifically on the interests of the labs. It found it increasing expedient to portray the leadership of OERI and the Department of Education as incompetent and politically motivated. Although this tactic probably benefited short-term CEDaR and lab interests, it continued to erode congressional confidence in general federal educational research and development and particularly undermined support for OERI. Moreover, the criticism fostered continued hostility and suspicion among OERI, CEDaR, and the education research community, ultimately damaging all parties involved.

Leadership of Chester Finn

Assistant Secretary Finn did much to reintroduce academic professionalism and leadership within OERI. Even those who disagreed with his views admitted that he was a highly talented, albeit opinionated and outspoken, researcher who brought high standards and expectations to OERI. He recruited other respected researchers such as Sally Kilgore, who was appointed as the OERI director of research (Mirga 1986). Finn's highest priority was the repair and improvement of the National Center for Education Statistics, a goal achieved with the help of Emerson Elliott (*Education Week* 1985a).[58]

Finn continued to question the wisdom of Congress's protection of labs and centers; moreover, he raised serious questions about the quality of work produced at those institutions—especially the labs. Under the able leadership of Christopher Cross, former ranking minority staff member of the U.S. House Subcommittee on Select Education, OERI convened a group of outside experts to review the work of the labs in the summer of 1987. As discussed in chapter 2, the Cross Lab Review Panel reaffirmed the regionality of the labs but suggested the need for a more national focus and expressed concern over the diminution of practitioner-oriented research at those institutions (Cross et al. 1987). While the Cross panel was rather reserved and tactful in its discussion of the role of the labs, Finn continued to disparage the quality of their contribution to educational improvement (Finn 1987).

Most directors of NIE and OERI had learned to be publicly circumspect about attacks on the labs and centers. However, Assistant Secretary Finn did not hesitate to issue frequent complaints about the lack of flexibility in OERI research funding—a circumstance due mainly to the congressional stipulation that the labs and centers were to receive the bulk of NIE/OERI funding, resulting in almost no money remaining for field-initiated research projects. While Finn directed some criticism toward the centers, he reserved his strongest attacks for the labs. At a congressional oversight hearing on OERI, he testified,

> The laboratories, in particular, have not been a very remunerative investment *per se.* This is not to say that they do nothing useful — they and their energetic Washington lobbyists are quite capable of finding hundreds of laboratory customers who will claim satisfaction with services provided by the laboratories. But I am saying that, given their present activities and configurations, and given the current fiscal constraints on the government, the laboratories represent a profligate use of OERI funds in relation to the benefit they generate. . . . This is so for several reasons. I have already mentioned that laboratory impact is amorphous and difficult to assess, and that these institutions simply cannot provide services to more than a few districts in our immense education system. But congressional protection of the laboratories and, to be blunt, the insatiable appetite of the laboratories for federal funds, have shielded them from any real competition from other forms of dissemination and technical assistance. As a result, they have become entrenched institutions whose primary goals seem to be self-perpetuation. (U.S. House 1988a, 171)

Congressman Major Owens (D-NY), chair of the Subcommittee on Select Education, shared some of Finn's reservations about the work of the labs and centers but asked why OERI did not redirect the agenda and activities of the labs toward more productive and useful pursuits. When Finn failed to answer Owens satisfactorily, Milt Goldberg, the director of Programs for the Improvement of Practice, admitted that the administration had relinquished its power to set the research and development agenda for the labs (U.S. House 1988a, 244). The exchange with Owens revealed the ambiguity within Congress itself over the direction of the labs and OERI's frustrating experience of receiving mixed signals from different legislators. On the one hand, at the instigation of CEDaR powerful senators like Hatfield and Schweiker and representatives like Obey and Williams protected the labs through appropriations report language. On the other hand, congressmen like Owens criticized OERI for failing to exercise appropriate leadership and stewardship over the labs. Consequently, OERI's administration of the labs and centers won it few friends and exposed the agency to continual micromanagement by certain members of Congress.

Summary

Overall, the Reagan years proved to be disastrous for NIE/OERI. Although the end of the 1970s had offered hope for improvements at NIE, the huge budget cuts of the early 1980s were devastating. The agency's losses in real dollars far outweighed the modest gains eked out in the late 1970s under the leadership of Hodgkinson and Graham. These large funding cuts contributed to NIE's further politicalization as CEDaR succeeded in soliciting from a few members of Congress protection for labs and centers from the largest budget cuts at the expense of other discretionary programs. Increasingly, the budget of NIE/OERI was mandated almost entirely by Congress, eliminating most other initiatives altogether. Moreover, this open and blatant use of political power by CEDaR to set the diminishing agenda of NIE/OERI portrayed the agency as less objective and less valuable a leader in educational research and development than otherwise. The split between CEDaR and the educational research community grew during these years, seriously eroding what little confidence the public placed in NIE/OERI.

The change in political leadership at NIE continued the trend of short-term, erratic leadership and signaled the arrival of individuals whose claim to office was often based on partisan activities rather than research or administrative capabilities. Moreover, some of these new leaders, responding in part to the budget cuts and personal, partisan ideologies, effected a surprisingly large reduction and turnover in NIE's professional staff. Such changes resulted in a demoralized and ineffective NIE/OERI staff, which inspired little confidence either in the research community or among education policymakers.

Directors like Curran and Sweet not only politicized NIE themselves, but they convinced other conservatives that the old NIE was neither as objective nor as neutral as it was portrayed by its proponents. They pointed to the liberal/leftist agenda of NIE during the 1970s, especially during the Carter administration, as evidence that the agency could not be trusted to oversee objective research. Challenging NIE's heavy reliance on social science, they questioned the usefulness of such an approach in resolving local educational problems. While these and other conservatives who controlled NIE in the early 1980s failed to persuade their opponents that the old NIE was politically and ideologically oriented, they did succeed in convincing some of the more conservative policymakers that the federal role in research and development was more complex and dangerous than previously suspected.

Both conservative and liberal members of Congress, reacting to the budget crises as well as the growing political turmoil at NIE, lost confidence in the agency and became increasingly prepared to interfere in its affairs by mandating its activities and questioning the integrity and motives of its staff. A series of small but highly visible shortcomings, such as the questionable operations at CEMREL and the ethical practices of Justiz, reinforced the image of a divided and inept agency.

As the Reagan administration drew to a close, OERI did exhibit hopeful signs, as it managed to carry out a fair and open laboratory and center competition, reorganize itself, and attract a capable and respected director such as Finn. Despite these significant improvements in the late 1980s, OERI retained its image as less effective and less respected than NIE at the end of the 1970s. Because it devoted so much time and energy to political and ideological battles during the first half of the 1980s and struggled throughout the decade with dramatically reduced resources, OERI failed to develop the major initiatives necessary to convince skeptical policymakers and the general public that educational research and development was an important and worthwhile investment of federal tax dollars.

IV. Labs and Centers during the Bush Administration

While the operation of OERI continued to be plagued by some of the chronic problems that had always faced the agency, observers noticed a few promising signs of improvement during the Bush administration. Under the direction of Christopher Cross and Diane Ravitch, OERI regained much of its former funding and even enhanced its intellectual reputation somewhat. Yet many, including some key congressional members, continued to see OERI as a troubled and ineffective institution.

New OERI Leadership

Leadership changes in OERI often resulted directly from the turnover of secretaries at the U.S. Department of Education. During most of the second half of the Reagan administration, it was headed by Secretary William Bennett, an outspoken, conservative intellectual who railed against the deplorable state of American education. Bennett used his post as a "bully pulpit" from which to persuade Americans to improve their public schools, chastising the teacher unions for resisting educational reforms.[59] When Bennett resigned as secretary of education in September 1988, his assistant secretary of OERI, Finn, also left (Rothman 1988).

President Reagan appointed Lauro Cavazos to replace Bennett. The former Texas Tech University president was selected in part because of the Republican need to appeal to Hispanic voters in the 1988 presidential election. Cavazos received warm support from most educators and politicians and proved less hostile to federal involvement in education than Bennett had been. Although some conservatives saw Cavazos as inferior in intellect and ideological orientation compared to Bennett, Bush decided to retain him as secretary (Miller 1988f).

Due to changes in the top leadership of the Department of Education, OERI remained uncertain and unstable. After Finn resigned, Goldberg served as acting OERI assistant secretary for only one month. Patricia Hines replaced Goldberg in October and served in that capacity for a brief five months. Hines, a former high school and college English instructor, was a conservative activist hired by Robert Sweet in 1982. She worked as an NCER staff member until 1986 and then worked in the White House on domestic policy under Gary Bauer (Miller 1988a).[60]

The appointment of Hines was seen as another attempt to reassert conservative control over OERI. Gerald Sroufe, governmental liaison for AERA, questioned Hines's research and management background (Miller 1988a). Joseph Schneider, executive director of CEDaR, criticized her appointment.[61] The new Bush administration, anxious to pursue a more moderate educational agenda, withdrew support for Hines's candidacy and designated Bruno Manno as acting assistant secretary. Manno remained in that post for six months (Miller and Viadero 1989; Walker 1989).

Finally, Secretary Cavazos appointed Christopher Cross, a moderate Republican with extensive congressional experience, as the next assistant secretary of OERI (West 1989). Cross was the former ranking minority staff member on the House Subcommittee on Education under Congressman Quie (R-MN), and he had also served in the executive branch. He had a well-earned reputation as a person who could work effectively with everyone. Cross had chaired the panel that conducted a review of the labs in the summer of 1987 and therefore was quite familiar with the operations of OERI.[62] He was confirmed quickly and enthusiastically by the Senate and did much to quiet temporarily the continuing congressional doubts about OERI.

Cavazos, who was increasingly viewed as a likable but ineffective secretary of education, was unexpectedly and unceremoniously forced to resign in December 1990.[63] As dictated by political etiquette, his major political appointees were also expected to leave to make room for the new team appointed by Cavazos's successor. Thus, despite Cross's visible successes at OERI, he resigned in May 1991 after being in office less than nine months (Baumann et al. 1991).[64] Manno was again named as the acting assistant secretary and served in this capacity for three months.

Lamar Alexander, former governor of Tennessee and a nationally recognized leader in educational reform, was named the new secretary of education. On the recommendation of Finn and others, Alexander nominated Diane Ravitch as the OERI assistant secretary in June 1991 (Licitra 1991l). Ravitch, one of the most prolific and distinguished scholars ever appointed assistant secretary of NIE or OERI, had been active in efforts to improve history instruction in the California public schools. Despite her controversial ideas about educational reform, her academic credentials and intellectual expertise were widely acknowledged. She was quickly and unanimously approved by the Senate (Blackledge 1991). Unlike Cross, however, she never established a close rapport with Congress—in part due to her political inexperience and in part due to her visible disdain for the behavior of certain of its members. Ravitch was also named counselor to the secretary and played a key role in the Bush administration's efforts to develop voluntary, national curriculum standards. She remained in her position until President Clinton took office in early 1993.

Thus, the leadership of OERI during the Bush administration presents a mixed picture. During some of these years, the outside perception of OERI was tainted by the appointment of the conservative Hines, who was widely portrayed as an unqualified partisan activist. Later in the Bush years, however, OERI was managed by two distinguished and able individuals, Cross and Ravitch. Personalities and abilities aside, perhaps the most disturbing pattern at OERI was the rapid turnover in leadership (it changed hands five times within that four-year period).

OERI's Funding Situation

OERI's overall funding situation improved considerably during the Bush administration, reversing the dramatic decreases of the early 1980s. Excluding the Library Programs, OERI funding rose from $78.2 million in FY89 to $286.2 million in FY93—an astounding 366 percent increase (214 percent in real dollars), the highest OERI budget since FY73.[65]

Most of the rapid increase in OERI's budget, however, was not in the research or statistics accounts but in the transferred or newly mandated programs designed to improve education. For example, the Javits Gifted and Talented Program, the Blue Ribbon Schools, and the Eisenhower Math and Science Program were added in FY89; Mid-Career Teacher Training and Educational Partnerships were acquired in FY90; and the Evaluation of Education Reform, the National Literacy Institute, and the Summit were added in FY91. In FY89, funding for the National

Center for Education Statistics, the labs and centers, field-initiated research, and ERIC comprised 98.7 percent of the overall OERI budget, with less than $1 million allocated for other activities. But by FY93 funding for these more traditional OERI activities accounted for only 52.8 percent of the overall budget ($135 million was allocated for the new programs). Thus, while the fiscal importance of OERI increased substantially during the Bush administration, the relative amount of funding devoted to NCES, labs, centers, ERIC, and field-initiated studies dropped sharply.

Within the more traditional OERI funding categories, the NCES budget increased the most sharply, rising from $31.1 million in FY89 to $78.9 million in FY93. The sizable FY87 and FY88 allocation increases permitted the substantial expansion of the statistical components of OERI. In real dollars, OERI spent more on the collection, preparation, analysis, and dissemination of statistical information than ever before. On the other hand, ERIC and field-initiated research saw only a modest gain in expenditures, the latter continuing as a minuscule, almost invisible part of OERI activities.

Funding for the labs and centers increased substantially during the Bush administration. Lab funding rose from $22.1 million in FY89 to $36.5 in FY93, a surprisingly large increase of 65.2 percent. Similarly, funding for centers rose from $17.8 million in FY89 to $27.7 million in FY93, a slightly lower but significant increase of 55.6 percent. Another interesting statistic indicated that center funding from FY83 to FY93 increased by 63.1 percent while lab allocations for the same period jumped by 136.6 percent. Most of the increases in center and lab funding resulted from congressional pressure on OERI and the earmarking of additional monies — particularly a sizable $4 to $6 million annual rural education initiative designated solely for the labs.

OERI's Policies toward the Labs and Centers

Although the overall OERI policy toward the labs and centers changed little during the Bush administration, a few interesting developments did take place. During the Reagan administration, Finn had emphasized the collection, analysis, and dissemination of statistics, dedicating less attention to research. Finn was particularly incensed by the continued, mandated existence of the labs regardless of their poor performance, and, although critical of the centers, he saw more value in their current and potential accomplishments (U.S. House 1988a, 255). In a rather controversial move, he decided to establish several minicenters, each funded at an annual rate of about $500,000. Although he was unable to persuade

Congress to change the structure of the labs, Finn did appoint a panel to evaluate the lab system; however, he left office before it had completed its analysis.

Cross continued the basic policies of his immediate predecessors with regard to the centers and labs but expanded the number of centers funded in the 1990 competition. With fourteen of the existing centers expiring in 1989, OERI's Office of Research planned to establish twelve new ones and considered another seven as possibilities. Many of the OERI career staff favored a smaller number of centers funded at a higher level. But Cross recommended that eighteen new centers be funded—for a total of twenty-five OERI-supported centers (Cross 1990).

Cross also presided over the successful lab competition of 1990. Under pressure from Congress, he expanded the number of labs from nine to ten. Although Cross approved some modest changes in the orientation of the labs, the overall system remained very similar to the basic outline codified in the 1985 reauthorization guidelines. Recognizing Congress's interest in dissemination, Cross emphasized both the labs' and centers' roles in dissemination.

Having witnessed the usefulness of the recommendations of the National Academy of Sciences in 1987 for restructuring NCES, Cross commissioned the same organization to conduct an independent evaluation of OERI (Licitra 1991g). Although the findings of the academy did not become available until after Cross departed, its recommendations aided Congress and OERI in reconceptualizing the role of the federal government in educational research and development. Indeed, the NAS recommendations were extremely influential in the subsequent reauthorization of OERI (Rothman 1992a; Licitra 1992).

The NAS panel recommended the reorganization of OERI's research efforts into three, four, or five R&D directorates. "Each directorate would coordinate R&D centers, field-initiated research programs, special studies, and linkages with the Reform Assistance Division" (Atkinson and Jackson 1992, 148). While the panel advocated the maintenance of centers, it also recommended larger institutions more focused on basic research as well as the development of more effective and rigorously tested methods of teaching and learning improvement (150–51). The committee also endorsed the continuation of the labs, suggesting ways to make them more effective in fostering educational reform. The report called for reorganization of OERI to oversee the labs' more effective work with the states and to pay special attention to subjecting the labs' work "to a quality assurance review" (152). The NAS committee offered other suggestions about these new institutions, including a controversial recommendation questioning the necessity or advisability of open competitions for labs and centers every five years (151, 153).

Analysis of the Labs and Centers

When Ravitch assumed the post of assistant secretary, she was not especially familiar with the work of the labs and centers but had heard from several sources that it was not uniformly high in quality or value.[66] She appointed me, a scholar from the University of Michigan, as her research adviser, assigning me the task of assessing the quality of the work of the labs and centers (Rothman 1992b). With considerable assistance from the OERI staff and the labs and centers, I investigated the quality of all the work produced by seven centers and five labs.

I first focused on the operation of the centers. In a preliminary internal draft in May 1992, I reported that much of the work of the centers was fragmented and uncoordinated. A surprisingly small amount of the OERI funds was actually spent on research — much of the money instead was expended on overhead, administration, and dissemination. The National Center for the Study of Writing and Literacy at the University of California at Berkeley, for example, actually spent more money on dissemination than on research. The quality of the work, which the National Academy of Science panel did not consider, was mixed.[67]

Ravitch also appointed Joe Conaty as the OR acting director and instructed him to improve the monitoring of the centers. Using information from my preliminary work as well as other sources, Conaty and the OR staff conducted a third-year review of the centers. Working closely with the centers, the third-year review was the most ambitious and effective such effort ever undertaken, leading to important improvements in OERI's working relationship with these institutions.

Eve Bither, the acting director of Programs for the Improvement of Practice, was an energetic and effective leader who substantially improved many operations of that unit but had little immediate effect on the operation and oversight of the labs. This occurred in part because, unlike the centers, the labs were not scheduled for a third-year review. Moreover, I was unable to turn my attention to the quality of work in the labs until late summer and did not complete my analysis of them until early 1993. Finally, the labs were more suspicious of and hostile to intensive OERI oversight than the centers had been. As a result, while Ravitch had initiated an in-depth review of the work of the labs, little progress was made before her departure on implementing changes in the existing lab system.

Congressional oversight of the labs and centers during the Bush administration also was mixed. Most members of Congress paid little attention to these institutions, though a few continued to support them rather uncritically and ensured that they received ample funds to continue or even expand their operations. At the opposite extreme, a relatively new congressman, Major Owens (D-NY), undertook the most active, albeit occasionally idiosyncratic, overview of OERI ever made. This review eventually culminated in the 1994 reauthorization of the agency.

While most members of Congress devoted scant attention to educational research and development, Owens dedicated considerable time and effort to OERI. A professional librarian, he had been elected to Congress in 1982 and focused heavily on the needs of his poor and minority constituents. He served as chair of the Select Subcommittee on Education until 1988. In April 1988, after holding two days of hearings on OERI, the majority staff of Owen's committee issued a draft report, which outlined a new vision for education in the 1990s. Although the authorization for OERI was not set to expire until 1991, Owens sought earlier reauthorization in order to introduce these changes.

Owens boldly proclaimed Congress's need to reclaim the original NIE vision: "to provide to every individual an equal opportunity to receive an education of high quality standards regardless of race, color, religion, sex, age, handicap, national origin or social class" (U.S. House 1988b, 1). Expressing disappointment at past and current OERI achievements, Owens called on the agency to fill a new treasure chest with gems of high-quality research (U.S. House 1988b, 2).

According to Owens, OERI's highly politicized nature proved to be a primary obstacle to adequate research and development: "In order for real progress to be made it is the Subcommittee's view that OERI needs to be depoliticized so that priorities can be properly identified and research activities can gain the kinds of credibility and support they merit" (U.S. House 1988b, 8). Throughout most of his hearings on OERI during the next seven years, he frequently reiterated charges of the agency's politicization (U.S. House 1989, 1). Therefore, he recommended the establishment of a strong policy advisory board, composed of representatives from some of the more active educational groups such as NEA and AERA, to oversee the operations of OERI.

Owens accurately portrayed the intensely partisan atmosphere of NIE/OERI in the early 1980s, but his assertion that OERI had remained equally politicized under the leadership of Cross and Ravitch is less convincing. He acknowledged that Cross had restored "professionalism" to OERI but continued to insist that the agency would benefit from a strong policy panel (Rothman 1991b).[68] In testimony before the select subcommittee, Ravitch, who clashed repeatedly with Owens over the desirability of his proposed policy board, expressed her exasperation at his repeated assertions about the political nature of OERI.[69] When she asked him to produce a single recent example of this politicalization, Owens failed to respond.[70]

After Ravitch's departure, Owens again introduced the issue of the politicalization of OERI, questioning Thomas Schultz, director of early childhood services at the National Association of State Boards of Education. Schultz, however, disagreed with Owens and minimized the existence of recent occurrences of politically oriented activity within OERI (U.S. House 1992c, 102–3).

These repeated clashes over the political depiction of OERI and the nature of the proposed policy board continued throughout the Bush administration. Owens, himself an intensely partisan and outspoken legislator, continued to portray OERI during the Reagan and Bush eras as a highly politicized and partisan institution. Although these charges provided a rationale for the fundamental changes he proposed for OERI, they also created a misleading and damaging image of the agency. Some policymakers, generally indifferent to OERI but vaguely familiar with the ideological controversies that had wracked it during the early 1980s, viewed these sharp exchanges between Owens and Ravitch as further proof of the continued ineffectiveness of and turmoil surrounding federally sponsored educational research. Moreover, continued charges of politicization persisted, weakening support for OERI just as the Bush administration began to rely more on the agency to oversee and fund some of its America 2000 activities (Miller 1991a, 1991b).

Despite the controversy, Owens did offer some useful recommendations on reorganizing the agency. He complained about the fragmentary nature of the current labs and centers and called for a large research institute for at-risk students (U.S. House 1988a, 7–8). Dissatisfied with the existing centers and labs, Owens felt the existing institutions provided insufficient help for minority and disadvantaged students. When Finn proposed the creation of a new at-risk center with annual funding of $1 million, Owens found himself in the anomalous position of opposing Finn in part because he felt the proposal was not sufficient to accomplish its goals. Owens, who had previously tried to mandate the continuation of the Center for Language Education and Research at UCLA, now tried unsuccessfully to halt the competition for the new at-risk center (Miller 1988c).[71] Johns Hopkins University earned the award and used it to establish the Center on Effective Schooling for Disadvantaged Students. Contrary to Owens's fears that the new center would be a waste of money, it became one of the most productive and effective OERI-funded centers in the early 1990s (Vinovskis 1992).

Rejecting the Johns Hopkins Center, Owens called for a new, large-scale, national center-laboratory whose primary initial responsibility would be to synthesize existing work on helping at-risk students (U.S. House 1988b, 37–38). Interestingly, his initial proposal for this new center-laboratory envisioned not a total reorganization of the existing labs and centers but the creation of another, somewhat larger institution designed to draw initially upon the works of the other units. Although some additional monies would be needed for minigrants and awards to fill gaps in existing knowledge, a large part of the funds would go to synthesizing and disseminating previously gathered information (39).

Owens continued to focus almost exclusively on creating a center-laboratory for the study of at-risk populations, while Arthur Wise, director of the Rand Center for the Study of the Teaching Profession and chair of the AERA Government and Professional Liaison Committee, lobbied for a more comprehensive and ambitious reorganization of OERI into several large, national, educational institutes. Criticizing the current organization of OERI for its failure to be mission or problem oriented, Wise in part modeled his proposed institutes on the organizational approach of the National Institutes of Health (U.S. House 1989, 66). He further expounded his views on the national institutes for educational improvement in an influential article that he co-authored for *Educational Research* in 1990 (Wise and Sroufe 1990, 22–25).

Owens continued to hold hearings on the establishment of a National Institute for the Education of At-Risk Students and received endorsements from legislators and researchers like James Comer, Edmund Gordon, and Linda Darling-Hammond in April 1991. Most congressional discussions, however, remained narrowly focused on the proposed at-risk national institute without proposing to reorganize the entire OERI structure. Indeed, Owens planned to maintain the existing centers and labs while adding only his institute for at-risk students (U.S. House 1991a, 1).

Owens introduced his bill to establish the national institute, which explicitly avoided introducing major changes in the overall OERI structure.[72] The language specified only the addition of a single, large-scale institute devoted to helping at-risk children. Calling for $50 million a year, the bill would direct the National Institute for the Education of At-Risk Students to develop a model for helping students in the poorest congressional districts (U.S. House 1991b, 8).

The bill outlined the broad duties of the institute but requested neither the creation of centers nor a fixed minimum to be set aside for field-initiated research. These requests would be submitted in later legislation.[73] The institute was to be subdivided into three units: a division of inner-city educational improvement, a division of rural educational improvement, and a division of minority language educational improvement (U.S. House 1991b, 9). The bill called for the establishment of a national institute board of thirty-three members who would oversee the agency and establish research priorities. The proposed legislation specified that board members would be chosen from a pool of nominees from "nationally representative children's advocacy or educational associations."[74]

While many scholars and policymakers concurred with Congressman Owens on the need for a national institute on at-risk children, few tried to explain why the new Johns Hopkins University center was flawed or inadequate, and few seemed to worry about the overlap and duplication that might result from the founding of the institute. Researcher Linda Darling-Hammond stated that "one of the things we have learned [from studying other agencies' research efforts] is that throwing money at problems does make a difference" (Rothman 1991b). And Arthur Wise called for an ambitious restructuring of OERI and the establishment of at least two national institutes (ibid.).

Rather than seeking a major restructuring of OERI, the Senate initially introduced S. 1275, a simple extension of OERI, but it was prepared to rewrite the legislation as necessary (U.S. Senate 1991, 189). Similarly, the Bush administration proposed a continuation of the existing legislation but suggested increased flexibility in the ways the agency could spend its monies, especially with regard to the centers and laboratories.[75] Despite the Bush administration's pleas for more flexibility in lab and center funding, neither the House nor the Senate indicated any willingness to grant this request. However, the impetus toward restructuring OERI into four or five institutes or directorates eventually succeeded in reconfiguring the agency.

Certain key members of the research community strongly endorsed and lobbied for the idea of multiple national institutes. Both Wise and Sroufe centered their OERI reauthorization proposal on the concept of multiple institutes (Wise and Sroufe 1990). Formally endorsing the plan, the AERA council directed its Governmental Professional Liaison Committee to work with the administration and Congress to enact this reorganization in early 1991 (25). The prestigious and influential National Academy of Sciences also supported the same approach in its lengthy, in-depth review of OERI in April 1992 (Atkinson and Jackson 1992).[76]

The Bush administration also came to understand the value of restructuring OERI into several national institutes.[77] One major education thrust of the Bush administration centered on developing and implementing voluntary national curriculum standards and assessments.[78] Secretary Alexander and OERI Assistant Secretary Ravitch were particularly committed to these reforms. When it appeared that the single national institute for at-risk students proposed by Owens might preclude adequate attention to curriculum and assessment, Ravitch argued for the creation of multiple research directorates — emphasizing the need for adequate funding for the one designed to handle curriculum and assessment.[79]

The new Bush administration's position on the creation of several large-scale research directorates was eventually accepted and expanded by the Senate. Slow to act at first, the Senate had less interest in the OERI reauthorization than did the House. The Senate was also split on the advisability of including the requirement for student testing that was favored by Sen. Claiborne Pell (D-RI). However, it was willing to accept Owens's call for an at-risk institute and an OERI advisory board, although it differed with Owens on some of the important details (Licitra 1991o). Given the limited contact between Senate and House staffs, the two reauthorization bills were developed somewhat independently — though lobbyists of the Bush administration and educational associations representatives provided indirect contact between the two chambers (Licitra 1991i).

Drawing upon the recommendations of the administration, the House, the AERA council, and others, the Senate Committee on Labor and Human Resources rewrote S. 1275 in March 1992 to reflect the growing consensus that OERI should be restructured into research institutes or directorates (U.S. Senate 1992, 13–14). The Senate bill required that a minimum of 15 percent of the money allocated to each directorate be used for field-initiated research and at least another third for one or two long-term national research centers (contracted for at least ten years). The proposed budget for the directorates was authorized at $70 million for FY93, with 50 percent of those funds for a national directorate on curriculum, instruction, and assessment (15).

Even before the Bush administration and the Senate moved formally toward national directorates for OERI, Owens had begun to gradually expand his focus from a single at-risk institute. In September 1991, he was still recommending the founding of one large-scale institute (Licitra 1991k). A month later, however, he introduced H.R. 3458, devised to reauthorize OERI. His new bill would create two new research institutes, one focused on at-risk children and the other on school governance. Although dependent upon the final OERI budget, each of the two institutes was to be funded with $30 to $50 million annually. Owens further recommended that OERI's new policy board was to receive no less than 5 percent of the agency's research budget and that the board, comprised of twenty-four members, would be required to review any contract or grant of $500,000 or more (Licitra 1991e).

Just before Congress adjourned, Owens introduced yet another version of the OERI reauthorization legislation (H.R. 4014), cosponsored with William Ford (D-MI) and William Goodling (R-PA). It called for the establishment of four institutes: an at-risk institute, a governance institute, an early childhood institute, and a student achievement institute. The bill also emphasized programs designed to help urban schools, the creation of a national education system, and continued support for the labs (Licitra 1991f). Because Owens's new legislation more closely resembled the AERA proposals, Sroufe, the AERA spokesperson, enthusiastically praised it (Licitra 1991f, 2).

Finally, on April 2, 1992, the Subcommittee on Select Education issued a report on H.R. 4014, which recommended the establishment of four national institutes (U.S. House 1992b, 44). Like the Senate version, the House bill called for more field-initiated research but did not mandate a particular amount or percentage of funds for this area. Unlike the Senate version, however, the House bill initially authorized $20 million for each of the four institutes—despite some differences of opinion in the timeline for establishment of each (the national institute for the education of at-risk students was given the first priority). Interestingly, the House discussion on the national institute for student achievement emphasized neither curriculum nor assessment, as did its counterpart in the Senate bill (U.S. House 1992b, 20–24, 44–65).

The primary difference between the two bills, the creation of an OERI policy board, proved fatal to its enactment during the Bush administration. Although both chambers created a board, the Senate version established it as a more advisory body than did the House language. Moreover, the House version specified that members of the twenty-person OERI policy board be selected from nominations made by selected research and educational groups—a provision vehemently opposed by the Bush administration, the Senate, and even the Republican members of the House committee (U.S. House 1992b, 26–44).[80] Although Owens, the chief architect of the policy board, offered to compromise in the closing days of the 102d Congress, his overture came too late and the legislation died without action (OERI bill 1992; OERI reauthorization 1992; Rothman 1992c; House passes 1992; Rothman 1992d; Reform bill 1992). Thus, although both the House and Senate reached a basic agreement on the restructuring of OERI into research institutes or directorates, differences over the nature and power of the policy board postponed any major changes in the legislation for another two years.

The House and Senate committees invested considerable time on the OERI reauthorization but focused almost exclusively on the centers and the proposed research institutes and directorates. The committee members devoted little attention during the hearings to the nature of the labs, although a few interesting issues did emerge. The House Subcommittee on Select Education gave its attention primarily to the reauthorization of OERI. Owens, the chair of the subcommittee, looked into the current operations of the centers in some detail but ignored almost entirely the operation of the labs,[81] several times stating that he anticipated no major changes in their current operations (see, e.g., U.S. House 1991a, 1). When confronted with evidence of the continued hostility between OERI and the labs, Owens professed ignorance of this rather well-known situation, suggesting that he may not have been kept fully abreast of developments in this area (U.S. House 1992c, 20–21).[82]

Although the House hearings touched only infrequently on the labs themselves, it is interesting to note the recommendations of the CEDaR representatives with regard to the proposed reauthorization. On the whole, they displayed a very thoughtful and broad understanding of the needs of educational research. For example, Preston Kronkosky, executive director of the Southwest Educational Laboratory, endorsed the overall plans for the research institutes, recommending constructive measures to strengthen H.R. 4014 (U.S. House 1992c, 62).[83] Unlike CEDaR's past positions, which often stressed the need for regional independence and autonomy, Kronkosky readily agreed that the labs should follow the research priorities stated in H.R. 4014 (61–62). Finally, he accepted the stress on dissemination in the bill but pleaded for a clearer, broader definition of that term.[84]

The effective participation of CEDaR in the larger discussions about the future need for educational research may have reflected in part the fact that the labs did not feel particularly threatened during the reauthorization process. This new attitude may have been influenced by the arrival of Deena Stoner, new executive director of CEDaR, who felt that the organization should play a larger, more constructive role in improving federal support of educational research and development.

CHAPTER 4

Restructuring and Reinventing OERI, 1993–97

Earlier chapters analyzed the origin and development of the regional educational laboratories and the R&D centers, with particular attention paid to the quality of their products, and investigated the extent and nature of congressional oversight of those long-standing institutions. Analysis of the labs' and centers' development over almost three decades was possible because these entities changed little with time — despite periodic fluctuations in popularity among education researchers and in the extent of federal financial and political support. Moreover, despite the larger organizational change in Washington, DC, as the National Institute of Education was absorbed within the Office of Educational Research and Improvement, major continuities continued to link the developmental and modern periods. The first three chapters carried the story only through 1992 to the new OERI reauthorization process, which called for a major restructuring and reorganization of that agency.

This chapter examines overall changes in OERI mainly from 1993 through 1997 to determine whether the proposed restructuring and reinventing of the agency had as much effect as some hoped and others feared. This chapter also scrutinizes the more recent fortunes of regional educational laboratories and R&D centers, albeit within the broader context of overall OERI developments. This larger historical perspective on recent changes at OERI will aid in developing recommendations for future improvements.

I. The Transition in OERI

OERI's March 1994 reauthorization significantly altered both the structure and some of the operating principles of the agency. With the return of a Democratic administration after a hiatus of more than a decade, educators and policymakers hoped for a more harmonious partnership between OERI and Congress that might result in major improvements within the agency. Yet changes at the agency, often unanticipated and unintended, weakened its ability to provide high-quality educational research, development, and statistics.

Emerson Elliott was named acting assistant secretary of OERI on January 22, 1993. Elliott was the commissioner of education statistics at the National Center for Education Statistics and was credited with transforming that organization into a highly effective and widely admired federal statistical agency (Harrison 1993; Sroufe 1995). Bush's few strictly political OERI appointees (the so-called schedule C appointees) were told to resign; however, Elliott asked everyone else to remain at their posts and to continue to function as they had before the election.[1]

In early March 1993, three names emerged as leading candidates for the position of OERI assistant secretary: David Berliner, professor of education at Arizona State University; Susan Furhman, director of the Consortium for Policy Research in Education at Rutgers University; and Sharon Robinson, director of the National Education Association's National Center for Innovation (Licitra 1993e). The White House passed over the two research-oriented candidates and nominated Sharon Robinson as the new assistant secretary of OERI, announcing her appointment in late March.[2]

Robinson earned a doctorate from the University of Kentucky in educational administration in 1979, served as a middle school and high school classroom teacher, and directed NEA's Instructional and Professional Division from 1980 through 1989. Since January 1990, she had directed the National Center for Innovation — NEA's research and development unit. When confirmed by the Senate in late June 1993, she became the first African American to serve as the assistant secretary of OERI (Hoff 1993).

Unlike her predecessor, Diane Ravitch, Robinson was not considered a major researcher or a distinguished scholar, but she was deeply committed to increasing the utilization of educational research in the classroom and improving teacher professional training.[3] Particularly interested in closer collaborations between researchers and classroom teachers, Robinson emphasized the value of teamwork. She downplayed the importance of expanding and revitalizing OERI's research staff but stressed the need for developing working partnerships between researchers and teachers. Providing equal public educational opportunities for all children was one of her primary goals — especially as this activity helped disadvantaged minority students to gain access to the resources and assistance needed for an adequate education. A dynamic and thoughtful speaker, Robinson received a rare standing ovation from the OERI staff at her first general agency meeting (Lictira 1993b).

Throughout her career as assistant secretary of OERI, Robinson tried to identify and serve the customers of the agency — parents, children, teachers, and policymakers. Somewhat reminiscent of former assistant secretary Christopher Cross, Ravitch's predecessor, Robinson emphasized the development of new strategies and better means of disseminating existing research to parents and teachers.[4]

As discussed earlier, disagreements over nature and powers of the proposed OERI policy board stalled the reauthorization of OERI in 1991 and 1992 (OERI bill 1992; OERI reauthorization 1992; Rothman 1992c, 1992d). With the arrival of the new administration, there was considerable optimism regarding a quick OERI reauthorization, but that hope died in 1993 (Licitra 1993c; Wong 1993; Schnaiberg 1993; Pitsch 1993). After much delay, a compromise was reached the following year. Rather than retaining the authority to develop and control OERI's long-term research agenda, the policy board was authorized to work with the assistant secretary to draft the agenda. Having settled these minor differences, Congress easily reauthorized OERI as part of the Goals 2000: Educate America Act on March 31, 1994, as Title IX of P.L. 103–27 (Pitsch and Schnaiberg 1994; Pitsch 1994; Schnaiberg 1994b; Licitra 1994).

The law called for the establishment of five national research institutes: the National Institute on Early Childhood Development and Education; the National Institute on Student Achievement, Curriculum, and Assessment; the National Institute on Education of At-Risk Children; the National Institute on Postsecondary Education, Libraries, and Lifelong Education; and the National Institute on Educational Governance, Finance, Policy-Making, and Management. The research institutes were authorized together at $100 million for FY96; at least 20 percent of those funds had to be allocated to field-initiated research and at least one-third to national research centers. The legislation also created a fifteen-member National Educational Research Policy and Priorities Board, calling for the establishment and implementation of high-quality standards for the conduct and evaluation of OERI research activities. Finally, the law mandated the establishment of the Office of Reform Assistance and Dissemination (ORAD), which was to include institutions and activities such as the regional educational laboratories, the Educational Resources Information Clearinghouses, and the National Diffusion Network (NDN).

The reauthorization of OERI was welcomed by most educators, policymakers, and researchers. Despite the earlier battles over the nature and powers of the National Educational Research Policy and Priorities Board, most observers were satisfied with the eventual compromise. And almost everyone thought that the restructuring of OERI was a step in the right direction, although some expressed concern about both the manner and the pace of implementing the new legislation (see, e.g., Sroufe et al. 1995).

II. Funding Increases and Staff Reductions

The previous chapter addressed the dramatic increases in overall OERI funding during the Bush administration. Funding for OERI continued to grow during the Clinton administration, although at a pace considerably slower than that of the previous four years. Overall funding rose from $286.2 million in FY93 to $398.1 million in FY97, a sizable 39 percent increase during those four years (the rate of increase in the previous four years had been a phenomenal 266 percent). Even in constant 1996 dollars, the rise in overall OERI spending from FY93 to FY97 was a substantial 25 percent (but still much less than the 214 percent constant dollar increase from FY89 to FY93).

The amount spent on the more traditional OERI programs (NCES, the centers and labs, field-initiated research, and ERIC) rose by only 25.3 percent from FY93 to FY97 while money for other, more recently added functions increased by 54.0 percent. As a result, the proportion of OERI funds allocated for the more traditional programs continued to decline (98.7 percent in FY89, 52.8 percent in FY93, and 47.6 percent in FY97).[5]

How one interprets the great expansion in OERI's nontraditional funding since FY89 depends in part on one's view about the current state of educational research and development. If one believes that there is already a "treasure chest" of well-researched information awaiting broader dissemination, then the direction of the recent changes in relative funding at OERI is welcome. But if one thinks that the amount of research and development is insufficient to provide much guidance for educators and policymakers, then the increasing focus on educational technology and dissemination might seem somewhat premature and misplaced. For example, in FY97 OERI spent approximately the same amount of money on new educational technology projects as it invested in the traditional centers, labs, field-initiated research, and ERIC combined. Given the recent sizable staff reductions, one might question the wisdom of a research-focused agency embarking on such new, large-scale initiatives — especially since many of them do not involve real research or development activities.[6]

In addition to the more modest increases in funding and shifts in the allocation of those monies, other important changes also took place. Congressman Major Owens (D-NY) in 1994 asked David Obey (D-WI), chair of the House Appropriations Committee, to include language in the FY95 appropriations bill that shifted educational research programs outside OERI into the jurisdiction of that agency (Schnaiberg 1994a). The House Committee on Appropriations report directed the Department of Education "to transfer the funding and management of research, evaluation and demonstration activities throughout the Department to OERI in the fiscal year 1996 budget" (U.S. House 1994a, 153). At first, Senator Thomas Harkin (D-IA), chair of the Senate Committee on Appropriations, did not take a position on the language mandating transfer of other research activities to OERI (Schnaiberg 1994a). After further deliberation, however, the Senate Committee on Appropriations also endorsed the consolidation of educational research within OERI (U.S. Senate 1994, 225).

The administration managed to persuade the House-Senate conference committee on appropriations to drop the language requiring the Department of Education to consolidate all of its research-related initiatives under the umbrella of OERI (U.S. House 1994c). But Congress established its point — it wanted OERI to oversee more of the federally funded research activities. While the department did not transfer other research programs as suggested, OERI did assure everyone involved that it would coordinate all research efforts within the department. Yet, except in the area of early childhood education, OERI provided little real coordination or consolidation of research activities within the Department of Education. Although several career officials were designated at various times to coordinate research-related activities within the Department of Education, most of them made only limited attempts to do so and did not achieve much success.

One of the most neglected subjects in OERI discussions is the recent OERI staff decrease and its impact on the functioning of the agency. The number of OERI employees was reduced by a sizable margin during the early years of the Reagan administration; this was followed by a small recovery in the number of full-time equivalent staff from 425 in FY88 to 448 in FY92 (a 5.4 percent increase).[7]

Department of Education staffing numbers during the Clinton administration have fluctuated. On the one hand, Congress expanded federal education funding and authorized the administration to staff new or existing initiatives such as the Direct Federal Student Loan Program. These developments increased the need for additional staff. On the other hand, the reinvention of the federal government was predicated in large part upon delivering existing services more efficiently so that the overall size of the federal government staff could be reduced. The net result in practice has been a small decrease in staff full-time equivalents at the Department of Education from 4,859 in FY92 to 4,655 in FY96 (a 4.2 percent decrease).

Although the overall size of the department staff has remained relatively stable, sizable and largely unnoticed shifts have occurred among the various agencies. The OERI was only one agency that lost a large proportion of its staff, moving from 448 in FY92 to 358 in FY96 (a decrease of 20.2 percent). The staff reductions did not end there; by March 1997, OERI had lost another 20 staff members (down to 338 FTEs). Thus, OERI's staff was smaller than it had been by approximately 25 percent when Assistant Secretary Ravitch left office in January 1993.[8]

An overview of the potential problems caused by the staff reductions is obvious when considering the amount of federal expenditures per FTE in OERI. While this is a complex ratio and by no means an entirely accurate indication of the amount of actual work facing the staff, this crude index does provide a useful perspective on the changes at OERI over time. In the early 1980s, each staff member at OERI represented in constant 1996 dollars approximately $170,000 to $200,000's worth of activity. The Reagan administration's major staff cuts were matched by reductions in agency spending, so that the burden of work from this perspective remained roughly the same. During the Bush administration, however, the large increases in OERI funding were accompanied by only modest staff increases so that by FY92 each individual in OERI accounted for approximately $975,000 in activities (in constant 1996 dollars) — four or five times as much activity as in the years of the Reagan administration. The continued increases in real expenditures at OERI coupled with the 25 percent reduction in staff means that each agency employee now represents $1.5 million's worth of activity (in constant 1996 dollars).[9] Thus, as the federal expenditures in real dollars in OERI have risen rapidly in the late 1980s and early 1990s, the availability of staff members to oversee these expenditures has dropped dramatically.

At the same time that the permanent OERI staff was reduced, another major staff shift occurred, but it elicited little attention from inside or outside the agency: the elimination of excepted service hiring. When NIE was created in the early 1970s, one of the most useful procedures granted to the agency was the option to hire highly qualified experts outside the regular civil service system for a three-year term (renewable one time). Critics charged that excepted service personnel were sometimes hired to circumvent the regular system or that the system was abused by politicians in order to hire unqualified friends. Despite these periodic challenges, excepted service continued as a useful practice (U.S. GAO 1987, 81–83).

In more recent years, excepted service has been almost totally discontinued at OERI. Congress was persuaded in 1994 to establish much more stringent criteria for hiring on excepted service roles. The new law still allows the hiring of scientific or technical employees for a three-year period, but it mandates competitions for those jobs and provides a fairly narrow definition of those qualified for application. Excepted service employers must now demonstrate that the scientific and technical needs cannot be met through the regular civil service system, an almost impossible task in principle given the current surplus of unemployed or underemployed behavioral and social scientists (Public Law 1994, sec. 912, c, 1).

The effects of this change in hiring criteria resulted in the elimination of almost all excepted service employees in OERI. In early 1993, approximately twenty excepted service employees served in OERI; in June 1997, only two excepted members remained — due primarily to the restrictions in the new law and the reluctance of OERI management to use this mechanism. Interestingly, there has been almost no notice taken and certainly little protest given by educational researchers or policymakers with regard to the elimination of this hitherto innovative way of bringing new ideas and people to OERI on a temporary basis.

One interesting and potentially very expensive staffing development is the effort by NCES to create a special outside contractor as a quasi-permanent source of professional and technical help. Many federal agencies already hire outside contractors to perform discrete tasks such as organize conferences, write position papers, and handle travel arrangements for invited speakers. This both helps the agency to focus on its primary work and overcomes government limitations on staff hiring. However, substantial overhead expenses often render these contracts with outside firms considerably more expensive than would be the case if the federal government were permitted to hire its own employees to do the work.[10]

Seeking to overcome recent FTE reductions, NCES created a separate entity in 1995 to help with its technical and statistical work — the Education Statistics Services Institute, or ESSI (U.S. House 1995, 1409–10). The institute was envisioned as a long-term adjunct of NCES that would work closely with the agency. In March 1997, approximately sixteen of the ESSI employees had their own offices in NCES — a rather unusual arrangement. Some raised complaints that ESSI personnel are in essence a new type of quasi-government employee and that their presence diminishes opportunities for advancement of regular federal career employees. Others have raised questions about the cost of the operation. Given the overhead for the operation, one rough estimate is that the actual cost of an ESSI employee may be approximately 40 percent higher than if NCES had put that individual on the federal payroll. Given the drastic staff reductions and the increasing volume of business in OERI, new mechanisms are necessary in order to handle the work of the agency.[11]

During the reinvention of OERI, adequate staffing for the agency was a major challenge. The office lost one out of every four employees from 1992 to 1997 — a devastating reduction under normal circumstances rendered even more difficult because OERI's overall responsibilities increased even as the organization was fundamentally restructured. As part of the general reinvention of the federal government, higher level staff members who had been with the Department of Education for a long time were offered a one-time bonus of $25,000 if they took early retirement. Approximately thirty senior OERI employees opted for this early retirement package, including some of the most experienced and valuable staff members. While the voluntary departure of these employees made it much easier to downsize the agency, it also eliminated competent middle-level managers who might have been particularly valuable in providing continuity and leadership in the restructured OERI.[12] Most of the employees who left were not replaced, and their departure left sizable staffing gaps in the smooth operation of the institution.

OERI's reductions provided considerable opportunities for the hiring of new employees. It is estimated that in recent years OERI has hired approximately seven to ten employees annually.[13] Some of these are recent college graduates entering federal service through the Outstanding Scholars Program. Staffing from this pool of recent graduates reduces the bureaucratic difficulties of hiring (it is much easier to process paperwork for an individual from the Outstanding Scholars Program than to employ someone from outside the federal government). While these new employees are often quite bright and capable, few have had extensive training and experience in research. Other recent staff additions have had prior government service, but most have had little training or previous work experience in research and development. As a result, despite continued staff hiring few new employees can be considered well trained, nationally recognized researchers and scholars.[14]

Staffing difficulties extended well beyond the reduction in numbers, the loss of senior-level employees, and difficulties in hiring qualified researchers. As OERI was restructured in 1994 and early 1995, the existing staff was shifted to the new positions. Staff disruptions might have been minimized by restricting the options available. For example, NCES employees could have remained in place since their unit was not restructured. The OERI authorities could have staffed the new institutes only with employees from the former Office of Research since the latter in essence had been dissolved to create the five national institutes. And certainly employees could have basically remained within their existing occupational categories in order to minimize dislocations. But Sharon Robinson was firmly committed to a major restructuring of OERI, which included giving all employees an opportunity to volunteer for any position in the agency (Robinson 1994a).

Many advantages were associated with allowing the employees to volunteer for whatever job they wanted and believed that they were qualified to handle. Many employees felt that their own career aspirations were finally being recognized and addressed by OERI. The federal employees' union was satisfied that the interests of its clients were protected, and therefore it cooperated fully with the management in implementing these extensive staff changes. And the opportunity to select one's place in the organization also gave everyone involved a personal sense of ownership in the restructuring of the agency.

But serious drawbacks to the staff selection process were also evident. Because the reorganization of OERI was still under way, management lacked a detailed sense of staff needs in each unit. Indeed, acting directors of the various units had just been announced—giving employees volunteering for positions an opportunity to consider future supervisors but not providing the new acting directors with adequate time to determine the specific personnel needs for their units. Moreover, because the employees were not rigidly constrained in the type of job classification they were permitted to seek, many lower level employees used the opportunity to move out of support positions into administrative and research jobs. Management might have exercised more control over the final decisions to match more closely the needs of the agency with those of the employees (as suggested in Robinson's September 8 memorandum). In practice, OERI allowed employees to take almost any position they desired—although informal discussions with the new acting directors undoubtedly guided the stated preferences of some. On October 26, 1994, Robinson announced that approximately 95 percent of the staff members had been granted their first choice of position (1994b).[15]

Heavy reliance upon employee preferences led to unanticipated imbalances in staffing the new OERI. Some of the designated units received more employees than planned—partly because employees wanted to work in those areas and partly because they often sought out acting directors thought to be effective and congenial leaders. While most employees stayed within their original job classification, some members of the support staff did attempt to improve their long-term career prospects by moving into administrative and research positions. The net result was a shortage of support staff. Thus, many higher grade employees had to type, make copies, handle mail, and answer telephones. At the same time, some members of the support staff moving into new positions lacked the experience or technical training necessary for those jobs.

The new OERI provided more than ample opportunities for training in team building and improving customer service. For example, Sharon Robinson placed Preston Foster, a White House Fellow active and influential in OERI, in charge of working with all employees to improve their customer service skills (Foster 1995).

Unfortunately, no comparable training was provided to the OERI staff in statistical and technical areas. While the assistant secretary repeatedly touted the value of staff training to further team activities and improve customer service, she did not emphasize the importance and necessity of employees developing the technical and statistical skills that many of them needed in their new positions.

Almost all of the employees had indicated job preferences and been reassigned by October 1994, but physical relocation was not completed until early 1995. While OERI experienced considerable pressure during 1994 and 1995 to restructure its fundamental operations, establish and work with the new National Educational Research Policy and Priorities Board, and develop a new research priority plan for the next five years, the number of employees available to work on these projects was reduced significantly. Almost all were preoccupied with rethinking their own career opportunities, and many devoted considerable effort to learning how to be better team members. Not surprisingly, the ongoing staff changes often significantly reduced the ability of OERI during these years to devote adequate time and attention to meeting some of the other challenges it faced.

III. Reinventing OERI

The activity requiring the most time and energy during Robinson's nearly four-year tenure as assistant secretary was the "reinventing of OERI." The impetus for OERI's reinvention grew out of recommendations made by the 1992 National Academy of Sciences study, mandates from OERI congressional reauthorization legislation, and directives from the more general efforts within the Clinton administration to improve government operations. While the restructuring of OERI was almost inevitable under the circumstances, considerable latitude was given as to the type and measure of effort invested in this undertaking. OERI chose to pursue an intensive and time-consuming strategy for reinventing itself. Whether the extra time and effort put into the reinvention were ultimately the best use of the agency's limited resources, however, is doubtful.

Little consensus exists among analysts on the specific components constituting the current "reinventing government" movement. Policymakers and scholars often emphasize different aspects of the movement, some in direct or indirect contradiction to each other. Despite this apparent discord, the Government Accounting Office conducted a useful review of the public and private administrative reforms, singled out the general causes for recent changes and then subdivided the managerial reforms into four categories (U.S. GAO 1994, 2).

The call for fundamental changes at OERI predated the reinvention of government movement. At the urging of Assistant Secretary Christopher Cross, a fifteen-member panel of the National Academy of Sciences convened to investigate OERI in 1991–92. The NAS report recommended redefining the mission of OERI, reorganizing the agency, and improving the methods by which work was being done (Atkinson and Jackson 1992, 4). The NAS panel further suggested the restructuring of the office, similar to the reauthorization legislation enacted in March 1994 (ibid.).

As discussed in chapter 3, Congressman Owens took the lead in drafting the OERI reauthorization legislation. He did not begin with an elaborate plan to reorganize the agency but focused on creating a large center to help at-risk students and develop a mechanism to shield OERI from undue political influence. However, as other participants in the policy-making process interjected ideas and suggestions, the reauthorization legislation expanded, ultimately mandating a fundamental restructuring of OERI. The new legislation required the creation of the National Educational Research Policy and Priorities Board, five national research institutes, and the national educational dissemination system. It also specified in considerable detail the characteristics and functions of each of these entities (P.L. 1994).

The reauthorization of OERI coincided roughly with the more general movement within the federal government to streamline operations. After only a few weeks in office, President Clinton designated Vice President Al Gore as head of the National Performance Review (NPR), an agency charged with reinventing the federal government. In the first of a series of annual reports from the National Performance Review, Gore summarized the rationale for this massive undertaking:

> The National Performance Review is about change — historic change — in the way the government works. The Clinton adminis-

tration believes it is time for a new customer service contract with the American people, a new guarantee of effective, efficient, and responsive government. As our title makes clear, the National Performance Review is about moving from red tape to results to create a government that works better and costs less. (Gore 1993a, i)

The effort to reorganize and reform the federal government was not new; nearly a dozen previously created commissions had attempted during the twentieth century to improve the performance of the federal government. Most of these, however, effected little lasting change.[16] The National Performance Review was modeled in part after similar efforts in private industry and was developed in a political climate that emphasized reducing federal expenditures and increasing government efficiency. With both managerial and political motives, the Clinton administration continued to stress the importance of reinventing government; thus, agencies such as OERI soon received directives to reinvent themselves.[17]

The National Institute for Education and its successor, OERI, had initiated periodic major restructuring within the agency. Most reorganization efforts sought to improve the efficiency and effectiveness of the office. But Grady McGonagill, an analyst of the 1977–78 NIE changes, pointed out other potential, but less obvious, benefits for incoming executives responsible to reorganize NIE/OERI. Reorganization provided (McGonagill 1981, 3):

1. A means of quickly learning a great deal about the personnel and programs of the agency
2. A way to acquire a sense of ownership of the agency, enhancing the capacity to represent it
3. A means of cutting the ground out from under critics by rendering criticism obsolete
4. A way of buying time to develop and initiate a political strategy for the agency
5. A means of realigning an agency's political commitments
6. A one-time opportunity to exploit the uncertainty and receptivity of agency staff to make changes that would later be resisted
7. A chance to introduce changes as part of a larger package that might be successfully resisted if introduced alone
8. An opportunity for the ceremony and ritual that satisfy unconscious and irrational purposes

Despite the obvious short-term attraction to reorganization, hindsight shows that many earlier NIE/OERI changes were questionable in terms of overall net benefits, especially since restructuring required so much time and energy perhaps better allocated elsewhere. When NIE was founded in the early 1970s, it experienced four reorganizations within a two-year period, contributing to the prevailing impression that the agency was unstable and in disarray (Sproull, Weiner, and Wolf 1978). The subsequent 1977–78 reorganization of NIE perhaps led to a more effective agency, but many participants questioned whether the improvements could have been introduced more effectively through gradual, incremental, less disruptive changes (McGonagill 1981). Similarly, Carl Kaestle's interviews with former participants in the OERI reorganizations of the 1980s revealed that many policymakers later regretted investing tremendous resources and effort in the restructuring of the agency (1993).

While a few members of the staff in 1993–95 were aware of the limited and disappointing results of the previous reorganizations, Assistant Secretary Robinson remained optimistic and enthusiastic about reinventing OERI. Given the legislative mandate and directives from the National Performance Review initiative, she had little choice but to embark on the restructuring. Yet Robinson's commitment to reinventing OERI extended well beyond meeting the minimal legal and bureaucratic requirements. She was genuinely excited by the prospect of working closely with her staff to restructure OERI. In fact, Robinson devoted an extraordinary amount of the agency's resources to orienting the staff toward team building and customer service. One of the few consultants she hired was Bruce Barkley, a University of Maryland adjunct faculty management specialist, who provided most of the customer-driven management training for the staff.[18]

For nearly a year, OERI participated in the reinventing process before the agency was reauthorized. As part of one of the thirty-eight reports accompanying the National Performance Review release in September 1993, employees outlined plans to "Build a professional, mission-driven structure for research" (Gore 1993b, 55). In the last three months of 1993, nine OERI working groups drafted background papers on the themes of the proposed five national research institutes, the proposed Office of Reform Assistance and Dissemination, professional development, technology, and the proposed National Library of Education. On December 7, 1993, Assistant Secretary Robinson convened a meeting with representatives from other units within the Department of Education to discuss how OERI could work with other involved parties on areas of common concern (Payer 1995).

After the reauthorization of OERI on March 31, 1994, reinvention activities within the agency gained more urgency and momentum. Based upon meetings with the senior program officers, on April 25, 1994, OERI issued its strategic plan, which set forth the agency's mission:

We *provide national leadership in the development and use of knowledge* to promote equality of opportunity and excellence in education for all learners. (OERI 1994, 1, emphasis original)[19]

After defining its customers (such as educators, researchers, policymakers, and parents), OERI defined four major goals for the office:

Goal 1. To expand the Nation's fundamental knowledge and understanding of education through research and analysis.
Goal 2. To provide statistics and research for monitoring, understanding and improving education.
Goal 3. To promote research-based reform at all levels of education.
Goal 4. To transform OERI into a high performance organization distinguished by customer focus and work satisfaction. (OERI 1994, 2)

At an OERI-wide meeting on April 26, 1994, with Secretary of Education Richard Riley present, Robinson presented the strategic plan to the staff and called upon all employees to participate in the reinvention endeavor (Payer 1995). Three weeks later, Robinson issued a written invitation to all OERI staff members to volunteer for at least one of the ten OERI reinvention teams.[20] A Planning and Implementation Council, chaired by Robinson, was also created to coordinate and facilitate OERI's reinvention activities. Dick Hays, the deputy assistant secretary, took responsibility for the day to day oversight of the planning and implementation process. By early June, the ten OERI reinvention teams were created and functioning.

At the same time that OERI organized itself into reinvention teams and sought help from other agencies in the Department of Education, its employees asked their customers for input and guidance. For example, on March 22, 1994, the assistant secretary met with the National Education Association and three dozen other education associations to solicit their views on OERI performance.[21]

While the ten reinvention teams drafted reports and made suggestions on the reinvention process, an influential OERI Coordination Team under the direction of Emerson Elliott was created on July 18, 1994.[22] The team was charged with digesting drafts produced by the other teams, addressing cross-cutting issues, and developing a short options paper that dealt with possible structures and characteristics of the new OERI. The Coordination Team completed its assignment on August 8, and its recommendations, only slightly modified, were then approved by the reinvention team facilitators at an August 10 retreat. Retreat participants issued fifteen statements that served as the basis for the subsequent reorganization and operation of the agency (Office of the Assistant Secretary 1994a).

At an OERI-wide staff meeting on September 8, 1994, Assistant Secretary Robinson revealed the new plans for the reorganization of OERI. In early 1993, OERI had four major divisions besides the Office of the Assistant Secretary (OAS): the National Center for Education Statistics, the Office of Research, Programs for the Improvement of Practice, and Library Programs. A fifth, the Fund for the Improvement and Reform of Schools and Teaching (FIRST), was a smaller unit reporting directly to OAS.

The new plan unveiled by Robinson was both more simple and more complex: divisions were more functional, but she recommended more of them. Rather than a single Office of Research, there were now five national research institutes. The National Center for Education Statistics remained the same, but Programs for the Improvement of Practice was renamed and reorganized as the Office of Reform Assistance and Dissemination. Library Programs was now subdivided into the National Library of Education and Library Programs. A new unit called Media and Information Services was created. The National Educational Research Policy and Priorities Board, which remained unappointed, was charted as working directly with the Office of the Assistant Secretary.

By the fall of 1994, OERI had created its new structure. The great accomplishments of the past year came at considerable cost because of the OERI staff time and effort needed to plan and then implement the reorganization of that agency. Moreover, much remained to be done on the reinvention efforts, including the reallocation of staff to new units and the development of the congressionally mandated research priorities plan (topics addressed later in this chapter).

IV. National Research Institutes

The centerpiece of the OERI reauthorization was the creation of the five national research institutes. While the proponents of these institutes had envisioned large-scale operations modeled after those in NIH, the actual amount of monies available was rather modest — $43 million for all of them in both FY96 and FY97, only about $10 million more than had been spent just on the R&D centers in FY95 (U.S. House 1996, 1388):

1. Achievement Institute, $12.9 million
2. At-Risk Institute, $12.9 million
3. Policy Institute, $4.3 million
4. Early Childhood Institute, $6.45 million
5. Postsecondary Institute, $6.45 million

The funds appropriated for three of the five national research institutes fell well below what many of its original supporters believed necessary to set up such an institution. Indeed, some national research institute supporters suggested that, given the small amount of total funding, OERI should have created, at present, only the Achievement Institute and the At-Risk Institute with a larger budget of $21.5 million each.

Despite these misgivings, the legislation mandated the establishment of five national research institutes and provided an extensive list of possible research topics for each, more extensive, in fact, than could be reasonably accomplished with limited funding. After considerable internal and external discussion, OERI developed its own, often unspecific, set of priorities for each institute.

Initially, the five national research institutes lumped most of their $43 million budget into the seven R&D centers (expanded to eleven centers by FY97). Legislation did mandate that the institutes invest at least one-third in the centers. However, in FY97 the institutes spent $31.15 million on them (57.7 percent), allocating $14.3 million to field-initiated research — 26.5 percent of the total institute funds. Only $8.55 million was slated for special studies, cross-cutting activities, fellowships, and peer reviews, 15.8 percent of the total institute budget (U.S. House 1996, 1388; U.S. House 1997, 1485). Thus, expenditures for the five national research institutes were more diverse than those of the former Office of Research, which had focused mainly on the R&D centers. Despite this diversification, the centers continued to receive almost 60 percent of the budget.

The last three decades have seen significant changes in the amount of annual funding for R&D centers. In the late 1960s and early 1970s, center budgets averaged between $3 and $5 million annually (in constant 1996 dollars). Over time, average center funding decreased sharply — in the late 1970s and early 1980s averaging between $2 and $3 million annually (in constant 1996 dollars). When the number of centers greatly expanded in the late 1980s, average annual funding for each center decreased again, reaching a low in FY91 of about $1 million (in constant 1996 dollars).[23]

In 1992, the National Academy of Sciences recommended that all R&D centers should be funded annually at no less than $3 million or

$3.35 million in constant 1996 dollars (Atkinson and Jackson 1992, 150–51). Other observers argued for even larger R&D centers, funded at perhaps $6 to $8 million annually (Vinovskis 1993a). Given the general consensus that the R&D centers in the early 1990s were both small and underfunded, coupled with specific NAS recommendations for at least $3 million minimum funding, Congress's mandate to fund the centers at a $1.5 million annual minimum was surprising and disappointing.

Total center funding (in constant 1996 dollars) remained relatively stable from FY92 to FY97. However, the number of centers fell by more than one-half in that time period. In FY92, there were twenty-two R&D centers, while five years later only eleven existed. As a result, the average annual funding (in constant 1996 dollars) of the centers more than doubled in size, from $1.28 million in FY92 to $2.76 million in FY97.

A review of current average expenditures is somewhat misleading, as most centers remain very small. Only two of the eleven extant R&D centers in FY97 received adequate annual funding: the National Center for Research on the Education of Students Placed at Risk ($5 million); and the National Center for Research on Education, Diversity, and Excellence ($4 million). Eight other centers operated on only $2.5 or $2.8 million each. Moreover, OERI recently allocated a twelfth R&D center only $1.5 million annual funding. Frequently, only half of all center funding went directly to research or development expenditures (the rest was spent in other areas such as dissemination, administration, and overhead costs); thus, it is likely that this serious underfunding limits actual research activities that can be attempted at these small R&D centers.[24]

Some strengths and weaknesses of the R&D centers are apparent in the newly released OERI third-year interim review, undertaken in 1998 and 1999, of nine of the twelve centers.[25] Each of the centers was assigned five to seven expert reviewers, who were provided with the original proposals, subsequent modifications, performance reports, and selected center publications or reports. Each center review included a two- or three-day site visit and resulted in a collective report from the review team (occasionally accompanied by individual reports). Reviewers commented on the quality of the center's work, its dissemination and outreach activities, and management issues within it.[26]

The results of the nine center reviews were summarized by OERI in a September 1999 report presented to the National Educational Research Policies and Priorities Board (OERI 1999). Individual center reports, however, were first made available to the public and policymakers only in April 2000 under the Freedom of Information Act (FOIA).[27] The OERI summary figured prominently in the NERPPB and policy-making discussions about the centers. However, that report stresses the positive accomplishments of the centers while downplaying some problems uncovered by the individual review teams. This occurred in part because the overall conclusions of many review panels are more flattering and enthusiastic than is warranted by in-depth analyses of projects and operations.[28]

Overall, the reviews of the nine centers were useful, interim assessments that suggest promising avenues for midcourse corrections. Although most reviewers were competent and thoughtful experts, not all were distinguished national scholars in their fields. Most center evaluations were serious, in-depth analyses, but a few reviews did not investigate as completely or thoroughly as others.[29] The reviewers interacted well with major publications and reports of the centers, offering both praise and constructive, sometimes penetrating, suggestions for future improvements. The analyses were limited, however, by the fact that the interim evaluations were forced to address work in progress rather than completed studies. Moreover, since the centers provided only "selected" research reports and publications, some of the smaller, less sophisticated, or unsuccessful studies may have eluded evaluation.[30]

One major disappointment in the third-year center review process was the lack of attention paid to the budgets, especially those of individual projects. This oversight rendered comment on the cost effectiveness or adequate funding for those particular endeavors virtually impossible. Considering the substantial funds typically allocated to administrative expenses, overhead, and dissemination as well as the large number of projects most centers support, the size of many individual projects was undoubtedly modest.

Although a few centers tried to coordinate various projects into a larger whole, many were unable to achieve this integration in practice since many centers worked with multiple, geographically dispersed partners. Thus, reviewers frequently commented that many individual projects were first rate but failed to work as a broad, cohesive unit. For example, the review team praised the work of the National Center on Early Development and Learning but pointed out that "the current center is focused more as a collection of individual research projects and there is a need for staff to step back and identify how they can move to a set of cohesive, related research activities that impact present and future practice and policy—i.e., a national center" (OERI Review Team, n.d. [NCEDL], 1).

Again, with a few notable exceptions reviewers found little evidence of systematic development, in which promising ideas or practices are rigorously tested and their impact in diverse and more typical classroom and school settings then evaluated. Instead, they complained that some center studies were conducted in unusual settings under the extraordinary leadership of the innovators, with little likelihood that such programs could be successfully incorporated in traditional schools. The interim review of the National Center for Improving Student Learning and Achievement in Mathematics and Science complained that "many of the curriculum projects that are used by the Center as test environments for identifying and validating design principles are idiosyncratic to the instructor and researcher and are situated in atypical sites far removed from mainstream classes. This makes transportability nearly impossible" (OERI Review Team, n.d. [Improving], 13). Moreover, projects were sometimes criticized for not attempting to translate research for use by teachers or policymakers. The reviewers of the National Center for the Study of Adult Learning and Literacy (NCSALL) concluded that "the projects, overall have a strong theoretical emphasis. Limited attention is paid, across the board, to how research will improve practice" (OERI Review Team 1999a, 10).

Although reviewers praised the work of the centers and offered suggestions designed to encourage midcourse corrections and improvements, they cautioned against anyone using the reports as a comprehensive or summary assessment of overall center operations. Many of the reviewers understood and were troubled by the fact that OERI considered using these interim evaluations as a major factor in deciding whether a center should be renewed for another five years. Not only was the review process not designed for such use, but the center work completed by the time of the third-year review was too limited and incomplete to provide sufficient information for a renewal decision. Moreover, Congress has not reauthorized the centers; nor have OERI and NERPPB developed a new and comprehensive research and development strategy for the future. Recent attempts by OERI to extend some center funding for another five years is both premature and inappropriate.

Although annual funding for many individual projects within the centers continues at only $30,000 to $50,000, the size of the field-initiated grants has grown considerably. The Postsecondary Institute, for example, funded six field-initiated studies in FY96, averaging $210,000 annually (the grants covered two and three years of work). Thus, an attractive feature of the center system, in principle, is its concentration of more research monies on a few large-scale, long-term projects than is usually provided to individual scholars through grants. Today, however, the situation may be reversed. Many field-initiated grants may be larger than individual projects conducted by centers.

The research plans for many of the individual projects in old R&D

center applications were poorly developed and unclear. These projects frequently devoted the first year to a review of the secondary literature, after which a more careful, detailed design of the subsequent research work was developed.[31] Moreover, center awards often included projects of very mixed quality, some parts excellent and some so weak that they probably would not have stood a rigorous outside peer review.

Successful field-initiated grants, on the other hand, focus and develop research proposals in order to win in the intense competition for individual funding. Because applicants are expected to be aware of secondary work in the field, there is less need to devote the first year of the project to a review of the existing literature before proceeding to original work. Most field-initiated grants are for only two or three years and can ill afford the luxury of reviewing secondary literature for the first year of a project before undertaking new research.

Since the center grants focused on a particular problem area, however, it was easier for OERI to target its resources to these sites rather than holding a relatively general, open-ended, field-initiated grant competition. The centers also provided an opportunity for researchers to work together on a common set of issues and required them to disseminate findings more broadly than most individual researchers are willing to do.

The advantages of the center approach might be duplicated, at least in part, by holding mission-oriented competitions for field-initiated research grants. That is, OERI might call for research on a particular area, such as summer learning or the education of pregnant adolescents, and then allow researchers to propose specific topics within that subject. Following the practice of many other federal research agencies, the institutes could convene the funded individual researchers to exchange ideas among themselves. The institutes might also synthesize the research results of these mission-oriented individual grants and disseminate the results among other researchers and educational practitioners. In order to administer and oversee a mission-oriented competition, OERI might hire a leading expert in that substantive area as an excepted service employee for three to six years. In any case, the advantages and disadvantages of funding research through individual grants or the existing R&D center system should be carefully evaluated in the near future and a beneficial alternative to current funding methods considered.

Because there are now fewer but larger centers, and because OERI was directed to develop a coherent, long-term research priority plan to guide its investments, one might imagine that there will be even closer integration of centers. Unfortunately, center attempts at integration have been rather disappointing. Faced with the slow development of an overall

OERI research priority plan, discussed later, the center competition was held well before the development of any coherent plan. And rather than working together closely to integrate the new set of centers each of the five institutes pursued its own agenda and interests independent of any other. Moreover, the competition announcement in the *Federal Register* for the seven centers lacked an overall framework or coherence, so that applicants for the competition and reviewers for each center treated them as isolated. Thus, while the set of eleven centers may be good individually, they are not conceptually or operationally integrated.[32]

One factor contributing to the lack of coordination among the five institutes, as well as among the other units within OERI, is that no one person is organizationally or intellectually responsible for the overall research agenda. Under the old system, all R&D centers were located within the Office of Research, headed by Acting Director Joseph Conaty, an experienced and respected researcher. Now each of the institute directors reports directly to the assistant secretary, who is able to offer only minimal supervision. Various ad hoc schemes have been tried in an attempt to improve coordination among the institutes, with occasional success. In practice, however, the system has become even more fragmented. The expected close coordination between the institutes and the rest of OERI has not materialized except in a few isolated instances.

Adding to the confusion and lack of research coordination among the institutes is the fact that OERI itself seems to have less intellectual leadership and direction than it did five years ago. Assistant Secretary Ravitch had been very interested and involved in the intellectual direction and research agenda of OERI; Robinson was less concerned with the research agenda and focused more on translating existing research findings for the agency's customers. As research adviser to the assistant secretary, I helped to coordinate OERI research activities, but upon my departure in August 1993 Robinson did not appoint anyone to replace me. She endorsed the concept of an OERI research adviser on several occasions; however, that position remains vacant.[33] Due to a lack of oversight, OERI is experiencing a major vacuum in the guidance of its intellectual and research activities. This gap has become all the more glaring because of the elimination of the Office of Research and the coordinating and leadership role that some of its directors played.

In terms of overall staffing, the institutes' experiences have been mixed. The five acting institute directors were selected from existing OERI staff; most of them had previous research experience, though few were still active researchers. Although OERI was expected to be able to recruit outside researchers as permanent directors, the final competition resulted in the appointment of only one outsider as an institute director.

Though OERI's staff had been reduced by approximately one-fourth since FY92, the staffs of the institutes in FY95 were approximately the same size as they had been in the Office of Research. Over time, however, the number of staff members in these institutes has decreased considerably. In June 1997, there were only 64 institute staff members, a substantial 15 percent drop from the 77 present in October 1994.

The institutes fared relatively well within OERI in that they possessed a generally competent leadership and sizable staffs, although they still lack an adequate number of trained and distinguished researchers. Some current staff members have had graduate-level training and experience in research, but most have not. Nor are there many nationally recognized scholars serving in the institutes. The distribution of the researchers among the institutes is also uneven. For example, until very recently the Early Childhood Institute had no experienced researchers on its staff even though its mission advocated a close working relationship with the research community. Moreover, several of the other institutes had only two or three researchers, hardly enough for a critical intellectual mass to carry out the research and development functions expected of them. Without the national intellectual leadership originally envisioned for the staff of the institutes, high-quality research and synthesis has not been produced as expected.

One primary objective of the institutes is the production of high-quality research and critical syntheses of secondary works that would prove helpful to policymakers and educators. So far, most of the institutes have produced only a few publications — usually directories of researchers and service providers, materials for parents, or limited analyses of some isolated issues (Gruskin, Silverman, and Bright 1997; Owens 1997; National Institute on Early Childhood Development and Education 1997). Regrettably, the shortage of active researchers in the institutes and OERI's lack of encouragement to its staff to write scholarly publications means that it may be unrealistic to expect broad-based analytic studies or syntheses from the institutes in the near future.[34]

Although the five national research institutes were to be the centerpiece of the new OERI, the agency seems to have relegated them to a secondary role. Despite the modest $43 million appropriations for the institutes for FY96, OERI did not request any increase in that budget the following year, preferring instead to request $250 million to support a new Technology Literacy Challenge Fund to integrate computer technology into the classroom (U.S. House 1996, 309–12). Congress allocated an additional $16 million to OERI in FY97. After considerable debate over how to spend the additional money, OERI designated $11 million of those funds for the institutes, most of which was invested in an additional center ($2 million), more field-initiated studies ($5.5 million), or special studies ($2.8 million) (U.S. House 1997, 1485).

As large new programs are added to OERI, the agency often decides to set them apart rather than directing the institutes to supervise the new activities. For example, although the Achievement Institute is concerned with improving the use of technology in the classroom and specializes in developing better tests, OERI decided not to have that institute oversee the new high-priority initiatives in educational technology or testing. In fact, personnel from the institutes are sometimes temporarily reassigned to work on new projects under the supervision of the newer unit, thus further diminishing the importance and function of the institutes. As a result, one might easily argue that in some ways the national research institutes now are less important and less central to the mission of OERI than the Office of Research was five years ago — a startling reversal of Congress's intentions for the new OERI. Even more surprising is the fact that the decline in the relative role of the institutes within OERI has gone largely unnoticed and uncontested by the educational research community and interested policymakers.

V.   Office of Reform Assistance and Dissemination

Throughout the long history of NIE and OERI, legislators and educators frequently criticized each agency for failing to disseminate research information to classroom teachers. These critics have often exaggerated the availability of reliable and useful research information about educational practices and have seriously underestimated NIE's and OERI's efforts to distribute that knowledge. Indeed, it could be argued that NIE and OERI have tried harder and obtained more success than many other federal research agencies in disseminating information to the public and practitioners (Atkinson and Jackson 1992, 128–29).

Prior to OERI's 1994 reorganization, OERI had actively sought to improve program development and disseminate the results through its Programs for the Improvement of Practice. The 1994 reauthorization of OERI created the Office of Reform Assistance and Dissemination, which assumed most of PIP's functions. ORAD has four divisions: the State and Local Support Division (SLSD), the Knowledge Applications Division (KAD), the Development and Demonstration Programs Division (DDPD), and the Learning Technologies Division (LTD).

Despite policymakers' and educators' repeated emphasis that ORAD should provide links between research and practice, staffing problems have hampered its operation. Whereas its predecessor, PIP, had 73 employees in 1990, ORAD had only 61 staff members in March 1997 (a 15 percent decrease). Thus, while Congress and the Clinton administration envisioned an expanded and improved level of dissemination and reform assistance through ORAD, the restructured operation had substantially fewer employees and had lost some of its most effective and experienced managers through early retirement during the buyout period.

Search for a Permanent ORAD Director

Perhaps an even more unsettling situation lay in ORAD's long-term operation without a permanent director. Eve Bither, hired by Assistant Secretary Ravitch in 1992 as acting director of PIP, was considered one of the more competent and effective OERI division managers.[35] When ORAD was created in 1994, she was named acting director; but a few of the Clinton political appointees still viewed her with some reservations simply because she had been appointed initially by Robinson's predecessor. When the position for the permanent director of ORAD was advertised, it was rumored that Bither would not be selected despite her impressive credentials and considerable OERI achievements and experience. Eventually, Bither also applied for and received in June 1996 the important position of executive director of the National Educational Research Policy and Priorities Board (New research 1996). Ron Cartwright, a highly effective and well-respected career employee, replaced Bither as acting director of ORAD, but his influence was somewhat limited since he had not sought the permanent position himself.

In the meantime, OERI placed an advertisement in the *Federal Register* for a permanent ORAD director at the senior executive service (SES) level. Several strong prospects applied, including two of the more capable in-house career employees, but OERI was especially interested in a particular outside candidate whose application initially was rejected by the Department of Education personnel office as unqualified for the high-level SES position. Rather than fill the position with someone else, OERI canceled the search.

The agency then rewrote and readvertised the position request and attempted to help the desired individual write a stronger application. While the candidate for the ORAD position was now included in the pool of potentially acceptable applicants, that individual still did not emerge as one of the leading candidates. That applicant, however, mobilized a large-scale outside letter-writing campaign to persuade the OERI management to appoint the applicant. The agency hesitated because the strongest candidates were still the internal applicants; at the same time, it was wary of antagonizing the vocal and active supporters mobilized on behalf of that particular candidate. Rather than face the politically difficult task of making a decision, OERI again canceled the competition. The position for the director of ORAD was then advertised a third time. Now determined to make an appointment, OERI hired Pierce A. Hammond, another outside candidate.

The lengthy search for a permanent director and the controversy surrounding the process seriously hindered the ability of ORAD to operate as effectively as it might have been able to do otherwise. The timing of this hiring controversy was particularly unfortunate because ORAD now needed strong long-term leadership to implement its new mandates. Moreover, while most OERI employees familiar with the hiring effort were initially sympathetic to recruiting an outside candidate for ORAD director, the management and resultant disarray of this competition created residual bad feelings among some career staff members.

One of ORAD's most important responsibilities was to guide and monitor the activities of the regional educational laboratories. Although the past had seen considerable controversy surrounding the regional labs, some observers were now hopeful that with a new administration a closer and more harmonious relationship might develop between them and OERI.[36]

The Policy Studies Associates Report

Congress reauthorized the regional educational laboratories along lines similar to those in the past but did provide for the possibility of expanding the number of labs from ten to twelve (although this expansion has not occurred). Following the conceptual scheme employed in other federal educational legislation in 1994, each laboratory was expected to "promote the implementation of broad-based systemic school improvement strategies." A lengthy list enumerated permissible tasks for the labs — ranging from the development and dissemination of educational research products to the provision of technical assistance and training for state and local educators. In the 1994 lab reauthorization legislation, Congress again ambiguously stated who was responsible for setting the research and development priorities of the labs. On the one hand, the labs were to be governed by their own regional boards. On the other, they were to respond to the needs of the federal government as set forth in the five-year lab contracts and were to coordinate their activities with other OERI units such as the national research institutes and the National Diffusion Network (NDN) (Public Law 1994, sec. 941h).

As OERI prepared for the 1995 lab recompetition, it had a considerable amount of new information about the laboratory system operation. My internal study of the quality of lab research and development, completed in June 1993, was widely distributed and discussed within OERI. While endorsing the overall concept of educational laboratories, I raised serious questions about them — ranging from their lack of national orientation to the uneven quality of their research and development efforts. While some lab directors challenged the study as too critical, other outside analysts wished that it had more candidly addressed the poor quality of the work produced by most labs. As an OERI consultant in 1994 and 1995, I continued to remind the agency of the need to improve the mission and functioning of the recently reauthorized regional educational laboratories (Vinovskis 1993a).

In preparation for the 1995 competition for lab contracts, OERI had commissioned a $750,000 three-year lab evaluation. Policy Studies Associates won that contract in 1991 and began work on perhaps the largest single evaluation of the labs (Turnbull 1991). Policy Studies Associates examined such aspects of the labs as their system of governance, collaboration with other institutions, development, and technical assistance.

Brenda Turnbull and M. Bruce Haslam drafted an interesting and useful description and brief analysis of how the lab governing boards commenced and operated, revealing considerable variation in practices among the ten institutions. In one of the more important sections, they discussed the OERI-lab interactions. Unfortunately, while this part of the report reviewed the 1985 and 1990 requests for proposals and raised useful questions, it did not investigate in sufficient detail the actual interactions between OERI and the labs. What happened, for instance, when the interests of the labs, as stated by either their governing boards or their management staffs, conflicted with the directives from OERI (Turnbull and Haslam 1994)?

The final hundred-page report devoted most of its space and attention to interesting case studies of diverse lab activities. In the conclusion of the evaluation, Policy Studies Associates listed some strengths and weaknesses of current labs. Among the positive findings were the following characteristics:

> Participants in laboratory activities almost uniformly express satisfaction with the experience. Moreover, the presence of specific, common themes in their reports suggests that there are in fact distinctive strengths in the works of laboratories (whereas more global, vague praise would have suggested to us that participants were showing more politeness than discernment). . . . To our surprise, we also found that almost 40 percent of the participants in workshops or

recipients of products reported a change in behavior — usually a trial of "something new" on the job — as a result of the information provided by the laboratory. . . . Similarly, the information transmitted to policymakers or their advisors has often been put to work, according to the recipients. . . . "Quality" is a term with many meanings. Rather than try to define or judge quality ourselves, we asked participants for their assessments of the quality of specific examples of laboratory work, and most rated it high. (Turnbull et al. 1994, 88–89)

While Policy Studies Associates found high rates of satisfaction among the clients of the labs, they questioned lab responsiveness to local needs, the cost effectiveness of their work, and scientific rigor of lab self-evaluations:

Some of the products, processes, and assistance efforts proffered by laboratories reflect optimistic assumptions about the preferences or agendas of practitioners — in other words, they reflect the failure of marketing. . . . We have seen flawed marketing in the laboratories' development and attempted dissemination of many large, unwieldy compendia of research findings; in some efforts to enlist educators as volunteer disseminators of laboratory processes and products; in a few policymakers' perception that some laboratories are only willing to do work that advances a particular agenda; and in the assumption that particular organizations strategically situated to assist schools actually share a laboratory's agenda of school improvement. . . . Although we are genuinely impressed by the favorable comments that we gathered from participants in the laboratories' activities, we worry in some cases about the ratio between satisfied participants and dollars spent. Whether in a development activity that does not seem destined for second-generation dissemination at a reduced per participant cost, or in technical assistance for capacity building that has not yet resulted in trickle-down benefits beyond the organization directly helped, laboratories are sometimes prone to delivering very good services to very few participants. . . . Some of the field tests and other reviews brought to bear on laboratory activities embody systematic designs, formal documentation that captures findings, and commitment to use the conclusions — but most do not. There is a continual temptation to seek good news and favorable ratings; designs do not always capture a range of important effects and issues; and the developers or assistance providers sometimes forge ahead in the face of what should be clear signals to reconsider a venture. (Turnbull et al. 1994, 91–93)

Given the size and scope of the evaluation as well as its potential use in drafting the 1995 lab RFPs, OERI asked me, as its consultant, to review a preliminary draft of the final report in late November 1994. I did so, praising it as a "competent and thoughtful preliminary analysis that reveals the usual even-handedness and high professionalism characteristic of the earlier work by Policy Studies Associates" (Vinovskis 1994a).

My nine suggestions for improvement of the Policy Studies Associates report called for substantial changes in the final draft. Among my criticisms was the point that the "draft report is more of a descriptive cataloging of the activities of the laboratories than an in-depth and systematic analysis of their work." I encouraged the authors to examine the quality of the laboratories' own evaluations, which I discovered exhibited major weaknesses. I questioned the reliability and usefulness of many lab studies due to their biases in representativeness and use of inappropriate statistical procedures. In addition, I recommended that OERI give more attention to the relative cost effectiveness of the lab services—an issue that Policy Studies Associates had raised itself. But "perhaps the most serious and disappointing weakness of the entire report is the failure to provide any independent evaluations of the quality of the products produced by the laboratories"—especially since my own assessment of lab research and development, made available to Policy Studies Associates, had raised critical questions about the quality of much of that work (Vinovskis 1994a).

Many OERI staff gave considerable attention and support to my criticisms and suggestions about the draft final report of Policy Studies Associates. Yet, rather than addressing any of these or other suggestions, one month later Policy Studies Associates resubmitted their November draft as the final report with almost no changes. Perhaps even more remarkable and disappointing is the fact that OERI accepted the unrevised draft report as the final deliverable. OERI, which had spent three-quarters of a million dollars for this major study, should have required Policy Studies Associates to address the serious questions raised by its own staff and consultants before concluding the contract.

The 1995 Request for Proposals

OERI worked on the request for proposals for the regional educational laboratories during the second half of 1994 and continued in earnest until it was issued with an August 8, 1995, deadline. Rather than repeating the lengthy list of permissible lab activities, the new RFP required these institutions to focus most of their resources on supporting broad-based systemic reform efforts while simultaneously developing a specialized area of expertise (OERI 1995, 3).

The laboratories acquired two new goals: to bring together scattered successful reform efforts at the state and local levels and to scale up the existing successful reforms to make them adaptable to other areas. By the end of the five-year contract, the laboratories were to have achieved some fairly tangible and ambitious goals (OERI 1995, 9).

Although it was understandable that the RFP should harness the work of the regional educational laboratories to the Clinton administration's emphasis on systemic reform, the conceptual basis for that initiative was problematic from the beginning. The RFP required each of the ten regional laboratories to develop, test, and help implement systemic reforms. A more efficient and effective method would have entailed one coordinated lab effort to develop and test systemic reform models and processes. Considerable waste and duplication was likely to result from several labs assessing identical reform models, such as Success for All, or developing nearly identical educational improvements without using similar measures or procedures to facilitate more scientifically reliable comparisons.

Nor did the RFP include a coherent or clear definition of *systemic* or *comprehensive*. For example, was "opportunity to learn" an integral and essential component of system reform? Was the provision of social services to schoolchildren also an essential part of systemic reform? Moreover, the RFP contained internal inconsistencies in the meanings or practical interpretations of these words and phrases. Previously labs had interpreted the concept of systemic reform quite differently, and some had explicitly rejected the idea altogether. The use of different approaches, while correctly permitted and encouraged by the RFP, might lead to meaningless comparisons at the end of five years. If OERI wanted to test or develop several approaches to systemic reform, it should have done so more explicitly and rigorously for better assessment and comparison of the various approaches' relative merits. Without a systematic process for developing a coherent variation approach (including using some standardized measurement schemes), OERI could waste or misdirect a considerable amount of money and effort.

Similarly, what did OERI mean by "scaling up"? Would each of the labs devise its own definition and strategy? Was OERI especially interested in any particular aspect of scaling up, such as the relative costs and benefits of working in partnership with teachers? Would there be any planned comparisons among these different strategies and approaches? Were ten different, uncoordinated, and expensive efforts necessary to study scaling up — especially from an applied research and development perspective?

A more analytically sensible method may have been for OERI to subdivide the core lab activities into two broad categories: an applied research and development initiative focused on investigating and assessing systemic reform and scaling up and a set of services provided to states and local areas to help them implement systemic reform and scaling up.

Rather than allowing each lab to develop and implement its own applied research and development projects on systemic reform and scaling up, perhaps OERI should have required labs to create a more coherent and coordinated effort through the existing network. This coordination would encourage closer cooperation between the labs and the Planning and Evaluation Service (PES) in the Department of Education, which was also working on systemic reform and scaling up. Through this method, OERI would minimize unnecessary duplications and ensure that major gaps would be identified and filled. Initially, the labs would make their own suggestions about how to proceed, but their proposals would then be reviewed, negotiated, and coordinated.[37]

The second part of lab core activities — to assist state and local entities to implement systemic reform and scaling up — could have been handled in a more traditional manner. Each lab would work within its own region to provide the necessary services for its customers at the state and local levels. Some interregional lab coordination for this activity might be useful but not as essential as when developing new models and processes applicable in diverse contexts throughout the nation.[38]

The agency considered a more organized and coordinated approach to systemic reform and scaling up, and some staff members agreed with the conceptual and practical advantages of such an approach. But given the continued hostility of the labs, which preferred to take directions from their own governing boards and management, OERI was unlikely to adopt this alternate approach, even though it might have produced more reliable and useful results over time. Rather, OERI was likely to acquiesce to the insistence of the labs and their allies in Congress that even though these institutions operated under government contracts and received substantial amounts of federal funds they should remain relatively autonomous.

The RFP included several other improvements. It mandated periodic evaluations of the labs — including a much needed independent third-year review of all labs (OERI 1995, 14). The required quality assurance system for each lab was expanded and made more rigorous

(13). Another innovative idea was to set aside approximately $200,000 per year for each lab for an optional task 6, providing assistance to OERI. This allocation could allow OERI to provide more direct guidance for a small portion of the labs' activities and to compensate those institutions when they performed special tasks for the agency (26–27). Finally, the RFP called for each lab to create a specialty area of development (task 7) reflecting its own interests as well as those of OERI. The importance of task 7 was reflected in its accounting for one-fifth of the total points assigned by reviewers in the lab RFP. The idea behind this approach was to encourage each lab to develop an area of expertise that it could share with others across the nation (27–28).

While OERI might have improved the lab RFP in several areas, given the political and practical constraints it did a good job overall and made some useful improvements. Certainly, the RFP of 1995 was much better than those of 1985 and 1990. If labs carried out the specific requirements and recommendations of the RFP, their orientation and effectiveness would have improved.

Change and Stability at the Labs

When the National Academy of Sciences panel analyzed the labs in 1992, it stated that the "committee questions the advisability of competitions for RALs [regional assistance laboratories]. The laboratories competed in 1985 and 1990, and only one of the 19 incumbents was unseated in those two rounds of competitive bidding" (Atkinson and Jackson 1992, 153).

In 1995, however, two of the incumbents were unseated: Research for Better Schools (RBS) was replaced by the Mid-Atlantic Laboratory for Student Success (LSS) and the Regional Laboratory for Educational Improvement of the Northeast and Islands lost to Northeast and Islands Laboratory at Brown University (LAB). In addition, the Southeastern Regional Vision for Education was created in 1990. Thus, contrary to the NAS panel's prediction of almost no changes in the labs through the competitions, a 30 percent turnover has occurred over the last two. Moreover, the orientation of some labs may shift, as the two 1995 additions are associated with universities.

Besides the creation of three new labs, change has occurred through the departure of many longtime leaders of those institutions. Experienced and influential executive directors such as Dean Nafziger (FWL), C. L. Hutchins (McREL), Robert Rath (NWREL), John Hopkins (RBS), and Preston Kronkosky (SEDL) have either retired or been replaced. As a result, the present leaders of the regional educational laboratories are less experienced but also perhaps more open to instituting changes in their operations and to reconsidering their relationships with OERI.

Another recent and influential change has been the resignation of the executive director of CEDaR, Deena Stoner, now executive director of the Society of Research Administrators. Moreover, the Department of Education is questioning the legality of the previous relationship between CEDaR and the labs and centers; this may lead to a future restructuring of that connection.[39] How these recent changes in CEDaR will affect lab operations as a whole, and the labs' political influence with the 106th Congress and the Clinton administration, remains to be seen.

While significant changes have occurred in lab membership and leadership, there are indications that some of their overall goals and practices have remained essentially the same. When Republicans gained control of Congress after the 1994 elections, some observers anticipated more critical oversight of the labs, but lobbyists for the labs have operated almost equally effectively with the new Republican Congress. For example, CEDaR persuaded its congressional allies to transfer to lab funds the $10 million saved by eliminating the National Diffusion Network (NDN) in FY96. While some portray this change as a temporary transfer, most observers expect that the additional $10 million will become a permanent part of federal funding of the labs — just as the special monies for rural initiatives in the late 1980s were eventually incorporated into the regular lab budget.

Similarly, despite the apparent support of the labs and CEDaR for the new directions enunciated in the 1995 RFP, once they received their new contracts some of them balked at working on projects initiated by OERI (task 6). The OERI staff was caught off guard when it discovered that CEDaR had persuaded the House and Senate appropriations committees to try to repudiate the explicit terms of the 1995 lab contracts. As a result, Congress's appropriations reports insisted that all of the labs' work should be based only on priorities established through their own regional governing boards (see, e.g., U.S. Senate 1996, 205).

Many OERI staff members felt betrayed by both CEDaR and the legislators for their inappropriate and blatant interference with the recently awarded contracts. Many OERI career employees increasingly resented the recent close CEDaR-OERI working relationship, which discouraged or even prevented them from fulfilling their normal oversight responsibilities with regard to the labs.

Knowledge of the privileged and protected position of the labs within OERI was widespread and occasionally openly spoofed. At the retirement party for David Mack and Hunter Moorman, two highly respected OERI managers who had worked for many years with the labs and centers, the staff sang a specially written song, "Labs and Centers" (to the tune of "Love and Marriage"):

LABS AND CENTERS

Labs and Centers
They sure have organized
Their defenders,
And just like bread and butter,
We couldn't get one — without the other.

Centers and La-abs,
Centers and La-abs,
Everything we've ever had
Went up for grabs.
Outdoing the ancient magicians
They even survived our recissions.

Try, try, try to monitor —
It's a mass confusion.
Try, try, try to figure out
What they're doin' —
It's all illusion.

But Labs and Centers,
Labs and Centers
Hold us up like a
Pair of suspenders.
It's so governmental,
It borders on the transcendental.

Centers and La-abs
Centers and La-abs
They play their game
While we pay the tab.
They'll never lose their luster
And we can't have one;
We can't have fun;
We can't have none;
Without the other.[40]

The Decision Information Resources Evaluation

In April 2000, the Planning and Evaluation Service released its in-depth interim evaluation of the current regional educational laboratories, which provides interesting information about the operation of those institutions. The 1994 legislation reauthorizing OERI (Title IX, P.L. 103–227) called for an independent evaluation of each of the ten labs in the third year of their five-year contracts (covering the period December 1995 through December 1998). In August 1998, the PES awarded the evaluation contract to Decision Information Resources (DIR). Each evaluation was to examine the implementation and management of lab activities, the quality of its products and services, the utility of its contributions, and the impact of its interventions.[41]

Due to the delay in awarding the overall evaluation contract, it was not until April and May 1999 that DIR was able to develop its assessment protocols, select the peer reviewers, and schedule the evaluation teams to visit the ten sites. Additional time was required for the peer reviewers to draft their individual lab evaluations and for the labs to have an opportunity to respond. The individual interim evaluations were intended to provide OERI and the labs with the information needed to make midcourse adjustments, but even the preliminary results were not available until well into the fourth year of the five-year contract, leaving little time for any major changes. Besides, early in the planning process the "ED staff stated that while the findings may suggest minor modifications in the efforts underway at a given Lab, they did not expect the findings to have a major impact on any individual Lab's funding" (Pistorio, Jackson, and Newell 2000, 10). Although individual labs had received preliminary drafts of their outside evaluations in the spring of 1999, policymakers and the public were not provided with copies of the lab evaluations until April 2000. As a result, information from the interim lab evaluations was not available to policymakers during the Title I or OERI reauthorization hearings in the House and Senate during 1999 and 2000.[42]

Given the troubled history of NIE and OERI attempts to evaluate lab operations, educators and policymakers wondered whether PES and DIR would be able to conduct an in-depth, objective assessment of the institutions. Particularly critical was the issue of who would be recruited as peer reviewers and whether labs would be allowed to influence their selection. Unfortunately, the procedures for recruiting peer reviewers appear to have been biased toward those with more favorable views of the labs.

Nearly three hundred peer reviewer nominations were submitted by the lab directors, the Department of Education (PES, OERI, and NERPPB), DIR's Technical Work Group, and other educational, business, and professional groups (e.g., the Business Roundtable, the Pritchard Committee, and the NPTA). Although PES screened the pool of potential reviewers for possible biases or conflicts of interest, current lab consultants were allowed to participate (though not as a reviewer of the particular lab that had hired them as a consultant). On the other hand, some of the more knowledgeable but previously critical analysts of the labs were not even nominated, and no outspoken critics of the quality of earlier lab activities were included among the final thirty-four reviewers selected. The labs were allowed to veto some reviewers they regarded as unsuitable and to choose which nominees they considered particularly "highly qualified to serve as a peer review panelist, as well as those who would be a good panel chair." Indeed, even the contractors acknowledged that "peer reviewers were hesitant to be excessively critical in their written reports recognizing that their findings could impact the funding of the individual Laboratory or, potentially, the total Laboratory system" (Decision Information Resources 2000b, 5). As a result, questions linger regarding the extent of the independence and objectivity of the peer review selection process and the balance of views represented by the panelists—issues that PES and DIR should have addressed in their published documents.

Analyzing the entire operation of the labs with such limited resources and staff would have been an almost an impossible task for any contractor. In this case, it was especially so since most peer reviewers were initially unfamiliar with the various projects and operations of the labs. While DIR valiantly tried to provide training and somewhat standardized guidance for the peer reviewers in a very short time, it would have been a daunting task even under the best of circumstances. The magnitude of the lab operations made it virtually impossible for peer reviewers to provide in-depth and comprehensive assessments of all aspects of those institutions. As one evaluation team aptly noted: "The review panel brought many perspectives to bear on the work of the Lab and was an effective mechanism for examining its work. However, in some ways it is analogous to a group of people in a rowboat drifting past an iceberg and attempting to evaluate not only the eighth they can see, but also the seven-eighths below the surface" (Decision Information Resources 2000a, 2).

Since lab projects were of such large number and variety, DIR designed a sampling strategy focused on a few "signature works"—those major projects or service programs that best exemplified the work of the labs during the current contract period. Labs could nominate up to six signature works, of which the peer review teams assessed two. In addition, labs provided peer reviewers with selected samples of other programs, products, and services. The sampling strategy, while logistically necessary, resulted in review teams considering only a small, albeit important, portion of lab activities — activities that labs felt were particularly suitable for evaluation by outsiders.

Although the peer review panels conscientiously tried to evaluate the programs, products, and services of each lab, they often exaggerated the quality of those items in their summary comments. The assessment of the Appalachia Educational Laboratory, for example, concluded that "AEL is developing products and services of unusually high quality" (Decision Information Resources 2000a, 10). Yet the more detailed criticisms revealed that AEL's samples were often ones of convenience rather than having been purposefully selected. Major reductions in the sample size of some proposed studies were not explained, adequate baseline school and student outcome data usually were not collected and analyzed, student achievement data were largely missing, the special projects on rural areas needed a clearer and more contextual focus, and the completed works were rarely vetted in scholarly refereed journals. Given these thoughtful and constructive individual and collective criticisms, it is surprising that the peer reviewer team would still unanimously characterize AEL's work as being of "unusually high quality" (Decision Information Resources 2000a).

The purpose of these interim evaluations was to provide information that would help labs improve their ongoing work, not to render an overall summary judgment of the entire system of laboratories. As a result, DIR simply provided a brief, executive summary of each institution, which listed some of the major accomplishments as well as areas in need of future improvement. However, DIR did conclude: "In all cases, Laboratories were found to have met their contractual obligations or were able to justify changes in the scope of work or in the deliverables schedule. Similarly, all Labs were found to have more strengths identified than areas needing attention" (Pistorio, Jackson, and Newell 2000, 13).

While it is difficult to reach general conclusions about the labs, especially since they vary considerably, a close reading of the peer review assessments reinforces impressions from earlier studies and from discussions of these institutions in the 1980s and 1990s. The bulk of the lab activities seems to be focused on providing technical assistance or supporting limited applied research or policy syntheses; few labs undertake large-scale, systematic development. Much of the limited applied research would benefit from better design, more appropriate control groups, and more rigorous quantitative and qualitative analysis. Surprisingly little effort is being made by the labs to collect and analyze student outcomes — although many of these institutions agree on the need for such information. Even more research oriented labs such as WestEd provide few incentives or opportunities for their professional staffs to publish their work in refereed scholarly journals. Moreover, rather than critically assessing all of their contributions using rigorous social science standards, the labs rely disproportionately on customer satisfaction surveys to validate their work (and labs almost uniformly receive high marks from their clients). Thus, in some ways the labs are much more like the new comprehensive regional assistance centers, which provide regional research-based technical assistance, than the R&D centers, which attempt to provide rigorous, high-quality, applied and basic research for a national audience.[43]

Besides working with the regional educational laboratories, ORAD was also charged with identifying promising educational models, developing and testing them in different settings, and then disseminating that information. Unfortunately, the Department of Education in general, and NIE or OERI in particular, have failed to develop and rigorously test educational models (Slavin 1997; Vinovskis 1999e). Rather than supporting the systematic and rigorous testing of alternative educational models, OERI spent most of its monies on a series of small, short-term projects (including many of those funded through the labs and centers).

Although in mid-1994 OERI received and approved a plan for a large-scale, rigorous evaluation of systemic reform, it failed to develop and implement that proposal (Vinovskis 1994b). Therefore, the Clinton administration, focused on assessing the strengths and weaknesses of systemic reform, relied more heavily on the work of the Planning and Evaluation Service in the Department of Education — especially its recently funded Longitudinal Evaluation of School Change and Performance. OERI played a very minor role in these discussions, in part because it was not undertaking any large, scientifically rigorous studies of systemic reform. Thus, ironically, whereas OERI might have been a leader in the efforts to critically assess systemic reform in mid-1994, it failed to take advantage of that opportunity, encouraging the Department of Education to look elsewhere for intellectual leadership and assistance in assessing the impact of systemic reform.

VI. The National Center for Education Statistics

During the OERI reauthorization process, Congress devoted less attention to the National Center for Education Statistics than to other OERI divisions such as the national research institutes and the Office of Reform Assistance and Dissemination. Congress continued to view NCES as the primary federal agency for collecting domestic and international educational data (Office of the Assistant Secretary 1994c).

NCES was divided into four units: the Statistical Standards and Methodology Division, the Data Development Division, the Education Surveys Division, and the Education Assessment Division. It made effective use of advisory groups, including two key ones that were legislatively mandated: the Advisory Council on Education Statistics (ACES), which helped the commissioner on general policies and operating standards; and the independent National Assessment Governing Board (NAGB), which oversaw the National Assessment of Education Progress.[44]

During the 1990s, in which NCES made important and meaningful improvements, it also faced some serious challenges. Perhaps one of the foremost was Emerson Elliott's decision to retire at the end of his term as the first presidentially appointed commissioner of education. Elliott, one of the most experienced and effective federal career civil service managers, played an instrumental role in developing NCES into a first-rate statistical agency. Pascal "Pat" Forgione Jr., the former Delaware state school superintendent, was a good choice to replace him on July 1, 1996 ("Forgione" 1996). But Forgione, understandably relatively inexperienced in the federal government, did not yet have the extensive network of contacts that Elliott had built up during his three decades in the federal government. Nor did he have the close working relationship with many OERI leaders and middle-level staff members that Elliott had developed over the years. On the other hand, he appeared very knowledgeable and interested in the technical aspects of NCES work.

Another troublesome problem for NCES was the unexpected, dramatic decline in staff size. When the NAS panel called for doubling the size of the NCES staff in 1991, the agency had about 143 employees. By October 1994, its staff had decreased to 112, and by March 1997 it was still only 115 — an overall decrease of nearly 20 percent. Due to the open enrollment season in September 1994 and the buyout program for senior staff, it lost some technologically skilled and experienced employees. Partly in reaction to recent changes at NCES, some of the more competent staff members have left the unit to work elsewhere in OERI or in other parts of the federal government.

The general deskilling of the NCES research staff diminished an important source of recruitment for other parts of OERI. In the past, OERI has temporarily "borrowed" a few of the more accomplished NCES professionals to work on high-priority projects such as the new voluntary national education testing initiative.[45] In addition, while the new Education Statistics Services Institute provided help on some of the more technical aspects of NCES work it also created additional problems and increased some staff tensions that have yet to be resolved. Thus, Commissioner Forgione was faced with the responsibility of satisfying the mandated increased tasks for NCES with a considerably diminished and weakened staff.

Although the expectations and responsibilities of NCES have expanded substantially in recent years, it has not received adequate increased funding for its activities. Its funding rose dramatically from $19.5 million in FY87 to $85.5 million in FY93 (in constant 1996 dollars). But funding actually decreased to $80.6 million in FY97 (in constant 1996 dollars) — a 5.7 percent decline. As a result, NCES's ambitious data collection and dissemination agenda had to be implemented by a smaller staff with fewer real dollars.

Despite these new challenges, NCES has managed to increase the diversity and usefulness of its publications for multiple audiences while producing high-quality work. It is interesting to observe that when Assistant Secretary Robinson testified before Congress, most of the OERI publications she distributed to the members were from NCES rather than the national research institutes or ORAD. At a time when the other OERI units have great difficulty producing original research or critical syntheses of existing scholarship, NCES continues to make significant contributions not only to the collection of data but to its analysis as well.

It also has made some key contributions to redesigning the National Assessment of Educational Progress. Mandated by Congress in 1969, NAEP has administered national tests at grades 4, 8, and 12 for ten different subjects. The component of state-level NAEP tests, first administered and released in 1990, has expanded rapidly. In 1996, forty-four states voluntarily participated in the NAEP math assessment at grades 4 and 8 and in the science assessment at grade 8 (NAGB 1996, 5). The National Assessment Governing Board has called for an even closer linkage between the NAEP tests and state and local needs (NAGB 1996, 17).

In March 1997, the NAGB further announced a tentative national and state schedule for its tests until the year 2010. The national tests in the ten subjects would continue periodically, but they would be supplemented every two years by state tests in reading and writing or mathematics and science (NAGB 1997). In order to expand the number and type of tests and yet stay within the existing budget, NCES is considering alternative ways to design and administer the tests (Phillips 1997; Vinovskis 1998c).

While NCES and NAGB are providing new and expanded coverage of subjects such as reading, writing, mathematics, and science at the state level, they are neglecting important areas such as social studies. For example, national U.S. history or geography NAEP exams are scheduled for only 2001 and 2009 and the civics exams for 1998 and 2003; the world history exam will be given only in 2005. Moreover, none of the social studies subjects is now scheduled to be included in any of the NAEP state assessments (NAGB 1997; Phillips 1997).

The neglect of social studies is not unique to NCES. In its plans for national tests and its evaluation of the Title I program, the Department of Education has focused almost exclusively on reading and mathematics assessments. While Congress and the Clinton administration have frequently evoked the importance of improved K-12 education to foster good citizenship, they have provided little leadership or guidance in this area. Most of the public and policymakers appear to be unaware of this limited number of subjects to be assessed, and professional social studies organizations have not protested the relative neglect.[46]

Another area of improvement for NCES is the provision of more complete information on the economic status of students taking NAEP tests. For example, the 1994 U.S. history scores were reported by the race and ethnicity of the students but not by the income of their parents. One-half of all white students, 83 percent of black students, and 78 percent of Hispanic students performed below the basic level in grade 12 (NCES 1996, 34). Yet undoubtedly some of these racial and ethnic differences in knowledge of American history reflect possible difficulties low-income students encounter in school success compared to their more fortunate middle-class counterparts.[47] From reports based on race and ethnicity but not on family economic status, policymakers and the public have received a rather limited and misleading impression of some basic factors in elementary and secondary school students' differential performance on the NAEP national history test.

In order to obtain some indication of poverty status, NAEP plans to ascertain whether or not a tested student participates in the federally subsidized food lunch program. This unreliable index, however, needs to be supplemented or replaced with better indicators. Naturally, valid measures of parental income are difficult to acquire from elementary students. NAEP should experiment with alternative ways to retrieve that information (perhaps through a more in-depth questionnaire to a sample of the parents or through student school records, which may have information on parental characteristics). Rough estimates of parental income might be asked of 12th-grade students, who may know the approximate income of their families. In any case, NCES and NAGB need to seek more appropriate indicators of the economic well-being of the parents of their tested students.

An expansion of work in policy analysis would be a useful although potentially difficult new direction for NCES. Since its inception, NCES has performed policy analyses, but it has hesitated to broaden this work since it fears compromising its independence and objectivity through close identification with a controversial policy or a particular administration.

As NCES expands the use of NAEP data to the state level and works more closely with state and local officials, support for that agency may grow as the usefulness of its work becomes more apparent. At the same time, however, there are hidden dangers in this new approach. Political leaders may express dissatisfaction with the state results if they contradict the often more optimistic findings of a state's own educational assessments. Policymakers who want NAEP test results processed more quickly and presented in less technical language place pressure on NCES to work faster and create additional, less complicated reports. In addition, close work with state and local educational policymakers may require NCES to provide those officials with additional training and assistance. None of these problems are insurmountable, but each will require additional NCES staff and resources, which are in increasingly short supply at the agency. A final consideration is whether these more expensive, policy-oriented investigations will drain scarce resources from the more basic and traditional NCES data collections and statistical studies.

Increased policy analysis undertaken by NCES will also necessitate using more complex statistical techniques to ascertain the relative impact of various factors. While NCES has performed relatively well in collecting and accurately reporting data, it has used less than highly sophisticated statistical methods of analysis. Most NCES studies still rely almost exclusively on simple cross-tabulation of the data. Only recently have a few of the NCES analyses even employed multivariate statistics and more complex modeling techniques.[48] Also, few studies do an adequate job of reviewing and critically interacting with the secondary literature on the topic addressed.

As NCES tackles more sophisticated and complex policy analyses, it will face many additional challenges. Will it be able to hire more staff with the needed substantive knowledge? Presently, its technical research staff, with little requirement for expertise in particular subject areas, can easily move from one project to another. Requiring staff members to have substantive knowledge and statistical expertise not only increases hiring costs but usually limits the number of areas an individual can be expected to cover. Similarly, will NCES need to create additional advisory panels that have a more substantive orientation in order to help oversee this new work? Ideally, NCES would obtain some substantive expertise through close work with the OERI national research institutes, but this likelihood is diminished due to a shortage of first-rate researchers in those units. Thus, as NCES undertakes more substantive policy analyses it must reassess its staffing and organizational structure and perhaps better coordinate them with related developments in other OERI programs.

Finally, NCES' further venture into policy-oriented work will draw criticism from those who disagree with the particular initiatives. For example, the Clinton administration has actively promoted voluntary national tests for reading and mathematics. This initiative attracted considerable political support but also raised significant opposition. As OERI was responsible for overseeing test development, it relied heavily upon some prominent NCES staff members for assistance. In such situations, would critics of the tests attack NCES for becoming too involved in specific administration policies? Would these same critics attempt to withhold additional discretionary funding from NCES for fear that these monies might be spent on projects deemed too partisan or one-sided? The responsibility for developing a voluntary national test was shifted to NAGB (Vinovskis 1998c), alleviating NCES' immediate problems of handling a particularly controversial policy-related assignment. However, NCES is likely to face similar issues, which it will have to address carefully.

VII.   The National Educational Research Policy and Priorities Board and the OERI Research Plan

As discussed earlier, protracted controversy over the characteristics and power of the National Educational Research Policy and Priorities Board delayed the reauthorization of OERI by almost two years. Yet some members of Congers viewed the NERPPB as so important that they did not begrudge the delay to ensure the creation of a powerful and active OERI policy board. The final compromise created a strong advisory board, but its actual role in the agency would depend to a large degree on who was appointed to that group and how they would relate to OERI in practice.

Although the legislation featured the policy board creation and major OERI restructuring, the Department of Education delayed the appointment of the board. The legislation mandated the board to meet by May 15, 1995, but Assistant Secretary Robinson had hoped to have it appointed by November 1994.[49] Finally, on February 27, 1995, Secretary

Riley named fifteen members from over three hundred nominees. As mandated by Congress, five of the appointees had extensive experience in elementary and secondary education.[50] Another five were selected for their broad educational expertise and background.[51] And five were educational researchers who had been nominated by the National Academy of Sciences.[52] Many key educational lobbyists were enthusiastic about the quality of the appointments to NERPPB.[53]

The board held its first meeting on March 30–31, 1995. The members worked well together, demonstrating a healthy respect for the varied goals of OERI and their own diverse backgrounds. Kenji Hakuta, representing the research community, and John T. Sanders, reflecting the broader educational orientation of the board, were unanimously elected cochairs. The board also created four ad hoc subcommittees: Research Priorities, Regional Educational Laboratories, Standards, and Research and Development Centers (NERPPB 1995).

Some earlier critics of NERPPB had expressed concern about the quality of interactions between the board and OERI. But thanks in large part to the openness and personal effectiveness of Assistant Secretary Robinson as well as the full cooperation of the board members, a close and harmonious working relationship quickly developed between the two groups. John Christensen, a high-level, senior OERI professional initially designated as the federal liaison to the board, played a key role in facilitating NERPPB activities. Eve Bither, a former high school physics teacher, school administrator, and state school superintendent as well as the acting director of ORAD, was selected by the board to be their executive director in June 1996 (New research 1996). Both Bither's extensive experience in state and federal educational affairs and her ability to work effectively with diverse interest groups have helped to maintain a close and cordial relationship between OERI and the board.

A primary responsibility for NERPPB was to develop, in coordination with OERI, a five-year research priority plan for the agency. Unfortunately, most anticipated OERI expenditures for the next five years had already been planned and almost fully committed before the board members were even appointed. For example, at the first meeting several board members questioned the wisdom of allocating so much of OERI's funds to the labs and centers. They had inadequate time, however, to investigate and discuss these issues since the announcements for lab and center competitions were due in a few months.[54] Board members also were disappointed to learn that OERI had already committed its monies for the next five years without developing a preliminary long-range research plan. The lack of an overall plan was surprising because the agency had been periodically working on one for the past three years.

The legislation mandated that by October 1, 1995, OERI and NERPPB must publish a report specifying the agency's research priorities for the next five years. Yet NERPPB met for the first time in March 1995 and only then began to think about a research priority plan. Under these circumstances, OERI and NERPPB decided to publish a general research framework as an interim product by October and then provide more specific future research proposals over the following year.

In June 1995, the newly created OERI Research Priorities Planning Team presented NERPPB with a set of alternatives and recommendations on a series of important issues. One important question the planning team addressed was whether there should be an overarching perspective for the plan (Research Priorities Planning Team 1995). The team recommended having no overall framework for the five-year research plan. NERPPB accepted the idea in essence, and instead OERI developed relatively separate research plans for each unit. The unfortunate decision to neglect an overall framework continued to leave OERI's operations fragmented at a time when many policymakers had hoped to focus the agency's resources on a few major initiatives.

In early 1995, OERI almost accepted an alternative approach. In an OERI-commissioned essay, I developed a life course perspective that elicited considerable interest within the agency. The proposed framework offered a more dynamic and yet comprehensive approach and emphasized focusing reform efforts on the more crucial transitions in the lives of children (Vinovskis 1995a).[55] The life course framework was discussed widely within OERI and endorsed by many members of the staff. No alternative frameworks emerged during those meetings to challenge this approach, and some units adopted aspects of the life course approach in their own planning. But ultimately the lack of intellectual leadership at OERI caused most programs to continue to pursue their own interests and orientation without trying to fit their work within a larger context.

After eighteen months of crafting, the five-year research priorities plan for education research was released jointly by OERI and NERPPB in December 1996. The colorfully illustrated, 112-page plan, *Building Knowledge for a Nation of Learners,* enjoyed wide distribution. The report listed seven national priorities for research in education (Robinson, Hakuta, and Sanders 1996, iv):

1. Improving learning and development in early childhood so that children can enter kindergarten prepared to learn and succeed in elementary and secondary schools
2. Improving curriculum, instruction, assessment, and student

learning at all levels of education to promote high academic achievement, problem-solving abilities, creativity, and the motivation for further learning

3. Ensuring effective teaching by expanding the supply of potential teachers, improving teacher preparation, and promoting career-long professional development at all levels of education

4. Strengthening schools, particularly middle and high schools, as institutions capable of engaging young people as active and responsible learners

5. Supporting schools to effectively prepare diverse populations to meet high standards for knowledge, skills, and productivity and to participate fully in American economic, cultural, social, and civic life

6. Promoting learning in informal and formal settings and building the connections that cause out-of-school experiences to contribute to in-school achievement

7. Understanding the changing requirements for adult competence in civic, work, and social contexts and how these requirements affect learning and the futures of individuals in the nation

While these priorities are well stated and perhaps even inspirational, sections of the report offer little specific guidance on allocations of scarce research funds and energies. For example, the second priority calls for "improving curriculum, instruction, assessment, and student learning at all levels of education." But this section does not provide any suggestions for which subjects or at what levels of schooling educational efforts should be focused to help children learn better. Nor does the report effectively summarize what is known about this area from a research perspective or recommend what research gaps should be addressed in the next five or ten years. Moreover, the report even acknowledged that "in setting this agenda, the Assistant Secretary and the Board refrained from ranking the priorities" (Robinson, Hakuta, and Sanders 1996, 17).

The priorities do provide some general guidance, as in the emphasis on early childhood education (priority 1) and middle and high schools (priority 4). However, the report does not indicate why these three broad periods were selected for special attention while others were ignored. For example, many scholars and studies have suggested that K-3 education is a particularly important period for helping disadvantaged children. Indeed, OERI's continued assistance in the development of Success for All has indicated the importance of these grades in helping at-risk children.[56] Yet the national priorities seemingly slighted K-3 education without explanation. Was it because the board members thought that improving pre-kindergarten education and reforming middle and high schools had a larger impact on students than helping K-3 education? Or did they think we already know so much about K-3 education that no more research is needed in this area? And if K-3 education is not one of the highest priorities for OERI, why does the agency continue to fund Success for All?

Another example of neglected guidance is found in research priority 6, which focuses appropriately on the contribution of out-of-school learning experiences for the development of the child. Certainly this is a crucial area for further research, as studies have revealed the importance of learning outside the classroom. But the report's discussion of this topic focuses mainly on extracurricular activities, after-school opportunities, and parental involvement in school programs (Robinson, Hakuta, and Sanders 1996, 60–65). The report omits mention of the potential importance of summer learning and the problems that at-risk children have during the summer. Yet existing research suggests that lack of summer learning is a significant factor in explaining the relative disadvantage of learning for children from low-income families.[57] Thus, a reader might wonder how comprehensively existing research was consulted and incorporated in making these specific recommendations.

The general tone of the report also raises questions. Segments appear too complacent about the quality and quantity of existing research.[58] And, while the report stresses the need for future improvements, its defense of school achievements in the past quarter century seems somewhat strained and exaggerated (Robinson, Hakuta, and Sanders 1996, 10–11). Moreover, although the report appropriately emphasizes the problems that many minority students face today, it often and surprisingly ignores or downplays the negative impact of poverty on all children.[59]

Overall, while the national priorities report was clearly written and handsomely produced, it does not provide a very useful set of guidelines or suggestions for educational research for the next five or ten years. Many OERI staff members privately acknowledged that *Building Knowledge for a Nation of Learners* has had little effect even within the agency. In a recent OERI *Bulletin,* for example, Ramon Cortines, then acting assistant secretary, listed seven priorities of the department without mentioning the new OERI research priorities (OERI 1997, 2).[60] And there was little evidence that those in other units of the Department of Education or outside the federal government have paid close attention to its recommendations. While some responsibility for the shortcomings of the OERI research plan must rest with NERPPB, most belongs to OERI, which has struggled to develop and implement any sustained, in-depth intellectual agenda.

VIII. Development of Quality Standards for OERI Work

The 1994 legislation reauthorizing the Office of Educational Research and Improvement contained the useful provision of requiring it to establish high standards of professional excellence for its research, development, and dissemination products and activities. The close cooperation between OERI and NERPPB in drafting these regulations reveals their very important, but as yet little noticed, contribution to improving the quality of the research, development, and statistics sponsored and overseen by the federal government.[61]

The legislation regulated three phases for development and implementation of the standards for research conduct and evaluation. The first phase, to be completed within the first year, specified a peer review award process for the creation of grants, contracts, and cooperative agreements. By the end of the second year, OERI needed to formulate standards for the exemplary and promising practice programs. Finally, by the conclusion of the third year, the assistant secretary would develop standards to periodically evaluate the performance of all OERI-funded activities (Vinovskis 1997, sec. 912, 1, 2).

On the whole, OERI completed all three phases satisfactorily. The phase 1 standards, which are particularly related to those in phase 3, are the beginning point for all projects eventually funded by OERI (U.S. Department of Education 1995b). Although the phase 2 standards are thoughtful and quite important, they focus almost exclusively on the special exemplary and promising practice programs.[62]

The phase 1 standards provide procedures and guidelines for evaluating applications for grants, cooperative agreements, and proposals for contracts. As intended by Congress, the activities covered by the standards are broad and seemingly all inclusive. One major ambiguity not specifically addressed in the document is whether the work of NCES is covered by these standards. On the one hand, Congress did not explicitly exempt the work of NCES from these standards. On the other hand, NCES frequently has its own regulations, which are often more scientifically rigorous than those employed in some other OERI units.

Assistant Secretary Robinson enacted the policy that phase 1 standards be applied to all OERI programs. Secretary Riley then extended the phase 1 standards to all Department of Education activities. The policy decision to broadly apply these standards was commendable and seems to have been useful in practice.

Implementing phases 1 and 2 of the standards is not an overly onerous undertaking because the tasks are easily defined and logistically manageable. For example, rather than requiring a listing of all sets of criteria for every possible type of grant competition, the phase 1 standards simply provide a menu of criteria to choose from and permit flexibility in assigning weights to them. Since the criteria and assigned weights for any competition are available in advance, both the applicants and reviewers can clearly understand what is expected of them. In addition, programs can easily find a sufficient number of qualified outside peer reviewers since the large-scale grants have only a few applicants and the smaller ones are shorter in length and less detailed (hence requiring less time from reviewers). Moreover, peer review is not required for applicants requesting funding of less than $100,000.

The phase 3 standards are much more daunting in scale and scope. All grants, cooperative agreements, and contracts (not just those over $100,000) are to receive both an interim and a final evaluation. Given the great diversity of OERI projects, both in scale and type of activity, it will be difficult, if not impossible, to provide adequate criteria in the regulations without either resorting to a menu approach or subdividing activities by types of recipients or products. Programs that depend heavily upon outside peer reviewers may encounter difficulty in recruiting and compensating sufficient numbers of qualified individuals. Therefore, before drafting the final phase 3 standards, OERI should have developed an overall evaluation plan that would ensure adequate and efficient assessment of all its research, development, and dissemination funded activities.

OERI's overall process for developing the phase 3 standards also needs some review. The OERI staff and NERPPB did raise important factors, such as the development of an OERI quality assurance system, to extend the five-year center cooperative agreements without recompetition. They also succeeded in soliciting the views of some individuals who represented the interests of the centers and labs.[63]

But OERI paid surprisingly little, if any, attention to the difficulties involved in creating its own system for monitoring and evaluating all of its programs and activities. By separating in practice the drafting of the phase 3 standards from the development of program oversight procedures and practices, OERI and NERPPB may have inadvertently missed an important opportunity to investigate and resolve the difficult problems inherent in the creation of a viable quality assurance system. Did OERI and the board analyze the strengths and weaknesses of the agency's monitoring and program evaluation practices? Why has the NCES review system seemed to work better than those developed for the labs and centers? Have OERI and the board explored the particular quality control problems believed to have plagued educational research, and have they discussed how this might affect the phase 3 standards? And, in addition to hearing from representatives of the major institutions funded by OERI, should the Committee on Standards not have heard from some of the critics who have questioned the quality of much of NIE/OERI's work over the past twenty-five years? Thus, while the OERI staff and NERPPB made a good beginning in drafting the phase 3 standards, they should have also addressed some of these broader, related questions.

Finally, it is important that as much as possible OERI make efforts to rely in part upon the quality assurance systems developed by the grantees and contractors themselves (with the guidance, assistance, and oversight of OERI). These self-evaluation systems can be periodically assessed to ensure their viability and usefulness, thereby greatly reducing the cost and logistical problems involved in trying to create an overall quality assurance system. Otherwise, the cost and burden of the phase 3 standards may become too high to ensure their full development and implementation. Moreover, as the phase 3 standards are developed they should also be linked to the collection and synthesizing of information from the OERI-funded recipients. After all, the ultimate goal of trying to develop high-quality educational research, development, and dissemination is to use it substantively and effectively in improving American education.

IX. More Recent Developments at OERI

During 1997, some developments at OERI have raised concerns among its supporters. Robinson resigned as the assistant secretary after three and one-half years in office — one of longest terms of any head of NIE or OERI in the past twenty-five years. After this lengthy period of leadership stability, OERI reverted to the troublesome practice of numerous, short-term assistant secretaries. Although Robinson had earlier communicated her decision to leave, nine months later the White House still had not nominated a successor.[64] Instead, OERI had already experienced three acting assistant secretaries — Marshall "Mike" Smith, acting deputy secretary of the Department of Education; Ray Cortines, former superintendent of the New York City and San Diego schools and a special consultant to the Department of Education; and Ricky Takai, a professional staff member of the Planning and Evaluation Service of the Department of Education. Thus, in the space of less than one year OERI had four different assistant secretaries — the most changes ever in annual leadership in NIE or OERI. Fortunately, Kent McGuire, a program officer at the PEW Charitable Trusts' K-12 education reform and restructuring program, was nominated in late October 1997 and confirmed in 1998 as the next OERI assistant secretary (Lightfoot-Clark 1997).

In addition to the lack of continuity due to ever-changing leadership, there is growing concern that OERI may be losing some of its long-sought independence from presidential administrations and Congress. Usually, the White House nominates an individual from within NIE or OERI to serve as permanent acting assistant secretary. Yet it seems to many observers that the Clinton administration has selected as acting assistant secretaries those closely identified with the top political leadership of the Department of Education. These selections carry the troubling message that no one at OERI is qualified to serve even temporarily as acting assistant secretary of the agency.

Concerns about the Clinton administration's increasing use of OERI to support its more immediate educational agenda were fueled by its decision that OERI should use its own staff and discretionary funds to develop and oversee the voluntary individual national tests in fourth-grade reading and eighth-grade math. Many Republican and Democratic members of the House of Representatives have denounced the proposed national tests, insisting that Congress should first discuss and then authorize any such major educational undertaking before the administration proceeds further on this matter. Bill Goodling (R-PA), chair of the House Committee on Education and the Workforce and an ardent opponent of the tests, stated, "It's probably the most controversial issue to come before Congress this year" (Innerst 1997). It now appears that the administration and Congress have reached at least a temporary compromise on the national testing issue, which has removed OERI from the direct development and supervision of that highly controversial undertaking (Lawson 1997b).

Another question regarding the national tests revealed an interesting new perspective on the responsibilities of the National Educational Research Policy and Priorities Board. Congressman Jay Dickey (R-AR), in an appropriations hearing in March 1997, asked acting OERI assistant secretary Smith about the use of discretionary monies from OERI's Fund for the Improvement of Practice for developing the national tests. Dickey wanted to know if NERPPB had "deliberated on the priority and included it in their plan" (U.S. House 1997, 418). Smith acknowledged its absence from the OERI research priority plan but explained that, before the board had an opportunity to meet and discuss it, the administration had gone ahead with the proposal. Moreover, Smith indicated that according to his interpretation of NERPPB's responsibilities the board did not have jurisdiction in this area because

> the Priorities Board is a research board. The Fund for the Improvement of Education is not in the research side of the agency. Think about OERI having three sides, one's a research side, one's a side that does development and dissemination, and then there's the statistics side. It is in the development and dissemination side of the agency. . . . And the Fund itself gives broad authority to the secretary, in effect, to carry out activities, a wide range of activities, to improve the quality of education. (ibid.)

Upon further questioning, Smith stated that the secretary had the power to spend these discretionary funds "without referral to the board," but he promised to look further into that matter (ibid.).

The debate over the source of funds for developing the national tests revealed that the leadership of the Department of Education viewed the powers of the new board as rather limited. Apparently the department believed that the board's role was primarily to oversee only the research side of the OERI and not its development, dissemination, and statistical functions. This interpretation seems at odds with the general tenor of earlier congressional discussions of the proposed policy board and contrary to the spirit of Assistant Secretary Robinson's treatment of the NERPPB. Whatever the actual legal resolution, it may signal a shift in the nature of the future relationship between OERI and the board as new assistant secretaries are appointed.

Finally, questions about OERI's overall priorities have been raised by the recent heavy emphasis of OERI management on developing and implementing the voluntary national reading and math tests as well as other new initiatives like the expansion of educational technology. Some staff members fear that the new leaders may slight the more traditional research, development, and statistical activities in the national research institutes, ORAD, and NCES as their attention becomes focused on the more pressing needs of the Department of Education.

These recent developments involving the lack of stable leadership at OERI, the reduction in its relative independence from specific administration and congressional policy initiatives, and the overall establishment and implementation of its research and development priorities threaten to hurt the agency in the long run. Clearly, there is now a need for the new assistant secretary to take steps to protect the scientific integrity and relative political independence of OERI lest the agency again, unintentionally and unnecessarily, become viewed as too politicized.

CHAPTER 5

Concluding Observations

Having analyzed the work of the R&D centers and regional education laboratories, congressional oversight of these institutions, and the recent developments at the "new" Office of Educational Research and Improvement, we now turn to a summary of some findings as well as recommendations for future improvements. While there are no easy answers or solutions to the lack of adequate, high-quality educational research and development, OERI must begin to rebuild its capacity to do first-rate work. Assessing past developments of federally supported research and development and the reasons for their limitations is a vital and necessary first step toward improvement. This step is particularly important today since Congress, with the purpose of reauthorizing OERI, is again scrutinizing the federal role in fostering and monitoring educational research and development. Yet unless the next administration and the incoming 107th Congress are willing to work together in a nonpartisan fashion, many of the problems and deficiencies identified in this volume will remain unchanged. This unfortunate stagnation would continue to deny policymakers and educators the rigorous, scientifically sound guidance necessary to help all students excel in school and become productive and active citizens as adults.

The federal government has been collecting, analyzing, and disseminating educational statistics for more than 130 years. Over time, the focus has shifted from data gathering to an emphasis on research and development, with the purpose of finding more effective ways to educate children. Most academics and policymakers in the twentieth century, however, have not held educational research and development in high esteem.[1]

Policymakers have usually downplayed the value of supporting long-term research and development compared to providing immediate and direct assistance to local schools. When the sciences and social sciences were called upon to increase their contributions during World War II, the U.S. Office of Education scaled back its support of educational research and development (Featherman and Vinovskis 2001). However, as it became increasingly evident in the mid-1960s that the government lacked adequate knowledge to improve the schooling of poor children, the Johnson administration and Congress supported larger investments in long-term educational research and development (Jeffrey 1978; Kearney 1967).

The need for federal involvement in educational research, development, and statistics has increased today. Analysts and policymakers are slowly and reluctantly coming to acknowledge that many of the basic federal compensatory education programs established in the 1960s are not as effective as originally hoped. Large-scale, popular, federal educational initiatives such as Title I and Head Start probably do offer assistance for some disadvantaged students. But these programs have not provided the same educational opportunities for at-risk children as their more fortunate counterparts enjoy. Many of these federal initiatives are really only general funding mechanisms rather than specific programs proven to be particularly effective for helping children who live in impoverished homes and neighborhoods. Also, educators lack the detailed and reliable statistical information about schools that would assist them in formulating better policy alternatives. As a result, America has a growing need for better educational research, development, and statistics to improve schooling for everyone.[2]

Both the Bush and Clinton administrations have emphasized standards-based reform. The Clinton administration and the 103d Congress enacted the Improving America's Schools Act (IASA), which called for the close coordination of high academic standards, assessment measures, and curriculum development. Although the concept of the new systemic reform approach in IASA was plausible, it was not an empirically tested approach and critics have raised some serious questions about its efficacy. More definitive evaluations of the standards-based or systemic reform approach will likely reveal its inability to close the achievement gap between at-risk children and their more fortunate peers.[3]

Unfortunately, the federal government in the 1980s and 1990s has given little support to rigorous development and evaluation of alternative ways to provide disadvantaged children with better opportunities at the school or classroom level. As Robert Slavin has aptly stated,

> For decades, policymakers have complained that the federal education research and development enterprise has had too little impact on the practice of education. With a few notable exceptions, this perception is, I believe, largely correct. Federally funded educational R&D has done a good job of producing information to inform educational practice, but has created few well-validated programs or practices that have entered widespread use. (1997, 22)

Similarly, Ellen Lagemann's recent historical survey of educational research found that "too often, for example, when policymakers or practitioners have wanted research on a particular topic, they have discovered
that none exists" (2000, 240). Therefore, policymakers should consider
how the current OERI structure and practices could be altered to facilitate the support of more high-quality research and development.

A short chapter such as this cannot explore all important matters
related to improving OERI. Therefore, this conclusion will briefly address eight issues: the relative independence of federal education research, federal educational program evaluations and large-scale development efforts, the quality and quantity of the research staff, funding and
flexibility in the allocations of resources, the fragmentation of research
and development efforts, the quality of the research and development
produced, the intellectual leadership at OERI, and the role of politics in
the agency.

I. The Relative Independence of Federal
Education Research

Although policymakers and researchers widely agree on the need for
federal involvement in educational research and statistics, they have
reached less consensus on the optimum organizational location of that
effort. Mid-nineteenth-century educational reformers wanted a separate
cabinet-level department of education to signal the importance of a federal role in schooling. In 1867, Congress did establish a separate Department of Education (almost immediately reorganized and renamed as the
Bureau of Education), but it deliberately confined its responsibilities in
practice to gathering, analyzing, and distributing data on schooling. This
restriction seemingly emphasized the importance and autonomy of the
federal government's statistical and research activities (Kursch 1965;
Warren 1974).

As the Bureau of Education acquired new responsibilities in the
early twentieth century, its statistical and research activities gradually
received less internal attention and support. Calls for enhancing federal
involvement in education often justified themselves by emphasizing the
importance of gathering educational data. But once the federal government attained broader involvement, policymakers usually downplayed
the statistical activities in practice (see, e.g., Hennigsen 1987; Pickett
1967; Smith 1923; and Sniegoski 1994).

The Bureau of Education was reconstituted as the U.S. Office of
Education in 1930. As the agency grew rapidly in the 1960s, fear arose
that the statistical and research functions of USOE had been neglected

and mismanaged.[4] As a result, a separate National Institute of Education was created to provide more visibility and coherence for educational research in the 1970s. Unfortunately, strong congressional hostility toward NIE initially prevented the agency from fully capitalizing on the benefits of its new independent status (Dershimer 1976; Sproull, Weiner, and Wolf 1978).

When the Department of Education was being created in the late 1970s, NIE was transferred to a new Office of Educational Research and Improvement, where it eventually lost much of its autonomy and visibility. The incoming Reagan administration tended to be suspicious of social science research and program evaluations and tried to curb educational research and development (Glaser 1984; Zodhiates 1988). The OERI reorganization in 1985 further diminished the role of researchers and scholars within the agency, as the remnants of NIE became further submerged within the larger organization.[5]

Starting in FY89, the transfer of many new but less research oriented programs to OERI shifted the overall budget and focus of the agency still further from the original NIE concentration on research and development. In FY89, funding for the National Center for Education Statistics, the regional educational laboratories and R&D centers, field-initiated research, and the Educational Resources Information Clearinghouses made up 98.7 percent of the OERI budget. By FY93, these more traditional OERI activities composed only 52.8 percent of the overall budget, and by FY97 they had shrunk to 47.6 percent (Vinovskis 1998a, 25–26, 34–35).[6]

Given OERI's current limited research and development capabilities and disappointing past achievements, perhaps the time has come to reconsider the organizational location of the agency. Should OERI maintain its rapidly increasing number of programs or should it separate the research and development components from its other growing responsibilities? Congress has strongly recommended that the Department of Education consolidate even more of its research and evaluation functions into OERI. This may be a useful step — depending on which programs and activities are designated as research oriented and transferred to OERI.[7] At the same time, perhaps OERI should also focus more of its attention on research, development, and statistics by shedding some of its recently acquired but less research related program activities. In a surprising but refreshing move by the head of a federal agency, Assistant Secretary Kent McGuire recently stated in testimony before the Senate his belief that much of OERI's more service oriented programs should be transferred elsewhere within the Department of Education (McGuire 1999). Congress will make the ultimate decision about whether to follow up on McGuire's initiative toward sagaciously reorienting OERI in the direction of research and development.[8]

Some analysts have suggested the abolishment of the existing OERI program. The more research oriented components of the current OERI could then merge with some other federal agency such as the National Science Foundation while its more statistically oriented activities could be incorporated into another unit such as the Bureau of the Census. This plausible alternative is attractive because educational research and development would be attached to another, more scientifically rigorous and accomplished federal agency. On the other hand, the focus on educational research might diminish overall in another agency. Moreover, the links between practitioners and researchers may stretch too far if the direction and control of educational research are removed from the Department of Education.

Rather than only reorganizing research and development within OERI, we should simultaneously improve program evaluations located in the Planning and Evaluation Service. Therefore, it is time to reconsider the current structure of PES and OERI and develop an alternate plan that continues to build upon the best parts of the existing agencies while placing more emphasis on the independence, integrity, and excellence of units that deal with educational statistics, research, evaluation, and development.[9]

While past periodic restructuring of NIE or OERI has not always been beneficial, some key changes would be helpful. The political independence and objectivity of research needs to be reaffirmed and protected. Many have suggested setting up a completely independent research agency.[10] While there are some drawbacks to establishing an educational research agency outside the Department of Education, they would be outweighed by the benefits of the research unit's relative freedom from political interference and ability to institute more rigorous and scientifically sound research practices. Therefore, an independent national center for education research should be created.[11] It would best be directed by a commissioner of research, appointed for a six-year term, with a distinguished background in research, development, or evaluation.

Following up on the earlier recommendations of Congress and recent statements by OERI's assistant secretary, Kent McGuire, more of the Department of Education's research and small-scale development should be concentrated in the new national center for education research. At the same time, some of OERI's current technical assistance and more program related activities might be better housed elsewhere in the department. In particular, it would be helpful to transfer the current Office of Reform Assistance and Dissemination, now in OERI, to a new planning and dissemination (PAD) agency, which would replace the existing Planning and Evaluation Service. The new PAD would have responsibility for the department's planning and dissemination activities while transferring PES's current program evaluations to a new special evaluation and development unit (discussed in the next section).[12]

Besides improving federal education research, Congress should reauthorize and upgrade other, related agencies that deal with education statistics, the National Assessment of Education Progress, and the eight national education goals. This objective includes preserving and expanding the independence of the National Center for Education Statistics and appointing a six-year commissioner of educational statistics. Similarly, the National Assessment Governing Board should continue as an independent group and have additional resources available to improve the quality of the work it oversees. Policymakers should give NAGB even more authority over and responsibility for the design and implementation of NAEP programs. Finally, serious consideration needs to be paid to reauthorization of the National Education Goals Panel if that panel would still be useful for overseeing other federal/state education reform activities (Vinovskis 2000b).

Naturally, no easy or ideal answer will be found to the difficult but fundamental question of the optimal location for federal educational research. Both NIE and OERI have experienced repeated reorganizations, many of which involved considerable time and effort but yielded few real improvements. Therefore, one should be wary of yet another call for reorganization. Rearranging existing organizational boxes is needed less than creating a situation in which knowledgeable researchers can have more influence on how the goals of the agency are formulated and implemented. Thus, the power and influence of an agency is as important as its structure, although the two issues are by no means unrelated. While any major reorganization by itself will not solve the many difficulties besetting OERI today, such organizational alternatives should at least be explored because research and development have not fared well within the current OERI structure and practices.[13]

II. Federal Education Program Evaluations and Large-Scale Development Efforts

Federal education program evaluations and large-scale development efforts require reorganization within the Department of Education in order to produce effective educational research. Large-scale, systematic development is largely absent at OERI. Many of the research and development projects at the R&D centers and the regional educational laboratories continue to be undersized and uncoordinated, and the scientific quality of much of the existing developmental work leaves considerable room for improvement. At the same time, neither the PES nor OERI have a sufficient number of scientifically sound and educationally relevant program evaluations to provide educators and policymakers with the information they need.

Since 1985, PES has had the primary responsibility for conducting program evaluations. But given its limited funding and preoccupation with numerous short-term assignments it has been unable to produce many rigorous, in-depth evaluations in the last fifteen years.[14] The previous chapter revealed its difficulties in conducting an objective and comprehensive third-year assessment of regional educational laboratory activities. Similarly, its interim multimillion dollar evaluation of the effectiveness of the current Title I program, the Longitudinal Evaluation of School Change and Performance (LESCP), was unsatisfactorily conducted. Indeed, the analysis so far has been less detailed and statistically sophisticated than the roughly comparable work for the Prospects evaluation, which took place almost a decade earlier (Vinovskis 1999d).[15]

Moreover, the Department of Education has not always delivered timely and objective evaluations of its major programs. It appears that when it suits its policy purposes, PES has immediately publicized selective results from evaluations (such as that for Prospects), even before making the actual reports available to the public or policymakers. At other times, PES has delayed much too long in releasing evaluation results that may challenge current departmental policies such as LESCP (Vinovskis 1999d). Whether intentional or not, PES has often failed to release the results of major evaluations in time for decision makers to fully use the findings in their policy deliberations. The third-year evaluation of the labs, for example, was not released until April 2000, well after most of the hearings on the OERI reauthorization in the 106th Congress had been concluded. And, although the Clinton administration has decided to eliminate the comprehensive regional assistance centers, it still has not released the evaluation of those entities.[16]

Occasionally, OERI has also engaged in selectively releasing evaluations to affect policy-making. As was pointed out in the introduction to this volume, some OERI officials in 1993 attempted to suppress my critical assessment of the labs' and centers' quality of work, and the Department of Education never published the report or shared the information with legislators during the 1993–94 OERI reauthorization process. More recently, OERI was reluctant to release the third-year evaluations of the R&D centers, and therefore most members of Congress did not have access to the evaluations until after the conclusion of the OERI reauthorization hearings.

The need for scientifically sound and politically objective program evaluations and large-scale development projects necessitates the creation of a national center for evaluation and development (NCED), an independent federal unit that would initiate and oversee a serious evaluation and development program. This agency would handle the major evaluations of educational programs, especially those that have important policy implications. Moreover, it would sponsor and oversee large-scale development projects.[17]

A commissioner of evaluation and development, appointed for a six-year term, would oversee NCED. The professional staff in this evaluation and development unit should be knowledgeable and familiar with the latest work in rigorous program evaluations and large-scale development projects. The program and development effort should be overseen by an independent, objective group of experts that will not only provide technical assistance but will ensure that the design, implementation, and interpretation of the work is scientifically sound as well as useful to educators and policymakers. Moreover, this group would help to ensure that the evaluations and development projects produced under this unit are readily and equally available to everyone, not just to those who control the Department of Education at the time.

Program evaluations should vary according to the types of information needed. For the most rigorous and statistically reliable studies, researchers should consider the use of randomized-assignment control groups—although the much higher costs of these efforts will limit the number of studies employing this approach. Planned variation projects, building upon the early 1970s work in educational evaluation, can be profitably used in many other instances. And the staff of most other projects could routinely gather less costly information to provide local areas with guidance and feedback for necessary improvements (Vinovskis 1999e).

The proposed NCED should set up an initiative for soliciting and implementing large-scale, systematic development. Initially, this program might focus its energies on three to five long-term projects in areas such as developing reading improvement programs or helping at-risk children make a successful transition from early childhood programs into regular classrooms. Any organization, including the R&D centers and the regional educational laboratories, could compete for these demonstration projects. The open competition would not only spur existing educational research and development providers to produce better proposals, but it might attract interest from major social science research organizations such as the Manpower Demonstration Research Corp. (MDRC), the RAND Corp., or the Urban Institute.

While ordinarily Congress should assign the major, large-scale evaluations and development projects to NCED, some smaller and less policy sensitive programs might be handled by other agencies. For example, the national center for education research and ORAD could support smaller and more short-term development projects; and PAD and the national center for education research could oversee some of the smaller and more applied evaluation studies.

III. The OERI Research Staff

Over the years, OERI has struggled with a lack of adequate personnel to implement and oversee the operations of the agency. This deficiency is not unique to OERI. Recent efforts to "reinvent" the federal government have led to significant staff reductions even while aggregate federal expenditures continue to increase. The reinvention movement has helped to reorganize federal agencies and improve their customer service. But, while some staff reductions can be justified by improved efficiency, the cuts may have been too deep in areas such as educational research and development. At the same time that OERI's budget mushroomed in the 1990s, the agency lost more than 25 percent of its staff, including some of its most experienced and capable individuals (who were eligible for the new early retirement buyouts).[18]

The severe cuts in OERI research staff during the Clinton administration have been not only disappointing but quite unexpected. Assistant secretaries Sharon Robinson and Kent McGuire repeatedly pleaded for additional OERI staff, but their requests were turned down by the Department of Education. During the past eight years, the department has in essence reallocated OERI staff positions to other departmental activities such as the Direct Student Loan Program. Indeed, OERI staff cuts continue, with another reduction completed in early 2000. Yet earlier Secretary Richard Riley and Undersecretary Mike Smith had been considered unusually supportive of educational research, development, and statistics. Why, then, has the Department of Education slashed the staff of OERI more than that of any other major federal education agency?

Equally puzzling has been the almost total silence of the educational research community as the Clinton administration reduced OERI staff by more than 25 percent. Even the National Educational Research Policy and Priorities Board, which is responsible for overseeing OERI and making policy recommendations, has not seriously discussed or protested the sizable staff reductions. Nor have scholarly education associations such as the American Education Research Association and the National Academy of Education challenged the reductions in OERI's research staff. Further, most of the witnesses and educational organization representatives who testified before the 106th Congress on reauthorization did not question the Clinton administration's decision to reduce OERI staffing.

Unless the academic and educational communities as well as individual scholars consistently and firmly insist upon the need for an adequate amount of high-quality federal research staff, it is unlikely that any of the other proposed reforms in this volume will make much of a difference. While the recent loss of more than 25 percent of the OERI staff is deplorable, equally troubling is the absence of serious protests against this misguided policy by those who are considered to be strong supporters of educational research, development, and statistics.

As a result of the cuts, recent expectations for higher quality work at OERI are making even greater and perhaps somewhat unrealistic demands on a significantly reduced and less experienced staff. The challenges of conducting high-quality work in the Department of Education are particularly difficult because the general field of educational research and development is not as methodologically sophisticated or scientifically rigorous as in other social and behavioral sciences (Boruch 1998; Cook 1999). Therefore, the OERI staff members who initiate and implement federal initiatives in educational research and development need to be particularly well trained and knowledgeable to ensure that the work supported meets high-quality standards. At the end of the Bush administration, outgoing OERI assistant secretary Ravitch correctly noted the lack of first-rate researchers in the agency—a situation that appears to have deteriorated even further after she left in early 1993 (Ravitch 1993b).

There are several explanations for the absence of a distinguished research staff at OERI. First, most of the OERI assistant secretaries, not experienced or productive scholars themselves, have underappreciated the need for hiring well-established researchers. Most of the top-level OERI leadership positions have been staffed not by distinguished or active researchers but by civil servants. This staff constitution has made it nearly impossible to operate a first-rate federal research agency or to recruit well-trained academics.[19]

Second, the relative overall weakness of the field of educational research has created difficulties in identifying and hiring a well-trained and methodologically sophisticated professional staff at OERI. The agency has shown little interest in recruiting the often better trained scholars from the other social sciences and behavioral disciplines. The American Educational Research Association, which is more activist and less research oriented than many other social science professional associations, has exerted little peer pressure on OERI to hire more outstanding researchers.[20]

Third, the wholesale dismissal of many competent professionals during the early Reagan years significantly weakened the agency. And claims of subsequent periodic abuses of "excepted service" led to the more recent congressional and union opposition to this appointment process (Zodhiates 1988). Instead of providing a way to attract distinguished scholars to serve in the federal government for a few years, excepted service has all but disappeared today. This diminishment is unfortunate because the government's ability to recruit temporarily some of the more capable and knowledgeable researchers might assist OERI in meeting its changing educational research and development staffing needs.

Finally, instead of trying to recruit and retain the best-trained and most talented researchers, OERI has often promoted individuals within the agency who lack the necessary research skills or experience. The agency has not provided adequate incentives or opportunities for the professional staff to upgrade their research skills and knowledge; nor has it allowed them to continue doing much of their own professional work. Questionable hiring practices also have sometimes denied career employees equal opportunities for professional advancement and contributed to relatively low staff morale during much of the 1980s and 1990s. One result of these and other problems is the view among many distinguished researchers that OERI is not an attractive place to work (see Vinovskis 1998a).

Thus, while not everyone in a federal research and development agency needs to be an expert in research and development, a substantial proportion of the professional staff should have skills in these areas. And, for those not well versed in research and development, agencies should provide opportunities and encouragement for additional training. Unfortunately, in recent years OERI has failed to attract and hire the high-quality research and development experts needed if the agency is to fulfill its internal goals as well as its congressional mandates.

IV. Funding and Flexibility in the Allocation of Resources

Educators and researchers have repeatedly pointed out the lack of adequate federal support for research, development, and statistics. Given the unusually broad and ambitious agenda expected of NIE and OERI, they have a legitimate complaint. Much more money has been available for research and development in medicine and science than in education. Even compared to the other behavioral and social sciences, funding for educational research and development has trailed badly (see, e.g., Atkinson and Jackson 1992).

The National Educational Research Policy and Priorities Board, which was created in 1994 to advise OERI, has recommended that:

> Funding for education research must be increased dramatically. An interim target should be to reach the level proposed by the President's Committee of Advisors on Science and Technology of ½% of our nation's expenditures for elementary and secondary education—about $1.5 billion annually. This would be a feasible target to reach over a five year period. (NERPPB 1996b, vii)

Similarly, the Independent Review Panel on the Evaluation of Federal Education Legislation has criticized the lack of knowledge regarding the most effective programs and practices for helping disadvantaged children:

> We find it unacceptable that as a nation we spend hundreds of billions on education, but do not fund the research and evaluation necessary to assess the effects of that investment. Title I illustrates this problem. The nation spends several billion dollars each year on the Title I program, but since reauthorization the budget for evaluation has averaged only $5 million a year. . . . During the next reauthorization, we recommend a set-aside of 0.5 percent of program funds, half of which should be allocated for evaluation and the other half for research and development. In evaluation, we believe it will be imperative for the Department of Education to support studies that assess more definitively the achievement of students participating in Title I. . . . Paired with the set-aside for evaluation, an equal sum for research and development is needed to identify effective practices in the field, to build on theory, and to refine model programs for wider implementation. The demand for "best practices" is increasing, and the knowledge base needs to keep pace. A significant investment in research and development is the best foundation for the dramatic improvements in education that all the nation's children need and deserve. (Independent Review Panel on the Evaluation of Federal Education Legislation 1999, 20)[21]

Lack of support for educational research is partially due to the low regard for educational research and development on the part of educators and policymakers. Many of them believe that available knowledge already exists to improve schooling. They believe that, if anything, researchers should simply expand the dissemination of results from the "treasure chest" of earlier work.[22] Others more supportive of the need for additional research and development have a low opinion of the quality and relevance of much previous work. This lack of enthusiasm is compounded by the considerable difficulty even many sympathetic educators and policymakers have in citing examples of past successful work despite three decades of sizable federal expenditures in this area (Astin 1988; Kaestle 1993).

The problem of limited funding is compounded by a lack of focus and long-term commitment to supporting research and development.[23] In the past, members of Congress and educators attacked NIE and OERI for the lack of relevant educational research and development. They forced the agency to devote a relatively large percentage of its scarce resources to dissemination (compared to NIH and NSF) so that little was left for research and development. As a result, research and development expenditures were particularly devastated in the mid-1980s (U.S. GAO 1987). Yet the increased attention and monies spent on dissemination in the late 1970s and early 1980s, compared to those received by other federal research and statistical agencies, were not sufficient to protect NIE and OERI from unusually severe reductions in overall funding during the Reagan years (Justiz and Bjork 1988).

While NIE/OERI has had limited monies available for research, development, and statistics, Congress has hampered its ability to spend those existing funds efficiently and effectively. The agency has not had the freedom to decide how to distribute its own resources in order to achieve the general goals set forth by the legislators. Rather, since the mid-1970s a few members of Congress have allied themselves with some of the largest beneficiaries of those federal contracts and controlled the agency's spending of federal educational research and development funds. While Congress certainly has the responsibility and power to set the general policy goals for federal research and development activities, its specific and detailed efforts to micromanage NIE and OERI have been counterproductive for the nation as a whole. This is especially true because Congress has been unable to devote the type or quality of oversight of these activities necessary to ascertain the full impact of its legislative interventions. Particularly problematic is the frequent practice of inserting in congressional report language at the last moment major policy directives that have not been adequately considered through the regular authorization and appropriations process (see Vinovskis 1998a).

As Congress and the Department of Education look to the future, they should review the distribution of monies allocated for research, development, statistics, dissemination, and other activities. How much money is needed to achieve the projected needs and priorities of the proposed national center for education research for the next five or ten years? Does the optimal division of expenditures in OERI currently exist given those future objectives? And, within each subcategory of expenditures, is OERI using the best mechanisms for achieving stated objectives? For instance, how much dissemination money should be spent on ERIC compared to alternative ways of reaching educators and policymakers? What proportion of NIE and OERI's expenditures have been congressionally mandated and what have been the advantages and disadvantages of that approach? For example, has congressional ear-marking of funds for labs and centers during the past two decades been the best way to distribute and use agency monies? Should such earmark-ing continue in the future or are there more flexible and less intrusive ways to achieve congressional goals?

V.   Fragmentation of Research and Development Efforts

A persistent complaint about educational research and development is that they have been fragmented and oriented toward short-term proj-ects. Educators and policymakers usually want to address more topics than can be reasonably expected with limited funding. Rapid changes in leadership at NIE/OERI have contributed to the episodic and imperma-nent nature of much of the agency's work. While numerous long-term research and development plans have arisen, few have survived for more than one or two years, and even those that have survived did not provide adequate guidance and direction. During its first twenty-five years, NIE/OERI simply was not willing or able to create a short list of research and development priorities and then to adhere to them for any length of time. Even the recent OERI research priorities do not provide the detailed and focused direction that is essential for guiding future work in this field.[24]

Already OERI's research priorities, issued in 1997, are being sup-plemented by more detailed and focused suggestions from other groups. The National Research Council has issued a fifteen-year strategy for improving the usefulness of educational research (Olson 1999). The NERPPB commissioned the National Academy of Education to provide research priority recommendations (NAE 1999). And NERPPB itself has issued a set of new recommendations, stating that "the priority for research in education must be *high achievement for all students* and, within that domain, the initial emphasis should be on *reading and mathematics* achievement" (NERPPB 199b, iv, emphasis original). As the new, often competing sets of research priorities are debated and resolved, it will become evident how (and whether) OERI changes its funding of the existing labs and centers to reflect the new directions in research and development and whether Congress permits the agency to retain any discretion over the disbursement of research funds.[25]

The centers and labs established in the mid-1960s were intended to focus on a small set of long-term educational research and development problems. Unfortunately, neither the labs nor the centers fulfilled that initial vision. Educators and policymakers often gambled by creating a larger number of small centers and labs in the mistaken belief that additional monies soon would be provided so that these institutions could be properly enlarged. Efforts to fund long-term, large-scale, curriculum development projects were discouraged in the mid-1970s first by Congress and then by NIE. Responding to internal and external pressures, each lab and center usually funded twenty to thirty small, short-term projects, which seldom fit together into a coherent and sustained research and development program (Vinovskis 1993a). In July 1998, OERI and NERPPB convened a conference for the leaders of more than a dozen top educational research and development initiatives; these leaders candidly acknowledged that "OERI's centers and labs are not preeminent in the field, partly because they have lacked the resources" (Timpane 1998, 8).

Given OERI's continued fragmentation and its funding of numerous small projects, Congress and the Department of Education should reexamine their strategies for encouraging long-term research and development. How much has the fragmentation of research and development in NIE and OERI hindered their ability to make a lasting impact on educational practice? What proportion of lab and center activities should focus on larger and more long term research and development projects? Why is there often discontinuity between calls for more integrated, long-term projects during lab and center reauthorizations and the fragmented, small-scale projects actually funded? What methods will improve coordination and long-term planning in areas such as field-initiated grants?

The OERI was certainly a logical choice to sponsor and oversee high-quality systematic development, and on many occasions its recent assistant secretaries have expressed support for this type of work. So why has so little been accomplished? After three decades of frustration and mutual recriminations, the time has come to acknowledge that many of the R&D centers and regional educational laboratories have not been producing much high-quality, systematic development work (Vinovskis 1999e). As mentioned earlier, one part of the solution is the establishment of a separate program under the proposed national center for evaluation and development to solicit and implement large-scale, systematic projects.

Because much existing work of the laboratories provides research-based technical assistance to their regional clients, the labs and the department's comprehensive regional assistance centers should be merged and placed under ORAD. Since five of the labs already operate five of the fifteen comprehensive centers, this merger would eliminate wasteful duplication and provide more efficient and effective services. Some of the monies saved by the merger could be redistributed directly to the states and local school districts to provide more flexibility in acquiring the technical assistance they need (including purchasing additional services from the newly merged labs and comprehensive centers). These technical assistance funds could be channeled toward schools that not only lack the resources necessary to improve their operations but serve the most economically disadvantaged children.[26]

The five-year R&D centers should continue to play an important role in educational research within the new national center for education research, but they should be much larger and their work more focused. In order for centers to be both efficient and effective, instead of an annual budget of only $1.5 or $2 million, the minimum funding of an R&D center should be at least $5 million annually. Moreover, these centers should develop coherent, focused five-year research programs; they should not have twenty to thirty small-scale, uncoordinated projects scattered among a half dozen different institutions throughout the nation (Vinovskis 1999c).

In 1994, Congress sensibly increased the amount of funding for field-initiated research in OERI. The next reauthorization should expand it even further. At the same time, however, OERI should target some of its field-initiated research competitions on particular educational problems by developing more focused, mission-oriented initiatives. A useful model would be the mid-1970s and 1980s research and evaluation work on the issue of adolescent pregnancy and early childbearing conducted by the National Institute for Child Health and Human Development. The targeted competitions for educational research may be most appropriately staffed by distinguished outside experts who could join OERI temporarily as members of the expected service staff.[27]

VI. Quality of the Research and Development

Some have questioned the shift in the type of educational research and development funded by the federal government from historical and philosophical studies in the late nineteenth century to behavioral and social science investigations in the twentieth. While most educators and policymakers welcomed this change, some individuals in the early 1980s challenged the increasingly exclusive use of the behavioral and social sciences. The present debate focuses on the relative use of quantitative or qualitative methods and on the benefits of conducting case studies rather than large-scale and more systematic investigations.[28]

Much of the research and development work produced by educational scholars is regarded by academics in other behavioral and social science disciplines as second rate both methodologically and conceptually. The low opinion of the quality of much educational research and development is frequently shared by policymakers, who consider the work sponsored by NSF or NIH to be generally more rigorous and scientifically sound.

Despite recurrent questions regarding the quality of educational research and development, NIE and OERI have done little to assess the work of their grantees and contractors. The groups and panels that examined the labs and centers in the 1970s, for example, did not investigate the quality of their contributions (Campbell et al. 1975). Nor did the recent National Academy of Sciences study of OERI consider the quality of its products or the products of its funding recipients (Atkinson and Jackson 1992). A review of the statistical work done by NCES in the mid-1980s raised serious questions about its quality — although later evaluations of the subsequent work done by NCES have provided a much more reassuring picture of its products (Levine 1986). One recent evaluation of the quality of the centers' and labs' research and development painted a mixed but disappointing picture of the conceptual and technical soundness of much of their work (Vinovskis 1993a). And, as mentioned in the previous chapter, neither the third-year center nor the third-year lab interim evaluations provided an in-depth and thorough examination of the quality of their work. Moreover, the limited analysis of the quality of their research and development suggested that many of these center and lab activities need additional assistance and scrutiny.

Policymakers should pay more attention to the types and quality of studies supported by OERI to ensure that federal research and development monies are being well spent. Have research and development focused too much on contemporary problems using a behavioral and social science approach without adequate attention paid to historical and philosophical analyses? How should quantitative and qualitative methods be used in educational research and development? Should educational evaluations employ more randomized-controlled experiments? What are the proper roles of case studies and large-scale investigations? How conceptually and technically sound are the OERI-funded studies? What can be done to enhance the quality of the work in educational research, development, and statistics?

Although concerns about the quality of research and development had not been prominent features at NIE and OERI, the 1994 legislation took an important step forward by calling for OERI, in consultation with NERPPB, to establish "standards for the conduct and evaluation of research" (Public Law 1994, sec. 941, h7). Both OERI and NERPPB have risen to that challenge, issuing strict quality assurance standards (NERPPB 1999a). They also commissioned a thoughtful and useful analysis of the peer review system (August and Muraskin 1999). Moreover, the Department of Education and OERI have been involved in an ongoing third-year review of the centers and labs, which many hope will consider the quality of their research and development products.[29] It is too early to know how effective OERI has been in improving the quality of its research and development work, but at least the agency now is addressing this important issue.

VII.   Intellectual Leadership at OERI

Federal involvement in educational research, development, and statistics has often suffered from unstable and weak intellectual leadership. Some outstanding and distinguished leaders have served in NIE and OERI, but some appointees have credentials based more on their political experience than on their distinguished educational and research achievements. Moreover, the rapid turnover of NIE directors and OERI assistant secretaries has restricted much-needed continuity or stability for the agency. During just the four years of the Bush administration, five individuals served as assistant secretaries. More recently, OERI has had four assistant secretaries in less than one year. Particularly lacking during much of the past three decades has been the type of intellectual leadership needed in a major federal research and development agency (see Vinovskis 1998a).

OERI has also often lacked strong intellectual leadership in its middle management research positions. While the past directorship of OERI's Office of Research oversaw the operation of all the centers, the five national research institutes created in the 1994 legislation presently operate independently and without adequate intellectual coordination.

Moreover, three of the five institute directors recently decided to leave OERI, raising some questions about the attractiveness of the agency's research leader positions and further diminishing the already depleted number of researchers in the institutes. Finally, while recent OERI assistance secretaries announced plans to appoint a distinguished research adviser for the agency, that post has remained vacant throughout the Clinton administration.

The Department of Education and Congress should examine some of the questions raised about the leadership and staff of the agency. Why have NIE and OERI had such a rapid turnover in leadership, and what can be done to provide more stability and continuity? How well have NIE and OERI handled the repeated interruptions in leadership, and what might be done in the future to make such transitions not only less frequent but less disruptive? What would be the essential attributes of a U.S. commissioner of research, statistics, or evaluation and development? What are the most important characteristics of a professional staff at any distinguished federal research, development, and statistics operation, and how well have these characteristics been reflected in the ever-changing composition of employees at NIE and OERI? Given the labor-intensive nature of the work expected at agencies such as NIE and OERI, what should be the size of the professional staff and how does this match what has been available over time? Why have NIE and OERI offered inadequate intellectual leadership in educational research, development, and statistics? And what must be done to improve the amount and quality of intellectual leadership in the future?

VIII. The Role of Politics in OERI

An important and troubling issue that has received little analysis is the charge that NIE and OERI have been too political. Compared to much of the work in medicine and science, school reforms and improvements are by their very nature more controversial and political. The education and socialization of children involve highly sensitive decisions not only about how students should be educated but about what they should be taught. The Bureau of Education was historically charged with helping to improve state and local schooling, and NIE has been committed to promoting excellence and equity in education. The appointees to these offices in the early 1980s had what conservatives deemed a liberal, activist federal research and development intervention agenda with respect to state and local education. Conservatives reacted to this intervention without realizing that their own role in education was also politically motivated.

Many observers have condemned the more blatant and transparent political controversies of the early 1980s (e.g., Resta 1988), but the more fundamental and subtle issue is how much and what kind of separation should exist between the immediate policy interests of any administration or Congress and the independence and integrity of NIE or OERI. While almost everyone involved agrees that the proposed NCED and national center for education research should critically investigate and evaluate the strengths and weaknesses of alternative educational policies and procedures, how much of their research and development agenda should be focused on those short-term policy-related questions? The mission statements of NIE and OERI have had strong educational reform components. But how should the leaders and staff of OERI interpret their responsibility to support any particular set of current reforms advocated by policymakers in the executive or legislative branches — especially when little bipartisan agreement exists on what educational reforms or improvements are needed?

In recent years, observers have tended to accuse OERI of engaging in politics. Diane Ravitch, an OERI assistant secretary in the Bush administration, rejected that accusation during her tenure and continues to reject it today, but she acknowledges that the perception remains and continues to hurt the agency:

> The overriding weakness of federal education research is a lack of trust, on the Hill, in the press corps, and among the public. When I was at OERI, I was told repeatedly by Congressional staff and members that the agency lacked any credibility, that it was thoroughly politicized. This reputation made it hard to recruit top-flight researchers. Based on my own experience, I did not believe it is true today. But certainly this perception is commonplace. Today, there is still a widespread perception that the federal research agenda reflects the political needs of the party in power or the interests of professional educators and researchers. (1999)

While all federal agencies engaged in research and development are involved in the political process, some members of Congress have been particularly intrusive in the area of education. Chester Finn, one of the original supporters of NIE, clearly expressed the inappropriate and inordinate involvement of Congress in educational research and development:

> Congressional people have no business setting research agendas. They create research agencies. They fund research agencies. They don't tell it what to do. They can tell it how much money to spend,

yes. They don't tell the director of the National Cancer Institute which drug to test on which forms of tumor. They have not told the director of the National Science Foundation, to my knowledge, how much money to spend on particle physics versus solid state metallurgy. . . . Congress is far more intrusive in the management of federal education programs than it is in the management of federal science research programs. But NIE, because it is overseen by the education committees and subcommittees, and so on, is stuck with the same mind set, the same political culture if you will, as Title I, where in fact it should be treated the same as NSF or NIH. (quoted in Breedlove 1996, 163)

Also needed is an open and candid discussion of the proper role of interest groups in guiding the operations of a federal research agency. In agencies such as NIH and NSF, academic and other outside interest groups have often attempted to influence general goals and lobbied to secure the necessary federal funds.[30] In the last two decades, some institutions of higher education have increasingly sought congressional earmarking of funds for special projects (Cook 1998). But most outside involvement has focused on providing support for a particular NIH division or for a solution to cure a specific disease (such as acquired immune deficiency syndrome [AIDS], cancer, or heart disease). Much less frequently have these outside groups or their congressional allies attempted to mandate the details of how research monies should be spent or which institutions within an agency should receive the federal assistance allocated to the agency. And when outside attempts to interfere in the day-to-day operations of other federal research agencies have occurred, strong protests usually have arisen from those agencies, the academic community, and members of Congress committed to protecting research objectivity and integrity.[31]

The troubled history of NIE and OERI with influential outside interest groups like the former Council on Educational Development and Research (CEDaR), which lobbied on behalf of the regional educational laboratories, suggests the need to explore this topic more openly and deeply. While politics inevitably will arise in any federal research and development operation, the extent and nature of that political involvement needs to be carefully monitored and contained lest it compromise the ability of the agency to do scientifically objective and efficient work. The periodic congressional micromanagement of NIE and OERI, often at the instigation of CEDaR, seems excessive and inappropriate in setting and implementing a scientifically sound and educationally effective research and development program.

Congress and outside interest groups have not been the only potential threat to the relative political independence of OERI. The Reagan administration made efforts to replace many OERI staff members who were viewed as too liberal ideologically (Zodhiates 1988). More recently, some have raised concerns about the Clinton administration's efforts to further its more immediate educational agenda by using OERI staff and discretionary funds to develop and oversee the proposed voluntary individual national tests in fourth-grade reading and eighth-grade math. Fortunately, that issue now appears to have been resolved, as the administration and Congress have reached at least a temporary compromise on the national testing issue, removing OERI from the direct development and supervision of that highly controversial undertaking (Innerst 1997; Lawson 1997a, 1997b).

Similarly, observers have questioned the Clinton administration's decision to not renominate Pascal "Pat" Forgione Jr. to a four-year term as commissioner of educational statistics to oversee the operation of the National Center for Education Statistics in OERI. Forgione was widely regarded as a conscientious and effective leader of NCES, and the agency's Advisory Council on Education Statistics had urged Secretary Richard Riley to reappoint him.[32] The reason given for not reappointing Forgione was his tardiness in filing his income taxes.[33] Although the administration strongly denies the allegations, some Washington insiders suspect that Forgione doomed his candidacy by publicly protesting Vice President Gore's inappropriate intrusion during the release of the national NAEP reading scores.[34] Whatever the motives, the entire unfortunate episode has raised additional questions about the relative political independence of NCES and OERI and has reinforced the call for additional protection of such agencies from political interference.[35]

Finally, the issue of a liberal bias in some educational research, development, and evaluation work should be addressed. Conservatives have frequently complained that academics, especially in the field of education, and the NIE and OERI staffs are often disproportionately liberal and biased in favor of more federal involvement in local schools. While conservatives have sometimes underestimated the attempt to maintain objectivity engaged in by all good scholars in their educational research and program evaluations, they are right to point to a general liberal bias at many major schools of education (with some notable exceptions).

Some conservatives and liberals allow their personal ideologies to intrude upon their more research-based analyses. Questions about the effectiveness of federal interventions such as Title I or Head Start have stimulated strong ideological opposition from some liberals who support those initiatives. On the other hand, the issue of school choice is often as much a philosophical and ideological disagreement between liberals and conservatives as it is an empirical question of how to provide the best services for at-risk children. Yet a disproportionate liberal bias continues at colleges and universities in most social sciences in general and education in particular. As a result, organizations not specifically conservatively oriented are less likely to fund or publish critical studies of the federal role in education because some liberal peer reviewers in the field of education, implicitly or explicitly, are less sympathetic to such critical analyses or the more conservative scholars who propose them. Conservative scholars and foundations can be just as opposed to supporting contrary views, but they tend to have fewer supporters and resources in academia than do their opponents.

Even those sympathetic to an improved and expanded federal role in education research can find themselves under attack for pointing out the shortcomings and weaknesses in existing programs. Indeed, some peer reviewers who opposed a more candid and critical analysis of current federal education endeavors tried to discourage foundations and publishers from supporting the investigation that has culminated in this book. Fortunately, other, more open-minded and objective peer reviewers have stepped forward and endorsed this project—even when they disagreed with particular parts of my analysis. If educational research and evaluations are to provide needed critical and objective analyses, more efforts should be made to increase the intellectual diversity in academia with regard to educational issues as well as to ensure that a peer reviewer's personal orientation, conservative or liberal, cannot in practice jeopardize or veto potentially worthy projects.

IX. Conclusion

Since the mid–nineteenth century, a general consensus has emerged that the federal government should play a key role in collecting, analyzing, and disseminating educational data and exert some responsibility for supporting educational research and development. Today, awareness is growing among the public and policymakers of the need for better research and development to help improve schools.

For more than three decades, the federal government has intermittently tried to create more rigorous and systematic educational research and development. The R&D centers were developed in 1964, and the following year Congress authorized the regional educational laboratories. Although periodically these institutions have experienced changes in their focus and operations, they have been among the major recipients of federal research and development expenditures since the mid-1960s. Although the monies allocated to research and development have never been adequate, from FY64 through FY98 the centers and labs spent substantial funds (in constant 1996 dollars): $1.16 billion and $1.59 billion, respectively. While the reasons for the shortcomings in these and other federal educational research and development programs are complex, the bottom line is that the public and policymakers still have not received the adequate and reliable information needed to ensure that all our children have a real chance of succeeding in school.

The history of federal educational research and development during the past three decades strikingly reveals thoughtful but often repetitive suggestions for making improvements. Almost every person involved in these discussions calls for more research funding; better trained researchers; more permanent and distinguished NIE or OERI leaders; more strategic planning to meet the needs of classroom teachers and students; more long-term, coherent research and development projects; scientifically sound research and development that is useful to practitioners; and preservation of the intellectual and political independence of the agency. Indeed, most of these recommendations have found their way into the legislative language of the agency's periodic congressional reauthorizations.

Yet what has been accomplished at the end of each reauthorization seldom matches the stated expectations and promises. Structural weaknesses in the design of the agency, inadequate funding, and periodic excessive congressional micromanagement partly explain the deficiencies. But some responsibility for the agency's shortcomings also rests with its own leadership over the past twenty-five years; NIE and OERI directors have not always attempted to recruit distinguished researchers or insisted upon high-quality work from all of the agency's grantees and contractors. Nor have all members of the educational research community been sufficiently committed to making NIE or OERI a distinguished agency, especially if it meant sacrificing their own short-term interests by subjecting their federally sponsored work to more rigorous evaluation or facing more frequent competitions for funding.

Thus, the issue during the present reauthorization of OERI is not just how to restructure the agency but how to ensure that the ideas put forth in the legislation will be carried out. In many ways the legislation that reauthorized OERI in 1994 was quite good and reasonable, and many of the shortcomings that subsequently appeared might have been corrected administratively. Perhaps a large part of the problem rests with how the legislative suggestions and directives have been implemented. As a result, some policymakers are becoming impatient with listening to the same, familiar promises of improving research and development in the near future when not enough has been done during the previous four or five years. Unless educational policymakers and researchers are prepared to make the often difficult decisions and sacrifices necessary to make OERI a first-rate, high-quality, research and development operation, some policymakers may consider shifting some current OERI monies and responsibilities to research and statistical agencies outside the Department of Education. The Senate Budget Committee Task Force on Education, for example, seems to have limited confidence in OERI's ability to produce necessary high-quality research and development:

> Unfortunately, it is often difficult to discern good research from bad. The precursor to OERI was the National Institute of Education (NIE). Modeled after the National Institute of Health, which is widely respected, the NIE never realized the same success as its role model. The Task Force heard that OERI does not seem to be closing the gap either. Inadequate peer-review processes and a lack of good quality control measures stymies progress. Even the PCAST [President's Committee of Advisors on Science and Technology] group recommends that additional research on education and the use of technology in education be undertaken by "a distinguished independent board of outside experts." There seems to be little faith in our current education infrastructure to produce the needed research on policies and programs that work. (U.S. Senate Budget Committee Task Force on Education 1998, 25)

Finally, while a review of past and present federal strategies for educational research, development, and statistics discloses difficulties in making significant and lasting improvements, it also provides occasional examples of outstanding success. For example, in the mid-1980s the National Academy of Sciences was so disappointed with the statistical work of NCES that it recommended the dissolution of that entity if immediate corrective measures were not undertaken (Levine 1986). Faced with that harsh reality, a few dedicated and talented individuals accepted the challenge to revitalize NCES. Working closely with the appropriate OERI staff and several influential members of Congress, they managed within only a few years to create an organization now acknowledged to be a distinguished and effective federal statistical agency (Atkinson and Jackson 1992). With the challenges and opportunities OERI faces today, much more has to be done to make OERI a first-class federal agency. The task of reforming and improving OERI, though difficult, can be accomplished if both Congress and the executive branch are willing to work together in a bipartisan fashion to restructure the agency into one capable of providing the high-quality research, development, and statistics needed to help all American children thrive educationally in the twenty-first century.

Notes

Introduction

1. For an analysis of research at the OAPP in the late 1970s and early 1980s, see Vinovskis 1988.

2. On the perceptions of policymakers and the public of the quality of educational research, see Kaestle 1991.

3. Since we are both educational historians and had met at academic conferences, Ravitch was familiar with my work. However, we did not establish a close working relationship prior to my tenure at OERI. My training in the social sciences, together with my quantitative and qualitative work in American history, provided a broad background from which to examine and evaluate various kinds of research. Moreover, she was anxious to engage someone outside the mainstream educational field who might not hesitate to criticize the commissioned research if necessary. She was not then acquainted with my previous experience on the staff of the U.S. House Select Committee on Population in 1978 and service as a frequent, long-term consultant to the OAPP and the Office of Family Planning (OFP) in the DHHS from 1981 to 1985. My tenure with Congress and DHHS afforded me experiences that proved invaluable in understanding the tasks at OERI. Since my job at OERI did not involve working with Congress, I did not participate in legislative activities within the agency during my tenure there.

4. Because I was familiar with the academic community, I began my analysis with the centers and then turned my attention to the laboratories. After completing the analysis, I had tentatively planned to study the National Center for Education Statistics (NCES), followed by the field-initiated research. Given the extended time required to complete the study of the centers and laboratories (in part due to other assignments I received) and the change in administrations, I completed only the analysis of the quality of research and development at the centers and laboratories before my return to the University of Michigan in August 1993. Therefore, my final OERI report contained only an analysis of the centers and laboratories rather than a series of individual OERI research and development studies as originally planned.

5. Prior to joining OERI, I had only a vague, incomplete understanding of the operations of that office or of the system of research and development (R&D) centers and regional educational laboratories that it funded. In order to become familiar with OERI, I initiated discussions with its staff and reviewed

briefing materials assembled for the panel that studied it for the National Academy of Sciences. Gradually, I developed a preliminary strategy for investigating the research and development funded by the office.

6. Particularly useful were my experiences as the coordinator of the OERI three- to five-year planning process during 1992. These provided me ample opportunity to work closely with the wide array of research and development activities within OERI as opposed to those associated solely with the centers and laboratories.

7. Prior to the November 1992 presidential election, however, my colleagues at the University of Michigan had asked me to chair the Department of History, and I agreed to do so. Unable to postpone that commitment, I returned to the university for the 1993 fall term. In the two years that followed, OERI engaged me to consult with it on a frequent and regular basis. This experience provided ample opportunities for me to continue working with the agency and allowed me to participate in designing and implementing the "reinvention" of OERI.

8. After several years, OERI distributed the report, or excerpts from it, to interested parties upon request or to potential grantees or contractors.

9. Since I was still employed with OERI either as a research adviser or a consultant during the years before the report was published, I did not try to share a copy of it with anyone in Congress. Although one member of Congress possibly received a copy of the report, he or she did not share it widely with colleagues or use it in congressional deliberations, hearings, or reports. Following the OERI reauthorization, and after leaving the employ of OERI as a research adviser or consultant, I met with some congressional staff members to discuss the materials that had been available to Congress during the 1993–94 reauthorization. Those with whom I spoke indicated that they had not received a copy of my report on the centers and labs.

10. These broader changes and their effect on the laboratories and centers operation are discussed in the first three chapters.

11. On the recommendations of the panel, see Independent Review Panel 1999. On my work on federal compensatory education programs, see Vinovskis 1999a.

12. I presented testimony on Title I before the House Committee on Education and the Workforce (April 14, 1999) and on OERI before the Joint House Committee on Education and Workforce and the Senate Committee on Health, Labor, and Pensions (June 17, 1999), the House Science Subcommittee on Basic Research (October 26, 1999), and the House Subcommittee on Early Childhood, Youth, and Families (April 12, 2000).

13. The difference stems partially from the 103d Congress's heavy reliance upon the National Academy of Sciences report on OERI (Atkinson and Jackson 1992). Unfortunately, the NAS panel did not consider the quality of the work produced by the centers, labs, or OERI. Members of Congress and their staffs did not appear to notice this important omission. The NAS panel, however, did make useful recommendations on other issues, which were incorporated into the 1993–94 reauthorization.

14. Ideas presented in chapter 5 grew out of comments given at the Brookings Institution conference in May 1999, where the material was first presented. I am especially grateful to Thomas Glennan Jr. and Carl Kaestle, who offered thoughtful written comments on my paper. It was published as "The Federal Role in Educational Research and Development" (Vinovskis 2000a).

Chapter 1

1. The information on center funding is based on data from an OERI draft document "Center Funding History, 1964–1992" (October 1, 1991). Since that document lacked some data from early years, I have tried to update it with information from other sources such as annual congressional appropriations hearings. While the general funding levels and trends are probably correct, some minor inaccuracies in the figures for some R&D centers may exist. The cost of living information is from the U.S. Department of Commerce index of consumer prices.

2. For a useful summary and discussion of the early federal efforts in research, see Dershimer 1976. For a nice summary of the broader changes in educational research in the twentieth century, see Lagemann 1997.

3. For an analysis of the passage of Elementary and Secondary Education Act (ESEA) of 1965, see Bailey and Mosher 1968.

4. For details of the data on center funding, see note 1.

5. For an analysis of the activities of educational research centers in the 1960s, see Sieber 1972.

6. For a very useful analysis of the activities of that task force, see Kearney 1967.

7. For example, the congressionally mandated panel that assessed the centers and laboratories in 1979 concluded that "The Panel finds virtue in maintaining the distinction between the purposes of laboratories and centers" (Panel for the Review of Laboratory and Center Operations 1979, iv).

8. From the inception of the National Institute of Education, disagreements often brewed regarding the role it would play in disseminating the results of its work to local schools. While Elliot Richardson, secretary of the Department of Health, Education, and Welfare, minimized the role of NIE in directly disseminating research findings to local educational institutions, some members of the House Select Subcommittee on Education stressed the importance of NIE being more involved in dissemination (U.S. House 1971a).

9. See note 1 for a discussion of the data sources for these calculations.

10. In late 1989, the OR considered three options: fund twelve centers, fund five larger centers, or fund nine medium-sized centers. There was strong support within OR for the funding of five centers with an annual average budget of $2 million (in current dollars), but that suggestion was rejected. The five centers would have been: Student Learning; Families, Communities, and Young Children's Learning; Middle Grades and High Schools in the Inner Cities; Learning to Teach; and Education Policies and Student Learning. Instead, OR continued

with the idea of twelve centers, with an annual average budget of less than $1 million, later expanded by the addition of seven centers for consideration.

11. The authorities opted to fund the original twelve proposed centers, the Dissemination and Knowledge Utilization Center, and as many of the other centers as funding would allow. The Center for the Teaching and Learning of the Arts, which was to be cosponsored with the National Endowment for the Arts (NEA), was dropped because NEA decided not to support the project. Eventually, OERI funded eighteen of the final proposed set of nineteen centers.

12. The National Research Council study did not investigate in any detail how the funds of the existing centers are utilized or how much money remains for research once overhead, administrative costs, and dissemination expenses are paid.

13. Note the larger center size proposed by the Campbell group in comparison with the recent recommendations of the National Research Council.

14. The panel recommended that NIE enter into long-term agreements with seven of the existing nine centers and seven of the eight laboratories.

15. For an analysis of the creation of the U.S. Department of Education, see Radin and Hawley 1988.

16. Ironically, as shown later in the chapter, much of the work of the centers is fragmentary and noncumulative. Hence, the rationale for establishing stable centers seems less persuasive in light of the current functioning of those institutions.

17. For an excellent analysis of the historical and current disrespect for research in education, see Kaestle 1991.

18. The National Research Council's proposal of work in August 1990 specifically stated that "the study will include a close look at the institutions and activities supported by OERI for the conduct of education research, particularly the labs and centers."

19. For convenience, centers will often be referred to by the designated name of their primary location. The Center for Research on Effective Schooling for Disadvantaged Students, for example, will sometimes be referred to simply as the Johns Hopkins Center.

20. In order to examine the quality of research, it was advisable to select centers in operation prior to 1990 so that an ample set of research products was available for inspection. Therefore, some of the new centers funded in 1990 or thereafter were systematically excluded from more detailed scrutiny. One might object that since all of the centers investigated existed prior to 1990 the analysis is biased toward more successful centers that were able to win in the next round of competition. The inclusion of two former centers, unsuccessful in the 1990 bid for funding, helps to correct that potential bias.

21. The OERI center monitors assembled the relevant materials from their own files. Most of the written materials for the five ongoing centers were produced in the five-year period prior to 1990.

22. Special attention was given to the FY92 budgets because they contained more detailed information about the budgets of the individual research projects. During the period 1985–90 most centers did not provide detailed budget breakdowns for individual research projects.

23. The 1985 original application as well as the 1988 renewal packets were examined for most of these centers. In addition, the 1990 grant applications for most centers were examined.

24. My visit to the Berkeley Center occurred on June 5–6, 1992, the UCLA Center on June 7–8, the Johns Hopkins Center on June 17, the Rutgers Center on July 13, and the Pittsburgh Center on August 20.

25. A copy of her letter as well as my specific reactions to her criticisms can be found in the appendix to Vinovskis 1993a.

26. Information for the more detailed examination of the FY92 budgets came from the application for continuation, parts 1 and 2. The data were analyzed manually because the computerized OERI Project Management Information System (PMIS) did not provide the type of categories about research expenditures necessary for this analysis.

27. Thus, four of the five largest centers were used in this analysis—including the UCLA Center, which received the $2.7 million. It is important to note, however, that almost all of the five centers were considerably smaller in the period FY86 to FY90. Average funding in FY90 was $1.14 million (in current dollars) and $1.68 million in FY92—a 47 percent increase. The UCLA Center in particular experienced the largest increase in funding, from $1.0 million in FY90 to $2.7 million in FY92. As a result, although these five centers were relatively large in FY92 compared to the others, they were much closer in size to the other centers prior to FY91. Therefore, the products available from that earlier period are more typical and representative of the other centers at that time.

28. This percentage was not the rate of indirect costs but the proportion of the total funds expended for this item. The rate of overhead based upon the overall direct costs of these five centers was 38.1 percent. Since any given center interfaces with the several colleges and universities that participate in its activities, the indirect rate for each of them varied substantially. One difficulty with OERI's computerized PMIS is that it does not always permit the analyst to distinguish indirect and direct costs. For example, in PMIS printouts the direct and indirect costs were distinguishable for the primary site institutions but not for the subcontractors. Although this information was usually available in the original budget application forms, the computerized PMIS did not make the distinction. Another problem stemmed from the centers' failure to provide detailed information on the subcontractors' budgets. In these few instances, it was necessary to contract the center to obtain the necessary information.

29. Most centers did provide data on the costs of administration and dissemination, but some did not distinguish between the two (and sometimes, of course, these were difficult to separate entirely since some project administrators were also very active in disseminating the results of their centers' research). Moreover, since some research project budgets also include money for dissemination, that amount was estimated using information from the distribution of activities as reported by the centers on project input forms for continuation budgets. Naturally, these activities' distributions were only approximations, and therefore the final figures for dissemination are only estimates.

30. It should be noted that the Johns Hopkins Center did devote a substantial

amount of effort to dissemination, but it did not charge OERI for that activity. Therefore, the variation in the amount of money spent did not always reflect the actual amount of effort made since the source of the funding for these activities might vary from one center to another. For example, some administrative costs in one center might be paid by the indirect costs while comparable services at another center might be charged directly to OERI.

31. In fact, the Johns Hopkins Center charged OERI very little for administering the center compared to centers with a lower indirect cost rate. Some centers worked very hard to reduce the overall amount of indirect costs in order to allocate more money to other activities. Sometimes this was done by categorizing research expenses such as supplies under administrative costs (if administrative costs were not subject to indirect costs). Other centers tried to house facilities off campus in order to lower indirect cost rates. Reducing indirect costs could have had a very large impact on the amount of money available for research, but centers were reluctant to publicly discuss their tactics to reduce expenses because this might have upset university officials interested in increasing indirect costs.

32. The figures provided indicated only the amount of OERI funds spent on research. Some centers supplemented OERI monies with cost-sharing contributions of salaries, services, or space. For example, the Rutgers Center contributed an additional $123,530 for their research projects—about a one-sixth increase over the OERI-funded portion of the research budget. The overall budget of some of the centers was also supplemented by outside funding. While OERI contributed $859,413 in direct research funds at the Rutgers Center, its actual research budget was $2,156,327 (including over $100,000 received from another of the OERI-funded centers). Interestingly, the proportion of NIE/OERI funds awarded to the Pittsburgh Center declined considerably over time (1975, 82.6 percent; 1984, 56.3 percent; 1988, 29.7 percent; 1993, 12.8 percent). Most centers, however, appeared to be more heavily dependent upon OERI funds than either the Rutgers or Pittsburgh Centers.

33. The Johns Hopkins Center listed twenty-five individual research projects, but some of these were small subprojects of a larger effort. If one compares the Johns Hopkins Center research projects to those of other centers, the actual number of different projects probably would be similar. For example, the UCLA Center listed only a few larger projects, although in practice many were composed of several efforts.

34. Naturally, if centers used cost sharing or outside funds to supplement their OERI-funded research projects, the distributions reported here would have exaggerated the number of small research projects. However, most of the centers did not appear to use their outside funding to supplement individual OERI-funded projects (although the new projects created may complement the work conducted on an OERI-funded project). Moreover, while cost sharing certainly may have enhanced the size of some of the smaller research projects, its overall effect was probably unlikely to alter the general picture significantly.

35. The recent National Academy of Sciences study of OERI discovered that the principal investigators of the research spent only an average of one-fourth of their time on their center-funded work (Atkinson and Jackson 1992, 65).

36. Information on the types of research activities came from the project input forms for FY92. For any particular research project, it was expected that those who completed the forms could split the allocation of the budget activities among the seven categories rather than having to characterize them as one type or another. As mentioned previously, these forms were completed by personnel at the centers and reflected their judgment of how much of the research effort was devoted to various activities. In some cases, the center employee who filled out the forms did not show the estimates to the researchers themselves. When this was pointed out during my site visits to the centers, the employees were given the opportunity to redo any previous estimates. Only the Rutgers Center provided new estimates and executed a major revision, which included moving "some of the communications, supplies and clerical dollars from dissemination and institutional activities" (Fuhrman 1992). The figures used in this chapter are revised estimates provided by the Rutgers Center staff. Naturally, these are only crude estimates and should be treated as such. Moreover, the definitions of each category may have varied from one project to the next and from one center to another. Nevertheless, they provided a rough and useful approximation of the distribution of research activities in the centers.

37. The definition of *basic research* was not always clearly or consistently employed by OERI and the centers. For example, the Rutgers Center initially categorized 8.3 percent of its projects as basic research; however, after consulting the principal investigators of the individual research projects and rethinking their answers on the PMIS forms, they categorized 37.7 percent of their projects as involving basic research (much of this change stemmed from the shifting of activities of policy studies and evaluation to basic research).

38. The terms *basic research* and *applied research* were not necessarily the best way to characterize the type of research done at the centers. Perhaps we should borrow from the Social Science Research Council (SSRC) the phrase "mission-oriented basic research." The SSRC defines *mission-oriented research* as "research in which practical concerns guide scientists' choice of topics. The research is conducted, however, in ways that do not necessarily yield immediate or directly foreseeable applications" (Featherman 1991, 75). Most of the work done at the centers under the rubric of basic research would be more accurately described as mission-oriented basic research since each center has a clearly defined mission. Interestingly, the concept of mission-oriented research was employed by educational scholars in the early 1970s.

39. The decreasing importance of development in general at NIE and OERI is discussed in greater detail in the analysis of the quality of research and development at the OERI-funded regional educational laboratories in chapter 2.

40. While the Pittsburgh Center has conducted important and innovative basic research in the area of math and cognitive structures, it required more than a decade to move into the developmental phase of this undertaking. Perhaps we

need to explore ways of speeding up the process from basic research to the development of more effective teaching practices.

41. While centers may choose to investigate almost any topic, they retained several implicit assumptions in overall approach. For example, most educational problems and topics were approached from a current perspective, with relatively little attention given to historical considerations.

42. "The nation does not need yet another entity to conduct research on the processes of teaching and learning science, nor can such research be done adequately for the amount allocated to OERI's science content center. What is needed is an organization committed to assimilating the results of today's fervent activity, and creating bridges without which no coherent, integrated contribution will be made to science teaching and learning" (National Center for Improving Science Education 1987, 3).

43. Given the limited funding, the recent National Research Council study also questioned the wisdom of spreading the research activities of each center across several universities (Atkinson and Jackson 1992, 65).

44. The UCLA Center's various works on assessing history may seem somewhat disconnected and sporadic to the outside reader because the broader underlying research strategy for this area had not been explicitly stated. However, in my visit to the UCLA Center that larger vision became evident in talking with Eva Baker, one of the center's codirectors. Moreover, in the subsequent continuation application the UCLA Center aptly clarified its overall themes and visions.

45. The interesting critical analysis of cultural literacy studies by the UCLA Center appeared to be more of an isolated project than a part of the broader research strategy. In other words, after reading the findings and inquiring as to the logical follow-up to the study, I discovered that none had been planned.

46. For an analysis of these four case studies and more detailed information about each, see Fuhrman and Elmore 1992; Fry, Fuhrman, and Elmore 1992a, 1992b; Dolan 1992; and Fuhrman, Fry, and Elmore 1992. The reports of the four case studies themselves were basically descriptive and deliberately nonanalytic. The justification for not providing more analysis within each of the case studies was that they are intended to be used for teaching purposes and the author(s) wanted students to do their own analyses and draw their own conclusions. Unfortunately, since the four case studies did not include an appendix with more detailed information regarding the conflicting views of the participants, their usefulness for teaching purposes was limited. Moreover, the Rutgers Center reanalyzed the data used by South Carolina to decide which schools to deregulate but did not provide those data in the case study or cite that report in the publication.

47. Despite the absence of much information about the educational impact of the takeovers, the authors appeared to draw rather strong conclusions regarding their value (Fuhrman and Elmore 1992, 27–28). Indeed, the two case studies hint that they used some positive, short-term educational benefits as a result of those takeovers (Fry, Fuhrman, and Elmore 1992a; Dolan 1992). Given their

decision to not follow up on the educational impact of these takeovers, perhaps the authors should have been more circumspect when concluding that takeovers lack any educational benefits.

48. There has been relatively little interaction and coordination, for example, between the history projects at Berkeley and UCLA.

49. For example, while the Pittsburgh Center had several projects that involve the analysis of teaching history, the projects were not coordinated among themselves. This occurred in part because the individual researchers were from different disciplines and only used history as a topic for their analyses. Given the sizable investment in history at the Pittsburgh Center, the activities of these individual researchers should have been more coordinated so that they could build upon each other's efforts whenever possible. Moreover, researchers should have made more of an effort to involve disciplinary experts in their projects. Thus, the study of representations of the American Revolutionary era might have profited from the involvement of an academic expert on the American Revolution, who would have been more familiar with the recent scholarly work in this area (Beck, McKeown, and Sinatra 1989).

50. For a useful review of the value of synthesizing literature and the difficulties of implementing those findings in practice, see Tushnet 1992.

51. The center commissioned me to do a paper on the economy and education in nineteenth-century America and invited me to attend a national conference it sponsored (Vinovskis 1989a). While my temporary and rather minor involvement in this center's efforts could potentially introduce a bias into my reading of the rest of its work, I have tried to remain objective and have used the same standards for assessment that I have applied to the work of other centers.

52. For example, Jacob Mincer did a series of studies for them (Mincer 1989, 1990).

53. The Success for All program initially appeared to hope that it would improve the reading skills of every participant. It now appears, however, that a certain proportion of the most disadvantaged at-risk children still did not meet the minimal standards of success in school. As the Johns Hopkins Center staff put it, "Will Success for All ultimately bring all children to grade level reading? Given the program's commitment to avoiding retention and special education and to the fact that most Success for All Schools are in very disadvantaged neighborhoods, it seems unlikely that the program will truly ensure grade-level performance for every single child. However, the program does substantially reduce the number of children performing below level, and this effect is increasing with each successive year of implementation" (Center for Research on Effective Schooling for Disadvantaged Students 1992, 23).

54. Much has been written about the efficacy of Head Start, but most researchers now acknowledge that the results of most systematic evaluations of those programs are either inconclusive or problematic (Haskins 1989). Moreover, most of these evaluations have not taken into consideration whether the money expended on Head Start might be used more effectively for other educational efforts. Therefore, it was especially interesting that Robert Slavin and his

colleagues found that, among nine different interventions examined, tutoring proved to be the most effective — even compared to participation in a Head Start program (Slavin, Karweit, and Wasik 1991). For a broader discussion of our changing attitudes toward early education, see Vinovskis 1993b.

55. Despite the statistical limitations inherent in many of its studies, the Berkeley Center's own summary of its five-year work and achievements did not provide the appropriate caution about its findings. Rather, conclusions were presented in a much more definitive manner despite the fact that many were based on severely limited samples (Freedman 1990). The use of case studies can be an invaluable component of an overall research strategy, but efforts should have been made to develop findings that can be applied to other settings as well. For a discussion of the use of case studies, see Feagin, Orum, and Sjoberg 1991; and Ragin and Becker 1992.

56. The statistics employed in this study were not particularly sophisticated either — mainly just descriptive statistics and simple correlations. Moreover, although the final report mentions seventeen tables, these were not included in this report, making it more difficult for OERI or anyone else to analyze this work.

57. For an excellent discussion of the problems involved in doing quasi-experimental research for policy purposes, see Achen 1986.

58. For an analysis and discussion of the quality of research or development at the regional educational laboratories, see chapter 2.

59. An unsuccessful former center submitted a complaint that the winning proposal had gained an unfair advantage by submitting a proposal that was longer than permitted. As that discussion was still under way, I could not comment on it except to say that there did not appear to be any suggestion that the staff of the Office of Research deliberately favored one institution over another in the recompetition process.

60. Staff input in the decision-making process was excluded because OR employees were not allowed to be part of the formal review panel. While this system may be advisable in that it leaves almost the entire decision in the hands of outside reviewers, it was unsatisfactory because it may have excluded entirely some of the more knowledgeable and experienced professionals in the field.

61. Criteria for technical soundness included: "(1) The applicant demonstrates a thorough knowledge of current research and development concepts, theories, and outcomes and relates these to the proposed activities and mission of the center; (2) the adequacy of the research design and methodologies to address the research questions posed; and (3) evidence that, where appropriate, the perspectives of a variety of disciplines are used" (Office of Research 1990, 139).

62. This comparison of successful center proposals with field-initiated proposals was based upon my personal experiences in evaluating grant applications from agencies such as the National Endowment for the Humanities (NEH), NIH, and NSF. It was not based upon an analysis of the field-initiated proposals submitted to OERI.

63. Naturally, a more thorough and proper examination of this question would entail a review of all applicants — not just the successful ones. It is possible that the researchers and practitioners differed on the unsuccessful applicants so that the only ones that won were those acceptable to both parties.

64. When this study began, Milton Goldberg was the director of the office of research. He was replaced in July 1992 when he left OERI for another assignment.

65. The occasional excessive turnover in center monitors has been detrimental both to the centers and OERI. For example, the former National Center on Education and Employment had five different center monitors in two and a half years.

66. Even when Sally Kilgore tried to encourage center monitors to use the handbook, one division head simply refused to comply, telling the monitors reporting to him to ignore it.

67. Judith Segal, for example, coedited several books with scholars at the center that she monitors (Segal, Chipman, and Glaser 1985; Chipman, Segal, and Glaser 1985; Voss, Perkins, and Segal 1991). Of course, while the close intellectual involvement of a monitor with his or her center is to be welcomed and fostered, some objection might be raised that involvement diminished the possibility of the monitor maintaining an independent and objective perspective. While such a concern is legitimate, such dangers were probably far outweighed in practice by concerns about having a center monitor who is not intimately familiar with the subject and methodological issues involved.

68. Indeed, since most center monitors were only allowed one annual trip to either their center or a professional conference, some monitors choose to attend the annual conference and meet with the center director there.

69. Keith Stubbs and Ella Jones headed up an OERI task force to review and revise the use of the PMIS system.

70. There was considerable debate within OR and OERI on how much attention should be directed to the quality of the research and development produced by the centers. Initially, the third-year review plans did not call for a careful assessment of the quality of the center work, but the final instructions to the outside and inside reviewers specifically asked them to address the quality issue.

71. Since Congress had specified the total minimum amount of money allocated to the centers as a line item, surplus funds could not be transferred to some other noncenter activity at OERI (unless the total amount allocated to the centers by OERI had exceeded the minimum set by Congress).

72. Similarly, more than $200,000 of another center's funding were withheld until it provided a much more detailed and developed research design for one of its projects.

Chapter 2

1. The information on lab funding is based upon data from a variety of documents gathered at OERI. While a few minor discrepancies exist in the

various annual estimates of lab expenditures, the overall level and trend should be reasonably accurate. The cost of living information is from the U.S. Department of Commerce index of consumer prices.

2. For a useful analysis of the Gardner Task Force, see Kearney 1967. At the time Kearney did his analysis, he did not have a copy of the official Gardner report, but he was able to re-create the contents of that document from materials supplied by some of the participants. Indeed, his understanding of the labs based upon earlier documents and discussions with the participants almost mirrors what is found in the report's final draft.

3. Some of today's laboratories do try to maintain close ties to colleges and universities. For example, the Appalachia Educational Laboratory (AEL) has representatives from the colleges and universities on its governing board, works with them on their Colleges and Schools Program, and hires expert consultants from those institutions.

4. For a discussion of the Elementary and Secondary Education Act of 1965, see Bailey and Mosher 1968.

5. For a thorough discussion of the early debates over the nature and function of the labs within the U.S. Office of Education, see Dershimer 1976, 83–103.

6. While his public statements about the labs generally were laudatory, privately he seems to have been quite aware of the serious shortcomings in the functioning of many labs. For example, in a retrospective interview in the early 1970s, he observed that the labs "were going in all directions — service-oriented, research-oriented, giving grants to people who couldn't have gotten them in national competition, some behaving like state departments of education, others behaving like weak schools of education. A lot of trial and error" (ibid., 92).

7. For example, Chase pointed to the cooperation between the Research and Development Center at the University of Pittsburgh, under the direction of Robert Glaser, and Research for Better Schools, one of the local labs prominent in developing and disseminating individually prescribed instruction (IPI). While there certainly were some instances of close center-lab cooperation, Chase greatly exaggerated their prevalence and seriously underestimated the difficulties involved in getting R&D centers and labs to work together as a team.

8. Chase felt that centers were generally more focused in their activities than the labs. He applauded the recent efforts of the labs to redefine their missions more narrowly and focus their attention on a smaller number of projects and activities (1968, 18–21). The U.S. Office of Education also believed that the mission of the labs was to be focused (U.S. House 1967a, 227).

9. While the tension between regional and national labs did not disappear in the late 1960s and early 1970s, USOE and its successor, NIE, stressed their national orientation (Rossmiller 1975, 101–2).

10. In constant 1996 dollars, the annual $1 million cost of each development project would be $4.5 million. Thus, the minimum size of a lab that had at least three development projects would be about $13.5 million (in constant 1996 dollars).

11. John Fogarty, chairman of the House Subcommittee on Appropriations for the Department of Health, Education, and Welfare (HEW) and a staunch supporter of federal research, died in 1968. Moreover, Congresswoman Edith Green, chairperson of the Special Subcommittee to Study the Office of Education, began to attack the labs—primarily out of her belief that their staffs were overpaid. But the budget constraints due to the increased costs of the Vietnam War created a climate in which all domestic spending increases became more difficult (Dershimer 1976, 95–98).

12. For an excellent discussion of the problems of NIE and its funding, see Sproull, Weiner, and Wolf 1978.

13. Initially, CEDaR had not opposed the program purchase policy, but it did so when it became evident that the policy would fragment its institutions (Breedlove 1996, 30–31, 52–59).

14. Sieber illustrated the dangers of unconcern regarding the quality of the research being disseminated: "The extent to which faddism dictates the adoption of innovations of doubtful merit has been demonstrated in a recent study of virtually all big-city secondary schools. This study reveals that while 46 percent of these schools are relatively high in adoptions of innovations, most of the innovations adopted by *half* of these innovative schools are of relatively low quality (as judged by a national panel of secondary school experts). Clearly, quality remains as important an issue as quantity of adoptions" (Campbell et al. 1975, 90).

15. Richard Rossmiller also was the director of the Wisconsin Research and Development Center for Cognitive Learning. Richard Scanlon was the executive director of Research for Better Schools, Inc., of Philadelphia, Pennsylvania.

16. Jennings Randolph et al., "Letter to Harold L. Hodgkinson," January 27, 1977.

17. Hodgkinson acknowledged the previous hostility between NIE and the centers and labs and admonished the NIE staff to change its behavior (1977b, 1).

18. In a meeting on September 3, 1976, NIE and CEDaR had agreed that "no less than half of the Panel members will be educational practitioners (with an emphasis on elementary and secondary practitioners)" (Hodgkinson and Rossmiller 1976).

19. For an analysis of curriculum changes in the past, see Cuban 1979 and Kliebard 1979.

20. For a recent discussion of some of these efforts, see Atkinson and Jackson 1992, 25–45.

21. For an in-depth analysis of the MACOS project, see Dow 1991.

22. The working definition of *prototypic development* was the "design and production of an exemplary part of an instructional program (e.g., a one-week unit in a two-semester course) to serve as a model for continued development" (Hodgkinson 1997a, 109).

23. For a detailed analysis of the changes and turmoil at NIE between 1981 and 1983, see Zodhiates 1988.

24. Whereas many of the plans for the laboratories in the late 1970s and early

1980s stressed participation of the regional laboratory governing boards in setting the agenda, this report tried to balance national and regional interests and emphasized the need to arrive at a negotiated settlement.

25. For an analysis of the peer review process in the 1985 lab and center competitions, see Schultz 1988.

26. NIE's opposition to large-scale curriculum development stemmed in part from the early 1980s resurgence of hostility toward any federal involvement in this area. For example, at the 1983 Chicago public hearing on a national competition for the labs and centers, Louise Kaegi, a former teacher, indirectly challenged federal support for curriculum development by questioning the usefulness of values clarifications and affective education in the schools. Similarly, Rev. Hiram Crawford stated that "many teachers are alcoholics, dope addicts, sex symbols and engage in teaching value clarification and secular humanism, whose basic philosophy is communistic" (NIE 1983a, 177). Even more direct and vociferous attacks on federal support of curriculum development came at the Kansas City hearings, during which several participants questioned the NIE-supported work at CEMREL, one of the leading labs in curriculum development in the 1970s (NIE 1983b).

27. Due to the congressional mandate, the North Central lab faced competition in 1984 rather than 1985.

28. Just before Cross became the assistant secretary, as chairman of the Laboratory Review Panel he submitted a final set of recommendations for the 1990 RFP for labs. Most of the recommendations had already been made in the 1987 report of that panel. Many of the panel's recommendations were used in the writing of the 1990 RFPs (Cross 1989).

29. For an analysis of the changes in the 1990 RFP, see Stalford 1991.

30. Since it was important to study labs that had produced a considerable amount of research since 1985, this analysis excluded the newly established Pacific Region Educational Laboratory (PREL) and the Southeastern Region Vision for Education (SERVE). The five labs investigated had a slightly larger budget than those not studied, in large part due to the relatively small amount of funding for PREL ($1.6 million per year). The average budget for FY92 for the five labs studied was $3.7 million, while that for the five other labs was $3.3 million.

31. Task 3 included the applied research and development activities for the period FY91–FY95. These items were also examined for FY86–FY90, when they were included under task 4.

32. The labs' and centers' products are now deposited in the U.S. Department of Education Library for public access.

33. I visited the Northwest Lab on August 31, 1992; the Far West Lab on September 1–2; the Northeast Lab on September 16; the Mid-continent Lab on September 28; and the Southwest Lab on September 29. While the agenda for these meetings varied somewhat from lab to lab, most of the time was devoted to meeting with the staff members primarily responsible for applied research, development, and evaluation activities. In addition, I spent considerable time with

the directors of the labs and their executive committees, and in some cases I had a discussion with all of the staff members in a large meeting.

34. For details on the FY92 budgets for the labs, see Stalford 1992. The FY92 budget included an additional $4.16 million congressionally appropriated for the labs for the specific purpose of collaborating on a math and science initiative (under task 4). Aside from this $4.16 million, task 3 received 25.2 percent of the total FY92 lab budget, or 33.6 percent of the total lab budget, excluding indirect costs and fees.

35. Some have argued that due to OERI directives the labs have little control over how much money is spent on research and development. While OERI's deemphasis of research and development certainly has played an important role in ability of labs to respond in this area, the sizable variation among the labs with regard to the percentage of funds spent on task 3 suggests that they have considerable discretion in the allocation of their funds.

36. For information on the outside funding for the labs, see Stalford 1992. Since that document did not have data on the outside funding for SEDL, this information was obtained directly from that lab (65 percent of its FY92 funds were from non-OERI lab monies). Much of the outside funds for the labs come from other sources in the U.S. Department of Education (including some funds administered by other programs within OERI).

37. The project input forms are part of the OERI Project Management Information System (PMIS). Therefore, sometimes these forms will be referred to simply as PMIS forms.

38. The categories of the PMIS forms would have gained useful distinctions by the addition of an administrative-managerial subgroup and by more precise definitions or subdivisions of categories such as development. For the purposes of this analysis, it seemed appropriate to remove the indirect costs and fees from each of the projects in order to make the results more similar across the labs and more comparable to the analysis of the centers. Moreover, since most of task 1 was related to managerial and administrative activities, it was also removed from the analysis whenever possible. It should also be noted that the FY92 PMIS forms contained information from task 6 (early childhood education linkages), even though task 6 activities were actually funded by DHHS through OERI, but the FY92 PMIS information did not include any data from the $416,000 supplement for each lab's collaboration on math and science.

39. While a considerable portion of lab dissemination activities consisted of providing technical assistance to clients, not all service to clients (task 2) was categorized as dissemination by the labs. For example, the Mid-continent Lab (McREL was one of the few labs to fill out its PMIS forms by task) subdivided task 2 as 10 percent policy studies, 60 percent applied research, and 30 percent dissemination. Overall, according to PMIS, 85 percent of McREL's total dissemination budget was expended under task 2.

40. The comparisons of expenditure distribution between the centers and labs must be seen as crude and inexact — even though they used the same PMIS forms. For example, the centers excluded most management expenses (beyond

the indirect costs) from their PMIS breakdowns, while the labs probably included some of them. As a result, while comparisons of relative types of expenditures between the labs and centers are interesting and useful, they should be seen as only rough approximations of expenditures.

41. For discussions of the use of case studies, see Ragin and Becker 1992; and Feagin, Orum, and Sjoberg 1991.

42. For a summary and detailed discussion of this project, see Louis and Miles 1990. Although the Northeast Lab provided the primary funding for this project, the North Central Lab and the Far West Lab also contributed some assistance.

43. For a description and analysis of this project, see Jolly, Hord, and Vaughn 1990.

44. Using task 3 funds to support research syntheses were explicitly sanctioned and encouraged in the request for proposals for labs in 1990. One of the five illustrations of permissible activities under task 3 was "synthesizing R&D, or otherwise contributing to knowledge about the improvement of schooling, particularly for at-risk populations" (PIP 1990, 24).

45. The labs, using OERI funds, subcontracted with CEDaR for the production of these one-page summaries. The labs then disseminated the CEDaR summaries to their regional clients (sometimes adding some of their own research/ policy summaries). After receiving research and policy reports from the labs, centers, and other scholars or organizations, CEDaR evaluated them for quality and relevance in deciding which to use for their one-page summaries. While many of the OERI-funded R&D centers sent their materials to CEDaR, some refused to participate, perhaps not realizing that this was an OERI-funded activity.

46. Assistant Secretary Christopher Cross made plans to coordinate all publication activities undertaken or funded by OERI. Unfortunately, those plans never materialized and the entire coordinating effort was subsequently abandoned.

47. For example, the Mid-continent Lab subdivided all of its activities for the PMIS forms according to the six tasks. Task 1 was designated as 100 percent development.

48. For a discussion of the Onward to Excellence Program, see Blum, Yap, and Butler 1992.

49. For a description and discussion of the project on computers in the classroom, see Kell, Harvey, and Drexler 1990.

50. For example, the Far West Lab undertook a multisite case study evaluation of twenty-four Chapter I schools throughout the country with funding from OERI—but not from OERI's regional lab budget (Rowan et al. 1986; Rowan and Guthries 1988).

51. Under pressure from NIE (and its successor, OERI) in the early 1980s, the Far West Lab moved away from its emphasis on basic research and toward applied and developmental work. While the 1993 staff was less oriented toward academic and basic research than were its predecessors, many members ap-

peared to be relatively well trained and sophisticated in their methodological and statistical skills.

52. The response rate for the mailed questionnaires to the principals and teachers was 68 and 63 percent, respectively. Unfortunately, the Far West Lab did not try to ascertain what biases might have been introduced by this response rate (Amsler, Mitchell, Nelson, and Timar 1988, 3).

53. For details of the collaborative action research effort, see Crandall 1991. As of June 1993, the Northeast Lab still had not submitted any detailed research plans for its collaborative action research project.

54. In 1990, 625 schools participated in the Onward to Excellence Program; 292 had been involved with OTE for at least two years and therefore were eligible for participation in this impact study. Of these, 163 were in the School Improvement Network Directory, which became the initial database for this study. Naturally, one wonders what kind of biases might have been introduced by looking only at schools that joined the School Improvement Network. Researchers could design a study to sample some schools that did not join and compare them to those that did. It might make even more sense to develop an ongoing longitudinal analysis of all participants in the Onward to Excellence Program for both analysis and monitoring (a standardized questionnaire might be developed for each program to complete each year). For details of the impact study of the Onward to Excellence Program, see Blum, Yap, and Butler 1992, 1993.

55. Interestingly, when I discussed the conceptual and methodological shortcomings of this study with one of its authors, he readily agreed and explained that he and his staff had been constrained by the lack of time and funds available for this particular analysis. However, when I discussed the same issue with the Northwest Lab staff members responsible for evaluation, they defended the study as methodologically sound and adequate. The Northwest Lab's final study did not acknowledge or discuss the methodological shortcomings that OERI and I had raised with the staff in writing (Blum, Yap, and Butler 1993).

56. For additional studies of the complexity of the relationship between class size and student achievement, see Mitchell, Beach, and Badarak 1991; Mitchell, Carson, and Badarak 1989; Tomlinson 1990; and Word et al. 1990.

57. Moreover, one real danger is that many at the labs who understand and support more systematic research and development are among those who worked at the labs in the late 1960s and 1970s. As they retire, much of the commitment to and expertise in research and development will be lost.

58. Under section C of the plan of operation, the lab competition did ask "the degree to which the objectives of the project relate to the overall mission of the laboratory program and also special emphasis in this statement of work (at-risk students, rural small schools and early childhood education)" (OERI 1990, 6). But this was only one of ten subcategories under the plan of operation.

59. Near the end of this investigation, Charles Stalford received the assignment to direct the Eisenhower Math and Science Program within OERI. He was replaced by Marshall Sashkin, the institutional liaison for the Far West Lab.

60. Since laboratories are institutional programs rather than just projects, the

term *institutional liaison* is used (Educational Networks Division 1992). Since the handbook is a loose-leaf manuscript, it is not possible to cite the appropriate pages when this document is quoted. Diane Ravitch, the former assistant secretary for OERI, strongly objected to the word *liaison* for designating the staff members overseeing the R&D centers and preferred instead the word *monitor*. She thought that *monitor* implied a much more active oversight of the R&D centers than *liaison*. As a result, OR now calls its staff members overseeing the R&D centers monitors. Apparently, Ravitch has not made the same point about the individuals who deal with the labs, as they continued to be called institutional liaisons.

61. The handbook has been placed in loose-leaf binders so that it can be easily updated to reflect new regulations or activities.

62. About half of the lab team members have an advanced degree beyond a B.A. But few members have had much opportunity in recent years to be active researchers themselves.

63. Unfortunately, the third-year review in 1987 did not look at the quality of the work being produced by the labs.

64. In 1987, the Grants and Contracts Office did allow the five-year lab contracts to be subdivided into two components. However, the same interpretation was not given in 1992, perhaps in part because of staff changes in that unit.

65. The PIP did initiate an analysis of lab governance through a three-year contract with Policy Studies Associates.

66. Comments from some employees in PIP on the earlier draft report (March 25, 1993).

67. For a useful and thoughtful discussion of TQM and its limitations, see Sashkin and Kiser 1993.

Chapter 3

1. For an analysis of early federal involvement in educational research, see Dershimer 1976.

2. For an in-depth analysis of the Gardner Task Force on Education, see Kearney 1967.

3. For a discussion of the origins and passage of ESEA in 1965, see Bailey and Mosher 1968 and Meranto 1967.

4. For an examination of why this federal aid to education bill passed, see Meranto 1967.

5. For an excellent overview and analysis of congressional oversight, see Aberbach 1990.

6. For a useful analysis of the leadership and membership of the U.S. House Committee on Education and Labor from 1951 to 1984, see Reeves 1993.

7. As Congressman John N. Erlenborn (R-IL) stated, "I get the impression that we may have 20 regional laboratories and 20 different missions, because they don't seem to be too well advised as to what exactly their role is" (U.S. House 1966, 103).

8. See also ibid., 640, 950, 1052.

9. See also ibid., 954, 1024, 1273–74.

10. For a broader analysis of the passage of the omnibus Education Amendments of 1972, of which NIE was one part, see Gladieux and Wolanin 1976.

11. Using the Americans for Democratic Action (ADA) voting scores for 1971 as an index of the liberalism of members, the subcommittee received a score of 59 while the House as a whole had a score of 39. Democrats on the subcommittee had an ADA score of 79, while those in the House as a whole had a score of 53. Similarly, Republicans on the subcommittee had an ADA score of 29 while those in the House as a whole had a score of 20.

12. Attendance figures were compiled from the records of the hearings (U.S. House 1971b). Brademas and Green disagreed bitterly and often personally over the NIE bill. This antagonism became particularly relevant once NIE was created and Green had an opportunity to cut its funding from her new position on the House Appropriations Committee (Brademas 1987, 29–37).

13. Daniel Moynihan, for instance, called for about $250 million annually for educational research (U.S. House 1971b, 19).

14. Harold Howe endorsed the idea of maintaining the R&D centers, the laboratories, and other research activities outside of the federal government (ibid., 147).

15. While some have provided useful analyses of the overall context of the roll call vote on NIE, no one has conducted an in-depth, statistically sophisticated analysis. For example, see the very useful and thoughtful discussion of the vote by Sproull, Weiner, and Wolf (1978).

16. For biographical and political information about the members, see U.S. Congress 1971; Barone, Ujifusa, and Matthews 1972; and *Congressional Quarterly* (1972a, 1972b).

17. On the roll call vote, 210 representatives supported the amendment to create NIE, while 153 opposed it. In addition, 14 representatives indicated afterward that they would have supported the amendment and 10 others said that they would have opposed it if they had voted (some of these nonvoters had been paired against each other). In order to obtain the broadest and most accurate indication of the House division over the amendment, statistical analyses were conducted on the basis of the 224 representatives who voted or indicated their support for NIE and the 163 who publicly opposed it. The full details of the multiple regression analyses are available upon request from the author.

18. The definition of the census regions was taken from the classification by the U.S. Bureau of the Census. The unadjusted support for NIE in each of the regions was as follows: New England (73.9 percent), Middle Atlantic (76.3 percent), East North Central (73.1 percent), West North Central (57.6 percent), South (15.9 percent), Border (58.6 percent), Mountain (47.1 percent), and Pacific (71.4 percent).

19. The chair of the House Committee on Post Office and Civil Service had opposed the original version of NIE because it dealt with personnel issues. I therefore ran another multiple regression, which included whether a representa-

tive was a member of that committee. After controlling for the effects of the other eight independent variables, membership on this committee was a negative but rather weak indicator of support for NIE.

20. For an analysis of Senator Magnuson's career, see Scates 1997.

21. For example, see the comments of Senator Magnuson in *Cong. Rec.* 1973, 25, 32982; and 1974, pt. 23, 31241.

22. Green had opposed NIE from its inception, and her animosity toward Brademas made her opposition even more determined (Brademas 1987, 29–37).

23. For instance, David Obey (D-WI) criticized NIE for having such a broad, unfocused agenda (U.S. House 1974, 832).

24. "But he [Glennan] was probably the most miserable witness I have ever seen in my career in Congress, when he sought to justify $162 million. . . . He did not know what they were doing. He had no idea of what they were going to do" (*Cong. Rec.* 1973, pt. 24, 32982). Congressman Daniel Flood (D-PA) raised comparable questions in the House about the efficacy of Glennan's testimony (U.S. House 1972, 786).

25. Testimony of Richard Dershimer on behalf of AERA (U.S. Senate 1971, 398–401).

26. For a useful discussion of the origins of CEDaR, see Breedlove 1996, 23–31. The Conference for Educational Development and Research was soon renamed the Council for Educational Development and Research.

27. With funding from center and laboratory contributions, CEDaR operated a two-person information office in Denver, Colorado, in space provided by the Education Commission of the States. Funded by a budget of about $50,000, it initially focused on producing an educational development and research catalog, which featured center and laboratory products. Interestingly, Congressman Flood raised questions about the cost of the catalog and the use of federal funds to produce it (U.S. House 1971c, 902–14). On the diverse ways in which CEDaR skillfully managed to influence legislators, see Breedlove 1996, 117–57.

28. After the Strategic Air Command base at Glasgow, Montana, closed in 1968, the U.S. Office of Education was persuaded to establish a five-year National Career Education project to help retrain unemployed members of families in the area. While some representatives, such as David Obey, questioned the wisdom of spending approximately $10,000 per family, others, such as senators Mansfield and Magnuson, insisted that NIE do everything possible to support the Mountain Plains Project (*Cong. Rec.* 1973, pt. 25, 32989; U.S. House 1974, 836–39).

29. "The strongest organized voice in the environment at present is the consortium consisting of most regional educational laboratories and research and development centers (CEDaR, for the Council on Educational Development and Research). . . . In anticipation of continuing decreases in their share of NIE funds, the group has lobbied vigorously in Congress and with the other associations for explicit legislative direction to be given to NIE to continue their work. . . . And, in the service of their undenied self-interest, this group of institutions has been almost single-handedly telling the story of education R&D on Capitol Hill. . . . It

is fair to say that because of the important political advantage of the laboratories' and centers' geographic diversity, the present size of their budgets (which makes them significant installations in any Congressional district), and the sheer persistence of their campaign on all fronts, the CEDaR group members have been the single most important continuing pressure on policy at NIE" (Campbell et al. 1975, 35). For a detailed analysis of the role of CEDaR in Washington, DC, during these years, also see Breedlove 1996, 117–215.

30. "Some Members and staff on Capitol Hill simply wish that NIE would just clean up its public act, so that clamorous lobbyists would go away. Several on Capitol Hill have told us, 'Why can't NIE just arrange some kind of truce among these different groups? We're tired of getting calls and mail on this; NIE has to solve its own problems'" (Campbell et al. 1975, 37).

31. For example, Joseph Cronin, Illinois superintendent of education, praised the leadership of both Hodgkinson and Graham: "Somehow when Secretary Califano came in, he felt that he should have a clean sweep of all the people who had been associated with the previous administration. Despite the fact that I believe Director Hodgkinson was a registered Democrat, he went out with all the others, at about the time when a number of us felt that he was making the NIE work the way it was supposed to. So that was, in my mind, an unnecessary discontinuity, even though Pat Graham then came in and did a very excellent job" (U.S. House 1980b, 73).

32. For a thorough and thoughtful analysis of the 1977–78 reorganization of NIE, see McGonagill 1981.

33. The October memorandum outlined three lab and center funding scenarios depending upon the total amount of money Congress would appropriate for NIE. For example, "at an appropriation between $70–$90 million, the Labs and Centers will receive a minimum of $26 million" (Hodgkinson and Rossmiller 1976, 1).

34. The pending reauthorization legislation accorded labs and centers an important, but not exclusive, role in nominating members for the panel to review lab and center operations. The October memorandum also indicated that "no less than half of the Panel members will be educational practitioners (with an emphasis on elementary and secondary practitioners)" (ibid., 4).

35. "In our judgement, this document ignores the express intent of Congress that NIE establish a special relationship with regional educational laboratories and university-based centers. The provisions of P.L. 94–482 are intended to spell out the nature of that relationship, and not allow NIE to establish its own structure for 'special institutional relationships' for which laboratories and centers may qualify. We cannot emphasize too strongly that the relationship with regional educational laboratories and research and development centers, as they are presently established, is a unique relationship, and not part of an overall design for 'special relationships' with a broad range of institutions" (Randolph et al. 1977, 1). The signers of the letter were four of the nine Democrats and one of the six Republicans of the U.S. Senate Committee on Labor and Public Welfare, which reauthorized NIE.

36. "We all know that the history of the NIE/lab and center relationship has been fraught with distrust so that it is not surprising that our lab and center policies are received with some skepticism. What concerns me, however, is that we continue to fuel this paranoia by informally conveying anti-lab and center sentiments in our conversations and behavior. This behavior and the image it projects proves detrimental to the Institute since much of our difficulty with Congress and the labs and centers is due to the appearance and not the reality of our lab and center policies" (Hodgkinson 1977b, 1).

37. "It [their interim report] does not represent an attempt to evaluate the previous performance of the L/C's [labs and centers]; nor is it an attempt to judge the quality of individual projects proposed by the L/C's; nor does it propose specific terms for arrangements between NIE and individual L/C's" (Panel for the Review of Laboratory and Center Operations 1978, 1).

38. For example, Joseph M. Cronin, Illinois state superintendent of education, disagreed with the growing regional orientation of the labs and the earmarking of funds for them: "Keep the labs and centers lean and accountable. This principle, already established, needs reaffirmation. State and local school systems should be able to shop around the Nation for the products or insight or expertise these labs or centers have developed. I personally think the emphasis on 'regional service,' or lack thereof, was overstated in the 1979 panel report on labs and centers. . . . I don't believe that any set percentage of the appropriation should be earmarked for any university or any center for long periods of time. I think the best proposals, and the best people should be given the support needed to conduct research and evaluation studies" (U.S. House 1980b, 50).

39. For example, Ralph D. Turlington, commissioner of education of the state of Florida, suggested that "funds awarded through NIE grants and contracts should not be used, directly or indirectly, to lobby for the continued existence or favored treatment of special interests in the research field. Even the appearance of using such funds to lobby Congress or NIE should be avoided. We call for the closer oversight of this matter as it relates to NIE funded activities" (U.S. House 1980c, 135). Similarly, George A. Parry, a member of the board of CEMREL, charged that "payments were made to a lobbying organization [CEDaR]" (ibid.). Rather than looking much further into the appearance or reality of using NIE funds to finance CEDaR, Michael Timpane, the acting director of NIE, simply replied: "We believe that this [Parry's comment] refers to CEMREL's membership in CEDaR (Council for Educational Development and Research), which is a non-profit educational association under Section 501(c)(3) of the Internal Revenue Code. We have been informed by E. Joseph Schneider, Executive Director of CEDaR, that the Internal Revenue Service recently performed a thorough audit of CEDaR and concluded that it was not a lobbying organization. CEMREL's payment of dues to CEDaR as an indirect cost allowable under the federal cost principle was not questioned by the HEW auditors" (160–61). In other words, NIE thought that giving its money indirectly to CEDaR was not a potential problem as long as it was legal, despite the fact that almost everyone viewed CEDaR as one of the more effective small lobbying groups in Washington.

40. George A. Parry, member of the board of directors of CEMREL, charged

that "the problems of which I have become aware, and of which NIE should have been aware, relate to numerous questionable practices which have clearly reduced the funds available for CEMREL's mission: excessive travel advances of long duration have been given to the chief executive officer as well as to other officials which may represent legally improper loans; undocumented or misdocumented payments have been made to directors; undocumented travel expenses have been paid; excessive travel and entertainment expenses, including substantial foreign travel have been paid; unnecessary and excessive rental payments have been made; payments have been made to a high salaried employee, which, when combined with payments received from others, indicates that the employee was receiving full time pay from two organizations including CEMREL; improperly completed tax returns have been filed which fail to inform the government and the public of payments to directors and other transactions between the corporation and organizations with which officers and directors are or were affiliated; . . . substantial corporate funds have been kept in non-interest bearing accounts in a bank with which the chief executive officer is affiliated as a director; and many more" (ibid., 156–57).

NIE was clearly embarrassed by these charges and tried to minimize them as much as possible in a detailed response. Michael Timpane, as the acting director of NIE, argued that much of the wrongdoing had occurred during the program purchase phase of work with the labs and that under the new arrangement such financial mismanagement could not occur. Moreover, rather than praising Parry for stepping forward now to point out these shortcomings, Timpane complained that he had not contacted NIE directly or mentioned these faults to the members of the oversight panel, which had visited CEMREL (158–62).

41. The NIE also moved away from funding individual researchers as opposed to institutions. While 75 percent of NIE awards for FY80 were to individual researchers, that number dropped to 44 percent in FY84 (U.S. GAO 1987, 37).

42. Terrel Bell was acknowledged as a supporter of federal research at the time. For example, David Florio, director of governmental and professional liaison for AERA, stated that he "has fought for educational research. As long as Secretary Bell is there, we have an ally, although he's not a very strong ally" (*Education Week* 1982).

43. For an excellent discussion of NIE's political struggles during the early 1980s, see Zodhiates 1988.

44. The text of the closing passage reads: "I have taken only some of the steps needed to restore balance, but I have already been publicly accused of trying to turn the agency into a conservative propaganda mill. My successor, if there is one, will know from the day he arrives that the easiest way to pacify the Washington-based interest groups is to encourage, or at least tolerate, the ideological agenda which flourished under President Carter. . . . In the long run, the public interest will be better served if the Federal Government simply drops NIE's mission and concentrates on the neutral collection of factual and statistical data on education. The interest groups would lose, but the values of pluralism, democracy, and freedom would all gain" (quoted in Zodhiates 1988, 104).

45. While the appointment of Justiz satisfied most in the educational commu-

nity, conservatives opposed his nomination. Indeed, Sweet lobbied members of Congress on his own behalf but failed to stop the appointment of Justiz (ibid., 139–64).

46. Curran personally preferred supporting individual grants over institutional ones: "Real creativity almost always comes from individuals rather than institutions" (quoted in ibid., 84).

47. In Humphrey's words: "I also want you to know—and this is why I ask the question—that I and a number of members of this panel believe that the acting director, Mr. Robert Sweet, is a man well qualified, who has turned in an excellent performance, and who is absolutely in accord with the President's philosophy on education and the Federal role. We believe his performance merits continuation in his permanent position there. He is deputy director or some such thing—acting director—but his permanent position is deputy director, and we believe that he merits continuation. . . . So I want to put you on notice, respectfully, that the situation will be watched and will be read, I believe, as I have characterized—that is, if there is an attempt to oust him, that will be read as a change in policy, and that will not be well received by those who support the President's point of view on education" (U.S. Senate 1983b, 78–79).

48. Schneider evoked strong feelings, pro and con, throughout his long career with CEDaR. For a thoughtful and generally positive assessment of his role, see Breedlove 1996. Breedlove's useful analysis benefits from her active participation at NIE and NEA in the 1970s and 1980s and is based in large part upon interviews in the early 1980s. As her sympathies tend to be with the labs and centers, she presents a more positive assessment of the role of CEDaR than many other analysts, who question the relative usefulness and effectiveness of those institutions.

49. For a useful analysis of the lab and center competitions, see Schultz 1988.

50. Interestingly, although Congress was supposed to exercise oversight of NIE's management practices, almost nothing was said of the continued difficulties at CEMREL or the need for NIE to terminate its contract. Even when Congress mandated the creation of another midwestern regional laboratory, it did not refer to the particular problems of CEMREL.

51. An investigation found that Justiz had improperly used frequent flier miles to help purchase personal tickets for his family and that he had used the federal phones to call his father. He subsequently reimbursed the $82.50 worth of personal telephone calls and the 9,500 frequent flier miles (Mirga 1984).

52. Jennings stated: "This is the 18th year that I've been here, and it seems as if every year someone wants to rearrange the boxes on the organizational chart. Rearranging boxes is nothing but a waste of federal money that doesn't have much effect on the end product" (quoted in Mirga 1985).

53. Under the new plan, most of NIE's programs were to go into the Office of Research and most of the NCES statistical efforts were relocated in the Center for Statistics. Later, the Center for Statistics reverted to its former name, the National Center for Education Statistics.

54. Obey's efforts were blocked by the subcommittee chair, William Natcher

(D-KY), and by several Republicans who objected to his amendment (*Education Week* 1985b).

55. Michael Timpane, president of Teachers College, testified on behalf of AERA: "AERA has endorsed the broad outlines of the Secretary's reorganization and feels that it represents a substantial improvement over the previous structure" (U.S. House 1986, 108–9).

56. The five groups in the coalition were the American Association of School Administrators, the Council for Educational Development and Research, the National Association of Federal Education Program Associations, the National Education Association, and the National Parents-Teachers Association (NPTA).

57. Senator Paul Simon (D-IL) drafted language protecting the regionality of the labs (*Education Week* 1986).

58. For a useful summary and analysis of the change in research priorities during the Reagan years, see Clark and Astuto 1988, 65–89.

59. On Bennett's style and activities as secretary of education, see Miller 1988b, 1988c.

60. Hines was initially named the acting OERI assistant secretary and then the official head of the agency in January 1989 when Congress was not in session. Incumbents under such circumstances can remain in power up to one year before they must receive formal Senate approval (Miller 1989).

61. "I'm not surprised, given that the movement conservatives' long-term agenda is to place their people in office and to hold them there through the change of Administrations. We can only hope that the next Administration sweeps them all out" (quoted in Miller 1988a).

62. On the review of the labs by Cross, see chapter 2.

63. For details of how Cavazos was unceremoniously forced out as secretary of education, see Kolb 1994, 165–83. Some questioned the propriety of the way Cavazos coordinated his official travel plans with those of his wife (Miller 1991c; Baumann 1991).

64. Secretary Alexander was prepared to give the highly regarded Cross another post, but Cross decided to accept a position at the Business Roundtable (Licitra, Schumacher, and McGavin 1991; Licitra 1991a, 1991b, 1991h).

65. The budgets have been reconstructed from OERI documents and the annual House and Senate appropriations committee reports. I am indebted to Thomas Brown of OERI in particular for his assistance in assembling the recent budgets. For analytic purposes, in this and subsequent discussions of the overall OERI budget the funds for the Library Programs are excluded.

66. Somewhat like Cross, Ravitch stressed the importance of developing a more effective system for disseminating research findings (Rothman 1991a).

67. "As mentioned earlier, there has been considerable discussion, but almost no analysis, of the quality of research produced by the centers. Based upon a fairly extensive and systematic reading of the materials produced at seven of the recent centers as well as a more cursory glance at some of the products from a few of the other centers, it appears that the quality of the research produced is mixed—both among centers and within centers. Some of the research produced

is of very high social science quality while other work could be substantially improved and expanded" (Vinovskis 1992, 39–40).

68. As Owens put it, "with the sudden firing of Christopher Cross, Ed's Office of Educational Research and Improvement is again in danger of sliding down the slippery slope of partisan politics" (Licitra 1991j).

69. "Having heard these charges of politicalization again and again, I have taken to asking people if they would give me examples of politicalization. They always tell me something about what happened 10 years ago. I can't do anything about what happened 10 years ago, so I say to them, 'Tell me about something that's happening right now that I can change.' I'm still waiting for someone to give me an example.

"Sir, I believe these charges to be untrue. Repeating them over and over again does not make them true. They're a slander on the dedicated professionals in the Office of Educational Research and Improvement. . . .

"So I'm still waiting for any concrete examples of any instance of politicalization in the Office of Educational Research and Improvement. I will happily make any changes necessary, but I have yet to get a single example that I can do anything about because, as I said, I can't help what happened in 1982" (U.S. House 1992c, 5).

70. Ravitch did not oppose an oversight panel for OERI but only the size and the manner in which the board was to be selected (ibid.).

71. A House report on the 1988 appropriations barred the department from ending funding for the language research center, but that wording was dropped in the final congressional appropriations report (Miller 1988f).

72. Owens stated at the AREA annual meeting: "We are not proposing a radical restructuring to better promote educational research, development, and dissemination" (Rothman 1991b).

73. Instead of changing the existing OERI structure of the labs and centers, the bill simply proposed that the institute should "develop partnerships with relevant ERIC clearinghouses, the national research centers (particularly those addressing issues connected with the education of at-risk students), the regional educational laboratories, the Chapter One technical assistance centers, the desegregation assistance centers and the National Diffusion Network, in order to expand the dissemination and utilization of materials on education research and evaluation findings, policies and practices" (U.S. House 1991b, 12).

74. The list of groups authorized to nominate candidates seems somewhat eclectic and unusual. In addition to the National Academy of Sciences, the National Education Association, the American Federation of Teachers, and the American Educational Research Association, it also includes the Children's Defense Fund, La Raza, Advocates for Black Children, and the Legal Defense Educational Fund. Moreover, two of the five nonvoting ex-officio members of the board were the director of the Bureau of Prisons and the secretary of the Department of Defense (ibid., 15–17).

75. Lamar Alexander, the newly appointed secretary of the Department of Education, testified before the Senate in June 1991:

This flexibility is the second major aspect of our legislative proposal that I'd like to discuss today. We will propose various changes to enhance the Department's ability to respond with the appropriate information or assistance to the enormous changes we expect to see during the term of this reauthorization. The law currently requires that we spend at least as much each year for research centers, regional laboratories, field-initiated studies, and ERIC clearinghouses. Funding of each of these activities should be determined in the context of all that needs to be done. The current mandated minimums should not be replaced with new ones. . . . Along these same lines, we will propose to expand the types of entities eligible to compete for regional laboratory and research center awards. Currently, only non-profit organizations may apply to operate regional laboratories, and only institutions of higher education may receive research and development center awards." (U.S. Senate 1991, 197)

76. Although the NAS panel members did not formally interview Arthur Wise, they were well aware of his work and suggestions and used them in formulating their own proposals for several large-scale research directorates.

77. The narrow initial Bush administration bill simply maintained much of the existing OERI structure but with more flexibility on how the money could be spent. The administration bill also called for a major expansion of NAEP (Licitra 1991c, 1991d).

78. For a discussion of the development of these standards and assessments, see Ravitch 1995a, 1995b; and Rothman 1995.

79. Ravitch was also aware of the work and ideas of Arthur Wise, but she did not always follow his recommendations directly. In a meeting between Ravitch and Wise, the two disagreed rather heatedly about the desirability of the proposed OERI policy council recommended by Owens. As a result, they had less communication and interaction than might have been expected given the similarity of their views on the need for a few large-scale research institutes or directorates. On some of Ravitch's early views of the future of OERI, see Licitra 1991m, 1991n.

80. When the House Committee on Labor and Education submitted the report on H.R. 4014 on August 12, 1992, the Republicans acknowledged the merit of the bill but opposed the new board (U.S. House 1992a, 134).

81. The Senate paid even less attention to the labs than the House did during the reauthorization process.

82. It is more likely, however, that Owens only pretended to be unaware of the situation since he had followed the debates over the labs. Indeed, he had even visited the Northeast Laboratory for a closer look at its operation.

83. Indeed, CEDaR probably had the best understanding of the nature and need for development throughout these hearings.

84. He stated: "Mr. Chairman and members of this subcommittee, if you are going to place the regional educational laboratories into a dissemination component, please carefully define what you mean by that term. To us, dissemination means the transfer of ideas and products from their original sites to other sites. It

includes planning, designing, and conducting activities that lead to the application of research and development in meeting educational needs" (U.S. House 1992c, 65).

Chapter 4

1. Asking the schedule C political appointees to resign was a routine and expected event in these situations and did not arouse much question or anxiety among members of the staff. When President Clinton's schedule C appointees arrived, some of them privately questioned why OERI had not eliminated or at least isolated more of the excepted service employees appointed by Ravitch. But Elliott, and then Sharon Robinson, decided to retain and use Ravitch's nonpolitical appointees. There were occasions, especially at the beginning, when some of the Clinton newcomers were concerned about the loyalty and dedication of former Ravitch staff. Over time, it became clear that even some of the more visible and outspoken OERI supporters of Ravitch served the new administration ably and loyally.

2. In March, even prior to the public announcement of her appointment, Sharon Robinson was invited to some of the key meetings of the U.S. Department of Education (Licitra 1993a, 1993b). As Robinson awaited Senate confirmation, she was hired as an OERI consultant and started to work actively with the staff in May.

3. Robinson's dissertation was a modest but interesting study of school administrators and black student suspensions (1979). While she had delivered many addresses, her scholarly publication record was limited.

4. As mentioned earlier, Ravitch had also stressed the importance of dissemination upon her arrival at OERI, but by the time she left she concluded: "I learned that I was wrong in thinking that OERI needs to spend more money on dissemination. Until there is an adequate program of research to generate new knowledge, there is little point in pouring additional money into disseminating it" (1993a).

5. In these calculations, the funds for library programs have not been included since they are part of a separate congressional budget. If the funding for library programs were included in the overall OERI budget totals, the proportion of monies spent on the more traditional programs would be even smaller.

6. Moreover, there are concerns that the monies allocated for educational technology were not being well spent. When funds were used to buy equipment, too often teachers did not receive the necessary training to use the hardware and software properly (West 1995).

7. All figures on the changes in staff FTEs were provided by Sharon Taylor of Budget Services, Department of Education, on May 1, 1997. I am greatly indebted to Ms. Taylor for running the special tabulations of data on OERI and the other agencies that made this analysis possible.

8. Much of the staff increase of the Office of Postsecondary Education (OPE) was due to the Clinton administration's efforts to have the federal govern-

ment take over the operation of the Direct Federal Student Loan Program from the banks. While this shift in supervision may have reduced student loan costs, it also necessitated a sizable increase in federal staff. The number of FTE staff needed to administer the direct Federal Student Loan program rose dramatically from 20 in FY93 to 220 in FY94. The staffing requirements rose to 346 for FY96 and were expected to go to 520 by FY97. While some of the future increases for staffing the Direct Federal Student Loan Program were to come from projected reductions in Student Financial Aid (SFA), most of them came from staff reductions in other Department of Education agencies (U.S. House 1994b, 1219; U.S. House 1995, X–6).

9. Most earlier calculations of OERI expenditures have not included library program costs, which Congress treated separately from the OERI budget. However, to estimate the amount of money spent by the agency per employee in FY92 and FY97, the expenditures for library programs were added because the total FTEs included the individuals working in those programs. In the future, the budget and staff of the library programs, but not the National Education Library, will be located outside the Department of Education.

10. Various contractors have been employed by OERI over the years. For example, the Office of Research had a multiyear, multimillion dollar contract with the Pelavin Research Institute to provide needed services such as organizing conferences, assembling research materials, and commissioning background papers. Similarly, Professional and Scientific Associates worked for the National Educational Research Policy and Priorities Board to organize their workshops and meetings.

11. The estimate of 40 percent higher costs is based upon interviews with several individuals closely involved with that operation.

12. Among those who left are Jan Anderson, John Christensen, Milt Goldberg, Dick Hays, David Mack, Ed Mooney, and Hunter Moorman.

13. For example, in April 1995, OERI was authorized to hire eight new employees (Kunin 1995).

14. One difficulty is that the field of educational research and development is considered to be less strong than many other social sciences. For useful discussions of the "awful" reputation of educational research, see Kaestle 1993; Lagemann 1997; and Sroufe 1997.

15. When I discussed this with some of the senior OERI managers, they could not think of any employees not assigned to the office of their choice. Another high-level OERI manager characterized the entire process of staff job choice as "folly."

16. On earlier efforts to improve the performance of the federal government, see DiIulio, Garvey, and Kettl 1993; Kamensky 1996; Kettl and DiIulio 1995; and Hollings 1996.

17. On origins and development of the National Performance Review, see DiIulio, Garvey, and Kettl 1993; Frederickson 1996; Ingraham 1996; Kamensky 1996; and Thompson and Ingraham 1996.

18. While Barkley had little expertise in educational matters, he was well

versed in the current issues surrounding improved management practices. Despite strong skepticism among many members of the OERI staff about the amount of time and energy devoted to improving staff management skills, he was able to work closely and effectively with both the assistant secretary and the staff. For a summary of Barkley's approach to management, see Barkley and Saylor 1994.

19. This strategic plan was based in large part on the discussions held at a planning retreat with the OERI senior staff on April 20, 1994, and delivered to the department on April 25.

20. The ten OERI reinvention teams and their process leaders were: Strategic Planning and Budget (Jan Anderson), Management and Culture (Dick Hays), Office of Reform Assistance and Dissemination (Eve Bither and Laurence Peters), Research Institute and Agenda Setting (Joe Conaty and Laurence Peters), National Education Library (Ray Fry), Synthesis (Emerson Elliott), Coordination of Research and Development (Naomi Karp), Policy Support (Ed Fuentes), Office of the Assistant Secretary and the Board (Sandra Garcia), and Media Products (Judy Craig) (Office of the Assistant Secretary 1994b).

21. Special meetings were also arranged with over one hundred individuals representing approximately fifty organizations such as the Education Commission of the States, the Leadership Conference on Civil Rights, and the National Association of Secondary School Principals. In addition, the assistant secretary held conversations with the public in six school districts across the nation (Pinellas County Schools, Florida, April 22; Austin Independent School District, Texas, May 5; Seattle Public Schools, Washington, May 18; Chicago Public Schools, Illinois, May 20; Portland Public Schools, Maine, May 24; and Newburgh Public Schools, Oregon, November 10) (Payer 1995).

22. The other members of the Coordinating Team were Judith Anderson, Margo Anderson, Bruce Barkley, Ron Cartwright, Blane Dessy, Cynthia Dorfman, Christina Dunn, Lee Eiden, Elizabeth Farquhar, Ron Hall, Naomi Karp, Barbara Marenus, Robert Morgan, Elizabeth Payer, Sheryl Stein, and Maris Vinovskis.

23. On the changes in the size of centers over time, see Vinovskis 1993a.

24. At the same time, of course, OERI was under great pressure to find some of these smaller centers in order to provide coverage in areas seen as substantively and politically important.

25. Evaluations of three of the centers were not available because their funding cycle was substantially different from those of the other nine. The Center for Research on the Education of Students Placed at Risk was reviewed much earlier—using a very different set of criteria. Information regarding the July 1999 review of the Center for Early Reading Achievement was not included in OERI's summary report to the National Educational Research Policies and Priority Board. The Center for the Study of Teaching and Policy was scheduled to be reviewed in March 2000. That review was completed, but the review was unavailable in time for this analysis.

26. Details of the review process are provided in OERI 1999.

27. Apparently, OERI had not planned to release the individual interim

reports and did so only after some prodding from the House staff as well as myself. D'Arcy Philps and Christine Wolfe of the House Committee on Education and the Workforce and Martin Orland of OERI provided help in securing these reviews under the Freedom of Information Act.

28. For example, the thoughtful but appropriately critical review of the National Center for English Language Learning and Achievement (CELA) pointed out strengths of the center as well as its shortcomings (which included the lack of appropriate control groups when examining exemplary sites, the lack of data on student achievements and the communities in which students lived, and the lack of systematic summaries of extant research). Yet the report concluded that "the reviewers left with the sense that the Center's program of research is sound, representing a coherent and sustained program of rigorous research that will contribute substantially to our knowledge of the issues involved and will result in very valuable recommendations for the profession" (OERI Review Team, n.d. [CELA], 16).

29. Some reviews, such as the one on early childhood education, were extraordinary in terms of their coverage and discussion (OERI Review Team, n.d. [NCEDL]). A few others were less comprehensive or detailed in their discussions. For example, see OERI Review Team 1999b.

30. As chapter 1 pointed out, often even some of the best R&D centers had individual projects, especially smaller ones, that did not live up to the high standards usually evident at those units.

31. Not everyone agrees upon the need to have prior research designs for the center projects. At an OERI workshop, a former chair of the center directors' group argued against requiring centers to submit a detailed research design to OERI. This person felt that they were unnecessary and time consuming to develop. This was a minority view, however, as most other researchers and center directors did see the value of providing research designs for individual projects.

32. As discussed later, an alternative to this more sporadic and uncoordinated approach to creating centers is to use the life course framework that I developed for OERI in June and July of 1995. For more discussion of this alternative approach as well as a conceptual critique of the announcement in the *Federal Register* for the center competition, see Vinovskis 1999b, chap. 8, "A Life Course Framework for Analyzing Educational Research Projects."

33. At one time, Sharon Robinson announced that Edgar Epps, a recent OERI consultant from the University of Chicago, would serve as research adviser. However, Epps devoted little effort to this role and had relatively little influence on the coordination of OERI research activities.

34. Naturally, there are a few notable exceptions. For example, Clifford Adelman, a member of the Postsecondary Institute, is a major and innovative scholar who uses college transcripts (Adelman 1990, 1995).

35. Initially Bither was hired as an excepted service employee.

36. For example, Preston Kronkosky, executive director of the Southwest Educational Laboratory, testified on behalf of CEDaR at the OERI reauthoriza-

tion hearings that the Office of Research should be reorganized into several large research institutes and that funding for field-initiated research should be expanded substantially. He also endorsed the idea that the labs should follow the research priorities outlined in the legislation (U.S. House 1992c, 61–65).

37. On the efforts of the Department of Education to support development and evaluation, see Vinovskis 1999e.

38. As a consultant to OERI, I had raised these criticisms and suggestions (Vinovskis 1995b).

39. For a discussion of some recent problems facing the labs, see Hoff 1998 and Shokraii 1998.

40. This song was sung at an OERI retirement party held for David Mack and Hunter Moorman on December 17, 1996. The words to "Labs and Centers" were written by Cliff Adelman and are used here with his permission.

41. Altogether twelve volumes were produced—an executive summary, a discussion of the study design and methodology, and separate analyses of each of the ten labs. For an overview of the process as well as summaries of the ten lab reviews, see Pistorio, Jackson, and Newell 2000. I am indebted to Carol Chelmar and Sandra Furey for kindly providing me with hard copies of all twelve lab evaluations.

42. For example, I requested copies of any interim evaluations from the contractors and the Department of Education in September 1999. These evaluations were not made available to me until the afternoon of May 2—after my testimony at the final May 4 House hearings on OERI had been drafted and submitted.

43. The similarity between the labs and the comprehensive regional assistance centers is not surprising; indeed, five of the ten labs have won contracts to operate one. My knowledge of the assistance centers is based upon my participation in the advisory group to the Policy Studies Associates' evaluation of them.

44. On the activities of NAGB, see Vinovskis 1998c.

45. Recently, the OERI group working on the national tests have been disbanded, and the "borrowed" employees have returned to their regular posts.

46. As a member of the Department of Education's Independent Review Panel, I have periodically challenged members of the Clinton administration for their failure to provide adequate assessments of such subjects as civics, geography, and history. While my suspicion that these subjects are being deliberately slighted has been confirmed, no one seems to be taking action to remedy this problem.

47. Indeed, information on the differences in achievement by parents' educational level or student receipt of Title I assistance suggests that economic disadvantage may be a very powerful factor (NCES 1996, 36, 38).

48. For recent NCES studies that do employ multivariate techniques, see Decker, Rice, and Moore 1997; and Lippman, Burns, and McArthur 1996.

49. When the administration still had not appointed a board by early February 1996, a frustrated Robinson stated, "We're at a point where we really need the board" (Viadero 1995, 29). Similarly, Gerald Sroufe, the executive director

of the American Educational Research Association, agreed: "There is a point when you can't do anything until you do something else, and that something else is the board" (19).

50. The appointees were Patricia Ann Baltz, teacher, Camino Grove Elementary School, Arcadia, California, 1993 Disney Outstanding Teacher of the Year; Ann Blakeney Clark, principal, Alexander Graham Middle School, Charlotte, North Carolina, 1994 National Principal of the Year; Rudolph F. Crew, superintendent of schools, Tacoma, Washington; Robert W. Marley, elementary school teacher, Pearl Kessler School, Wichita, Kansas; and Claire L. Pelton, associate director, Advanced Placement Program, the College Board, and vice chair, National Board for Professional Teaching Standards (U.S. Department of Education 1995a).

51. The appointees were Gene Bottoms, director of the High Schools That Work program in thirteen southern states, Southern Regional Education Board; John T. Bruer, president, James S. McDonnell Foundation, expert in cognitive science and education; Joyce A. Muhlestein, specialist, Utah Center for Families, and member, National Parent Teacher Association's Health and Welfare Commission; Alba A. Ortiz, associate dean for academic affairs and research, College of Education, University of Texas, specialist in bilingual and special education; and John Theodore "Ted" Sanders, state superintendent of schools, Ohio (ibid., 1995a).

52. The appointees were Jomills Henry Braddock II, professor and chair, Department of Sociology, University of Miami; Kenji Hakuta, professor of education, Stanford University; Sharon Lynn Kagan, senior associate, Bush Center of Child Development and Social Policy, Yale University; Glenda T. Lappan, professor of mathematics, Michigan State University; and Edmund W. Gordon, distinguished professor of educational psychology, City University of New York.

53. Sroufe believed that "these are independent thinkers. I think some of the members would be hard-pressed to recite the words to the systemic-reform hymn of this Administration." And Deena Stoner, executive director of the Council for Educational Development and Research, praised the appointees by saying, "It looks like the kind of group that Congress intended it to be" (Schnaiberg 1995, 15).

54. Edmund Gordon, for example, "expressed for the record his unhappiness with the relative amounts of money that goes for labs and centers as opposed to the amounts available for discretionary work," and John Bruer called for further discussions of the entire matter (NERPPB 1995, 9–10).

55. A revised version of the essay was published in Vinovskis 1999b.

56. On the Success for All program, see Slavin, Karweit, and Wasik 1991; and Slavin et al. 1996.

57. On the importance of summer learning, see Entwisle and Alexander 1992 and Heyns 1978.

58. "The level of public interest in improving America's schools is unprecedented, a solid body of education research now exists upon which to build new knowledge, and evidence is mounting that past research has already led to

important advances in education practice" (Robinson, Hakuta, and Sanders 1996, 2).

59. The lack of focus on the negative impact of poverty appears to be one of emphasis since the authors are certainly aware of the powerful impact of socioeconomic status. For example, see ibid., 55.

60. Given the general nature of the OERI research plan, it can encompass the priorities of the Department of Education. The point, however, remains that the top OERI management does not view the OERI research priorities as being the real focus of the agency's activities.

61. Much of the discussion and language in this section draws upon a commissioned background paper prepared for OERI (Vinovskis 1997).

62. A preliminary draft of the phase two standards are available in the briefing book *Materials for Meeting of Standards Committee* (Bither 1996).

63. For example, see the useful, though somewhat one-sided, discussions at a Committee on Standards meeting held on December 5, 1996 (Committee on Standards 1996).

64. The Clinton administration's slow pace in replacing assistant secretaries is not confined to the Department of Education. The White House has not filled vacancies in more than a third of the top twenty-one jobs at the Department of Health and Human Services. For example, the post of the assistant secretary for children and families has been vacant for nearly a year (Stolberg 1997).

Chapter 5

1. On the federal role in education statistics and research after the Civil War, see Kursch 1965; Justiz and Bjork 1988; and Warren 1974. On the more general developments in educational research in the twentieth century, see Lagemann 1997, 2000.

2. On the effectiveness of federal compensatory education programs, see Barnett and Boocock 1998; Haskins 1989; Slavin et al. 1994; and Vinovskis 1999a.

3. For discussions of the new reforms, see Fullan 1996; Jennings 1995, 1998; Pogrow 1996; Ravitch 1995a, 1995b; Rothman 1995; Le Tendre 1996; and Vinovskis 1996.

4. For discussions of the state of educational research in this period, see Bloom 1966; Brim 1965; Carroll 1961; Coladarci 1960; Cronbach and Suppes 1969; and Good 1956.

5. Policymakers such as former congressman John Brademas and former secretary of education Terrel Bell would have preferred that OERI be abolished and all research and development activities placed in NIE (Brademas 1987, 76).

6. The budgets for OERI have been reconstructed from OERI documents and the House and Senate appropriations committee reports. I am indebted to Thomas Brown of OERI in particular for his assistance in assembling the recent budgets. For analytic purposes, OERI budget funds for the library programs were excluded since the unit was run quite separately from the other operations.

7. Congress has recommended transferring other research-related programs within the Department of Education to OERI, but little has been accomplished. While the Department of Education has affirmed that OERI now coordinates and oversees many of the other research-related activities, in practice OERI has not significantly increased its involvement.

8. Some individuals in OERI expressed surprise and strong disappointment regarding McGuire's proposal to transfer some of the nonresearch functions elsewhere. They believed that there is no reason why an agency such as OERI should not handle both research and more direct reform-oriented activities. While these critics may be correct in principle, in practice OERI has become so bereft of researchers that it should shed these more service-oriented activities in order to refocus the energies of the agency on research and development. Naturally, if as the more service oriented programs are transferred the full-time equivalents of their administrators are also shifted out of OERI, the overall benefits to the agency would be considerably diminished.

9. Details of this proposed reorganization of PES and OERI were presented at a House hearing on the reauthorization of OERI (Vinovskis 2000b).

10. For example, Christopher Cross, the former OERI assistant secretary, called for moving research and data collection from the current OERI organization to a newly created Agency for Learning—somewhat similar to the National Science Foundation and the National Aeronautics and Space Administration. Similarly, Diane Ravitch, another former OERI assistant secretary, has advocated a separate, independent, educational research agency. Several others have recommended a separate, but not totally independent, research unit under a U.S. commissioner of education.

11. In this volume the acronym NCER refers to the National Council on Education Research. The proposed national center for education research is written out in full.

12. Moving ORAD out of OERI and into the new PAD would allow those performing reform and dissemination activities to work more closely with other federal, state, and local education entities in encouraging the use of research-based information to improve education.

13. On the problems of reorganization, see Kaestle 1993 and McGonagill 1981.

14. On the difficulties of conducting systematic program evaluations in the Department of Education, see Vinovskis 1999e.

15. See also the reply of the Planning and Evaluation Service (PES 1999).

16. As a member of the advisory committee to the Policy Studies Associates's evaluation of the comprehensive regional assistance centers, I had an opportunity to read and comment upon the various drafts of that evaluation. The advisory committee reviewed a preliminary draft of the final report in September 1999 and hoped that the evaluation would be released early in 2000. So far, none of the evaluations have been released.

17. This proposal was presented at a recent House hearing on the reauthorization of OERI (Vinovskis 2000b).

18. The figures on changes in staff FTEs were provided by Sharon Taylor of Budget Services, Department of Education, in May 1997.

19. Naturally, a good OERI assistant secretary does not have to be a trained and experienced researcher, as several of the better assistant secretaries have demonstrated. However, he or she must understand and appreciate the strengths and weaknesses of the fields of research and development. Moreover, the secretary should have capable researchers on staff and in leadership positions to help develop and implement appropriate strategies for research and development.

20. On the general weakness of the field of education research and development as well as the poor reputation of its scholars, see Astin 1988; Kaestle 1993; Lagemann 1997; and Sroufe 1997.

21. It should be pointed out that I was one of twenty-three members on that independent review panel.

22. For a summary and refutation of this position, see the testimony of Diane Ravitch at a hearing before the Senate Committee on Health, Education, Labor, and Pensions (Ravitch 1999).

23. On the lack of interest in long-term educational research and development, see Brademas 1987, 14–48.

24. The recent OERI research priorities plan is not adequate and was not available to be used in the allocation of funds for most of the current R&D centers. For example, see Vinovskis 1999b, chap. 8.

25. The Senate Budget Committee Task Force on Education has raised questions about the structure and effectiveness of NERPPB. It has recommended that the model of the National Assessment Governing Board be used instead (U.S. Senate Budget Committee Task Force on Education 1998). For a discussion of the strengths and weaknesses of NAGB, see Vinovskis 1998c.

26. For a discussion of the Comprehensive Regional Assistance Centers, see Laguarda et al. 1997.

27. On the uses of research in the area of adolescent pregnancy, see Vinovskis 1989b.

28. For a useful review of the trends in educational research, see Lagemann 2000.

29. For a discussion of the difficult issues involved in ascertaining the quality of the work in these areas, see Vinovskis 1997, 1998b.

30. For a useful summary of the developments in the sciences, see Martino 1992.

31. On the abuses in the use of federal funds to support political activities of the nonprofit groups in science-related activities, see Bennett and DiLorenzo 1998.

32. "Pat Forgione is a strong and energetic leader of the National Center for Education Statistics. In his brief time in that post, he has accomplished a great deal. He has ensured the quality and timeliness of publications, vigorously pursued the use of the World Wide Web to make NCES statistics more widely and readily available, and reorganized his staff in ways that connect their talents and interests more effectively with the work to which NCES is committed. All the

while he has managed to have the agency respond successfully to an ever-increasing scope of work without increases in staff available to perform that work" (Porter 1998, 1).

33. "For the past eight years, Mr. Forgione said, he has applied for an extension before the April 15 filing deadline for federal income-tax returns. But each of the years until this one, he missed the Aug. 15 deadline granted under those extensions. He has not paid penalties or been subjected to criminal charges, he said, because each year he has been due a refund. . . . But the pattern has created an ethical cloud that administration officials did not want, he said. Mr. Forgione decided to withdraw his name from consideration last week so he can pursue other jobs" (Hoff 1999a, 3).

34. There was considerable controversy over the appropriateness of having Vice President Gore, rather than the commissioner of educational statistics, initially release the 1998 NAEP report card. Mark Musick, chair of the National Assessment Governing Board, was among those protesting that Gore's actions violated the established guidelines and procedures (Musick 1999).

35. For discussions of this episode, see Fox 1999a, 1999b; and Hoff 1999a, 1999b.

References

Aberbach, Joel D. 1990. *Keeping a watchful eye: The politics of congressional oversight.* Washington, DC: Brookings Institution.

Achen, Christopher H. 1986. *The statistical analysis of quasi-experimental experiments.* Berkeley: University of California Press.

Adelman, Clifford. 1990. *A college course map: Taxonomy and transcript data.* Washington, DC: Government Printing Office.

———. 1995. *The new college course map and transcript files: Changes in course-taking and achievement, 1972–1993.* Washington, DC: U.S. Department of Education.

Altonji, Joseph. 1990. Controlling for personal characteristics, school and community characteristics, and high school curriculum in estimating the return to education. National Center on Education and Employment, Technical Papers, no. 14, July.

Amsler, Mary, Douglas Mitchell, Linda Nelson, and Thomas Timar. 1988. An evaluation of the Utah Career Ladder System: Summary and analysis of policy implications. Far West Laboratory for Educational Research and Development, January.

Ashburn, Elizabeth, Conrad Katzenmeyer, Marty Orland, Ron Pedone, Ram Singh, and Ollie Moles. 1988. A handbook for OR center liaisons. Office of Research, August.

Astin, Alexander W. 1988. The decline in public faith in education research. In *Higher education research and public policy,* ed. Manuel J. Justiz and Lars B. Bjork, 147–56. New York: Macmillan.

Atkinson, Richard C., and Gregg B. Jackson, eds. 1992. *Research and education reform: Roles for the Office of Educational Research and Improvement.* Washington, DC: National Academy Press.

August, Diane, and Lana D. Muraskin. 1999. Strengthening the standards: Recommendations for OERI peer review. Summary report draft. National Education Research Policy and Priorities Board, January 30.

Bailey, Stephen K., and Edith K. Mosher. 1968. *ESEA: The Office of Education administers a law.* Syracuse: Syracuse University Press.

Balkcom, Stephen. 1992. *Cooperative learning. Education Research Consumer Guide,* vol. 1 (June).

Barkley, Bruce T., and James H. Saylor. 1994. *Customer-driven project management: A new paradigm in total quality implementation.* New York: McGraw-Hill.

Barnett, Steven, and Sarane Spence Boocock, eds. 1998. *Early care and education for children in poverty: Promises, programs, and long-term results.* Albany: State University of New York Press.

Barone, Michael, Grant Ujifusa, and Douglas Matthews. 1972. *The almanac of American politics, 1972.* Boston: Gambit.

Baumann, David. 1991. Cavazos says political naivete doomed his tenure at ED. *Education Daily* 24 (July 5): 1–2.

Baumann, David, Jordan Dey, David Harrison, Annette Licitra, D. S. Olney, and David Schumacher. 1991. Alexander plans shakeup among top ED officials. *Education Daily* 24 (March 29): 1.

Beck, Isabel L., Margaret G. McKeown, and Gale M. Sinatra. 1989. *The representations that fifth graders develop about the American Revolutionary period from reading social studies textbooks.* Pittsburgh: University of Pittsburgh, Learning Research and Development Center.

Bennett, James T., and Thomas J. DiLorenzo. 1998. *Cancer scam: Diversion of federal cancer funds to politics.* New Brunswick, NJ: Transaction Publishers.

Bither, Eve. 1996. *Materials for Meeting of Standards Committee, December 5, 1996.* Washington, DC: Office of Educational Research and Improvement.

Blackledge, Brett J. 1991. Senate panel approves Ravitch, Martin nominations. *Education Daily* 24 (July 18): 3.

Bloom, Benjamin S. 1966. Twenty-five years of educational research. *American Educational Research Journal* 3 (May): 211–21.

Blum, Robert E., Kim O. Yap, and Jocelyn A. Butler. 1992. Onward to Excellence impact study. Paper presented at the American Educational Research Association annual meeting, San Francisco, April.

———. 1993. Onward to Excellence impact study. Northwest Regional Educational Laboratory, February.

Bock, R. Darrell. 1989. Duplex design: Giving students a stake in educational excellence. Center for the study of Evaluation, Standards, and Student Testing, final report, July.

Boruch, Robert F. 1998. Randomized controlled experiments for evaluation and planning. In *Handbook of applied social science methods,* ed. L. Bickman and D. J. Rog, 161–91. Thousand Oaks, CA: Sage.

Brademas, John. 1987. *The politics of education: Conflict and consensus on Capitol Hill.* Norman: University of Oklahoma Press.

Breedlove, Carolyn Jean. 1996. Origins of a conflict: The National Institute of Education, the laboratories and centers, and the Congress, 1972–1976. Ed.D. diss., University of Illinois, Urbana.

Brim, Orville, Jr. 1965. *Sociology and the field of education.* New York: Russell Sage Foundation.

Britt, M. Ann, Mara Georgi, and Charles A. Perfetti. 1992. *Learning from history texts: Conceptual and text factors.* Pittsburgh: University of Pittsburgh, Learning Research and Development Center.

Burns, Robert B. 1988. Longitudinal analyses of student achievement in an innovative mathematics program. Far West Laboratory for Educational Research and Development, July.

Campbell, Roald F., et al. 1975. *R&D funding policies of the National Institute of Education: Review and recommendations.* Washington, DC: Department of Health, Education, and Welfare.

Carroll, John B. 1961. Neglected areas in educational research. *Phi Delta Kappa* 42 (May): 339–46.

Carroll, Thomas G. 1988. Theories of research and action. In *Higher education research and public policy,* ed. Manuel J. Justiz and Lars G. Bjork, 33–63. New York: Macmillan.

Center Funding History, 1964–1992. 1991. Working paper, OERI, Washington, DC, October 1.

Center for Research on Effective Schooling for Disadvantaged Students. 1992. Research on Success for All, chap. 7. Manuscript.

Chase, Francis S. 1968. *The national program of educational laboratories: An independent appraisal of twenty educational laboratories and nine university research and development centers conducted under contract no. OEC–3–7– 001536–1536.* Washington, DC: Department of Health, Education, and Welfare.

Child, Family, and Community Program. 1991. *ECEAP 1991 longitudinal study and annual report: Washington State's Early Childhood Education and Assistance Program.* Portland, OR: Northwest Regional Educational Laboratory.

Chipman, Susan F., Judith Segal, and Robert Glaser, eds. 1985. *Thinking and learning skills: Research and open questions.* Hillsdale, NJ: Lawrence Erlbaum.

Clark, David L., and Terry A. Astuto. 1988. Changes in federal education research policy. In *Higher education research and public policy,* ed. Manuel J. Justiz and Lars G. Bjork, 65–89. New York: Macmillan.

Coladarci, Arthur P. 1960. More rigorous educational research. *Harvard Educational Review* 30 (winter): 3–11.

Committee on Standards. 1996. *Transcript of proceedings of the National Research Policy and Priorities Board* (December 5). Washington, DC: ACE-Federal Reports.

Congressional Quarterly. 1966. *Almanac: 89th Congress, 1st Session, 1965.* Washington, DC: *Congressional Quarterly.*

———. 1967. *Almanac: 89th Congress, 2nd Session, 1966.* Washington, DC: *Congressional Quarterly.*

———. 1968. *Almanac: 90th Congress, 2nd Session, 1968.* Washington, DC: *Congressional Quarterly.*

———. 1972a. *Almanac: 92nd Congress, 1st Session, 1971.* Washington, DC: *Congressional Quarterly.*

———. 1972b. *Weekly report* 30 (April 29).

Congressional Record. 1966. 112, pt. 19 (October 5–6, 1966).

———. 1968. 114, pt. 14 (June 26); pt. 20 (September 5).

———. 1971. 117, pt. 30 (November 4).

———. 1973. 119, pt. 25 (October 4).

———. 1974. 120, pt. 16 (June 27); pt. 23 (September 16).

———. 1976. 122, pt. 26 (September 29).

Conklin, Nancy Faires, Carole Hunt, and Laura Walkush. 1990. Language development: A base for educational policy planning. Northwest Regional Laboratory, July.

Cook, Constance Ewing. 1998. *Lobbying for higher education: How colleges and universities influence federal policy.* Ann Arbor: University of Michigan Press.

Cook, Thomas. 1999. Considering the major arguments against random assignment: An analysis of the intellectual culture surrounding evaluation in American schools of education. Paper presented at the Conference on Evaluation of Educational Policies, American Academy of Arts and Sciences, Cambridge, MA, May 13–14.

Corbally, John E. 1977. Review of Resolution 18. National Council on Education Research memo, May 19.

Cotton, Kathleen. 1990a. Educating urban minority youth: Research on effective practices. Northwest Regional Educational Laboratory, November.

———. 1990b. Schoolwide and classroom discipline. Northwest Regional Educational Laboratory. October.

Crandall, David P. 1991. Annual report, 1 December 1990–30 November 1991. Regional Laboratory for Educational Improvement of the Northeast and Islands, December.

Cronbach, Lee J., and Patrick Suppes, eds. 1969. *Research for tomorrow's schools: Disciplinary inquiry for education.* New York: Macmillan.

Cross, Christopher T. 1990. Approval concurrence of the centers to be competed in the FY 90/91 national educational research and development centers competition. Memo to the Secretary of Education, January 22.

Cross, Christopher T., Joy Frechtling, Ernest House, Alexander Law, Gary McDaniels, and Carl Sewall. 1987. Report of the Laboratory Review Panel on the 1987 review of laboratories. Office of Educational Research and Improvement. October 6.

———. 1989. Report of the Laboratory Review Panel on the pending laboratory recompetition. Office of Educational Research and Improvement, April 28.

Cuban, Larry. 1979. Determinants of curriculum change and stability, 1870–1970. In *Value conflicts and curriculum issues: Lessons from research and experience,* ed. Jon Schaffarzick and Gary Sykes, 139–96. Berkeley, CA: McCutchan.

Decision Information Resources. 2000a. *Interim evaluation of the regional educational laboratories: NCREL evaluation reports.* Vol. 7. Houston: Decision Information Resources.

———. 2000b. *Interim evaluation of the regional educational laboratories: Study design and methodology.* Vol. 2. Houston: Decision Information Resources.

Decker, Paul T., Jennifer King Rice, and Mary T. Moore. 1997. *Education and the economy: An indicators report.* Washington, DC: U.S. Government Printing Office. NCES 97–269.

Dershimer, Richard A. 1976. *The federal government and educational R&D.* Lexington, MA: Lexington Books.

DiIulio, John J., Jr., Gerald Garvey, and Donald F. Kettl. 1993. *Improving government performance: An owner's manual.* Washington, DC: Brookings Institution.

Dolan, Margaret. 1992. State takeover of a local district in New Jersey: A case study. Consortium for Policy Research in Education, TC–008, April.

Dow, Peter B. 1991. *Schoolhouse politics: Lessons from the Sputnik era.* Cambridge: Harvard University Press.

Dyson, Anne Haas. 1987. Unintended helping in the primary grades: Writing in the children's world. Center for the Study of Writing and Literacy, report no. 2, May.

———. 1991. The case of the singing scientist: A performance perspective on the "stages" of school literacy. Center for the Study of Writing and Literacy, report no. 53, September.

Education Week. 1982. 1 (10 February): 7.

———. 1985a. 5 (September 25): 9.

———. 1985b. 5 (October 23): 10.

———. 1986. 5 (April 2): 2.

Educational Networks Division. 1992. Handbook for institutional liaisons. Office of Educational Research and Improvement, April.

Entwisle, Doris R., and Karl L. Alexander. 1992. Summer setback: Race, poverty, school composition, and mathematics achievement in the first two years of school. *American Sociological Review* 57 (February): 72–84.

Euchner, Charlie. 1984a. House committee seeks probe of N.I.I. bidding. *Education Week* 3 (February 29): 1, 18.

———. 1984b. Panel said likely to challenge technology center contract. *Education Week* 3 (February 1): 1, 15.

Feagin, Joe R., Anthony M. Orum, and Gideon Sjoberg, eds. 1991. *A case for the case study.* Chapel Hill: University of North Carolina Press.

Featherman, David L. 1991. Mission-oriented basic research. *Items, Social Science Research Council* 45 (December):

Featherman, David L., and Maris A. Vinovskis. 2001. Growth and use of social and behavioral science in the federal government since World War II. In *Social science and policy-making: A search for relevance in the twentieth century,* ed. David L. Featherman and Maris A. Vinovskis, 40–82. Ann Arbor: University of Michigan Press.

Finn, Chester. 1986. Strengths (and weaknesses) of peer review. *Educational Researcher* 15 (August–September): 14–15.

———. 1987. Memo, Office of Educational Research and Improvement, October 27.

Forgione is confirmed for top NCES post. 1996. *Education Week* 15 (June 19): 25.

Foster, Preston G. 1995. Note to all OERI employees. OERI memorandum, April 28.

Fox, Jonathan. 1999a. Forgione resigns post as top ED statistician. *Education Daily,* May 20, 1–2.

———. 1999b. Politics blamed for ouster of NCES commissioner. *Education Daily*, May 27, 1–2.

Frederickson, H. George. 1996. Comparing the reinventing government movement with the new public administration. *Public Administration Review* 56 (May–June): 263–70.

Freedman, Sarah Warshauer. 1990. Final report of the center for the study of writing. Berkeley Center, December.

Fry, Patricia, Susan H. Fuhrman, and Richard F. Elmore. 1992a. Kentucky's Program for Educationally Deficient School Districts: A case study. Consortium for Policy Research in Education, TC–005, April.

———. 1992b. Schools for the 21st Century Program in Washington State: A case study. Consortium for Policy Research in Education, TC–006, April.

Fuhrman, Susan H. 1992. Letter to author, August 14.

———, ed. 1993. *Designing coherent education policy*. San Francisco: Jossey-Bass.

Fuhrman, Susan H., and Richard F. Elmore. 1992. Takeover and deregulation: Working models of new state and local regulatory relationships. Consortium for Policy Research in Education, RR–024, April.

Fuhrman, Susan H., Patricia Fry, and Richard F. Elmore. 1992. South Carolina's Flexibility Through Deregulation Program: A case study. Consortium for Policy Research in Education, TC–007, April.

Fullan, Michael G. 1996. Turning systemic thinking on its head. *Phi Delta Kappan* 77 (February): 400–407.

Gardner, John. 1964. Report of the President's Task Force on Education. LBJ Presidential Library, Austin, Texas, November 14.

Garduque, Laurie, and David C. Berliner. 1986. Beyond the competition. *Educational Researcher* 15 (August–September): 19–20.

Gladieux, Lawrence E., and Thomas R. Wolanin. 1976. *Congress and the colleges: The politics of higher education*. Lexington, MA: Lexington Books.

Glaser, Robert, ed. 1984. *Improving education: Perspectives on educational research*. Pittsburgh: National Academy of Education.

Good, Carter V. 1956. Educational research after fifty years. *Phi Delta Kappan* 37 (January): 145–52.

Gore, Al. 1993a. *From red tape to results: Creating a government that works better and costs less—report of the National Performance Review*. New York: Times Books.

———. 1993b. *From red tape to results: Creating a government that works better and costs less—report of the National Performance Review, Department of Education*. Washington DC: Government Printing Office.

Gruskin, Susan. 1975. Monitoring manual. National Institute of Education, August.

Gruskin, Susan, Kim Silverman, and Veda Bright. 1997. *Including your child*. Washington, DC: U.S. Department of Education.

Hansen, Kenneth H. 1988. Early childhood education: Policy issues. Northwest Regional Educational Laboratory, May.

Harrison, Dave. 1993. Riley picks 11 to run ED offices pending nominations. *Education Daily* 26 (16): 1–2.

Harvey, Glen, Diane Kell, and Nancy Gadzuk Drexler. 1990. Research on computers and literacy development in primary classrooms. Final report, Regional Laboratory for Educational Improvement of the Northeast and Islands, July.

Haskins, Ron. 1989. Beyond metaphor: The efficacy of early childhood education. *American Psychologist* 44 (February): 274–82.

Heard, Alex. 1982a. Bill would halt N.I.E. contract cancellations. *Education Week* 1 (May 26): 8.

———. 1982b. Planned cancellation of N.I.E. contracts called permissible. *Education Week* 1 (May 19): 9.

Heard, Alex, and Thomas Toch. 1982. N.I.E. chief plans to cancel research contracts. *Education Week* 1 (March 31): 1, 11.

Hennigsen, Victor W., III. 1987. Reading, writing, and reindeer: The development of federal education in Alaska, 1877–1920. Ed.D. diss., Harvard University.

Herman, Joan. 1990. The effects of testing on teaching and literacy. Center for the Study of Evaluation, Standards, and Student Testing, Final Report, November.

———. 1991. High quality performance-based assessment. Center for the Study of Evaluation, Standards, and Student Testing, November.

Hertling, James. 1985a. E.D. official questions N.I.E.'s effectiveness, structure. *Education Week* 4 (March 27): 10.

———. 1985b. Finn to head reorganized research unit. *Education Week* 4 (August 21): 14–15.

———. 1985c. Lawmaker threatens to block new N.I.E. plan. *Education Week* 5 (September 18): 10.

Heyns, Barbara. 1978. *Summer learning and the effects of schooling.* New York: Academic Press.

Higgins, Lorraine, Linda Flower, and Joseph Petraglia. 1991. Planning together: The role of critical reflection in student collaboration. Center for the Study of Writing and Literacy, report no. 52, September.

Hodgkinson, Harold L. 1977a. NIE's role in curriculum development: Findings, policy options, and recommendations. National Institute of Education, February 8. (Prepared by Jon Schaffarzick and Gary Sykes.)

———. 1977b. The official NIE view of labs and centers. National Institute of Education memo, March 1.

Hodgkinson, Harold L., and Richard A. Rossmiller. 1976. Memorandum of agreement between NIE and labs and centers from the September 3 meeting. National Institute of Education memo, October 4.

Hoff, David. 1993. ED adds four Clinton nominees to Assistant Secretary Roster. *Education Daily* 26 (June 29): 4.

———. 1998. Critics say federal laboratories not charting a productive course. *Education Week* 18 (September 16): 1, 25.

————. 1999a. Renomination blocked, Forgione to depart. *Education Week* 18 (May 26): 3.

————. 1999b. Republicans vow to free NCES from political meddling. *Education Week* 18 (June 2): 18.

Hollings, Robert L. 1996. *Reinventing government: An analysis and annotated bibliography.* Commack, NJ: Nova Science Publishers.

Hood, Paul D. 1990. Responding to educational needs and opportunities for school improvement in the Far West: The fourth annual self evaluation report of Far West Laboratory Regional Programs, January.

House passes OERI reauthorization bill: Movement afoot in Senate. 1992. *Report on Education Research* 24 (September 30): 11.

Independent Review Panel. 1999. *Measured progress: The report of the independent panel on the evaluation of Federal Education Legislation.* Washington, DC: U.S. Department of Education.

Independent Review Panel on the Evaluation of Federal Education Legislation. 1999. *Measured progress: An evaluation of the impact of federal legislation enacted in 1994.* Washington, DC: U.S. Department of Education, April.

Ingraham, Patricia W. 1996. Reinventing the American federal government: Reform redux or real change? *Public Administration* 74 (autumn): 452–75.

Innerst, Carol. 1997. Goodling plans effort to stop national tests: Critics fear rise of national curriculum. *Washington Times,* July 31, A7.

Jeffrey, Julie Roy. 1978. *Education for children of the poor: A study of the origins and implementation of the Elementary and Secondary Education Act of 1965.* Columbus: Ohio State University Press.

Jennings, John F., ed. 1995. *National issues in education: Elementary and Secondary Act.* Bloomington, IN: Phi Delta Kappa International.

————. 1998. *Why national standards and tests? Politics and the quest for better schools.* Thousand Oaks, CA: Sage.

Jewett, Janet. 1991a. Effective strategies for school-based early childhood centers. Northwest Regional Educational Laboratory, December.

————. 1991b. School-based early childhood centers. Northwest Regional Educational Laboratory, July.

Jolly, Deborah V., Shirley M. Hord, and Marianne Vaughn. 1990. Developing indicators of educational success: The road to improvement in five schools. Paper presented at the American Educational Research Association annual meeting, Boston, April.

Justiz, Manuel J., and Lars G. Bjork, eds. 1988. *Higher education: Research and public policy.* New York: Macmillan.

Kaestle, Carl F. 1991. Everybody's been to fourth grade: An oral history of federal R&D in education. Final Report to the Committee on the Federal Role in Education Research, National Academy of Sciences, September.

————. 1993. The awful reputation of education research. *Educational Researcher* 22 (January–February): 23–31.

Kamensky, John M. 1996. Role of the "reinventing government" movement in federal management reform. *Public Administration Review* 56 (May–June): 247–55.

Kearney, Charles Philip. 1967. The 1964 Presidential Task Force on Education and the Elementary and Secondary Education Act of 1965. Ph.D. diss., University of Chicago.

Kell, Diane, Glen Harvey, and Nancy Gadzuk Drexler. 1990. Educational technology and the restructuring movement: Lessons from research on computers in classrooms. Paper presented at the American Educational Research Association annual meeting, Boston, April.

Kettl, Donald F., and John J. DiIulio, Jr., eds. 1995. *Inside the reinvention machine: Appraising governmental reform.* Washington, DC: Brookings Institution.

Kiesler, Sara B., and Charles F. Turner. 1977. *Fundamental research and the process of education.* Washington, DC: National Academy Press.

Kliebard, Herbert M. 1979. Systematic curriculum development, 1890–1959. In *Value conflicts and curriculum issues,* ed. Jon Schaffarzick and Gary Sykes, 197–236. Berkeley, CA: McCutchan.

Kolb, Charles. 1994. *White House daze: The unmaking of domestic policy in the Bush years.* New York: Free Press.

Kunin, Madeline. 1995. Critical hires. Deputy Secretary, Department of Education, April 17.

Kursch, Harry. 1965. *The United States Office of Education: A century of service.* Philadelphia: Chilton.

Lagemann, Ellen Condliffe. 1997. Contested terrain: A history of education research in the United States, 1890–1990. *Educational Researcher* 26 (December): 5–17.

———. 2000. *An elusive science: The troubling history of educational research.* Chicago: University of Chicago Press.

Laguarda, Katrina G., Karen P. Walking Eagle, Jeanine L. Hildreth, Theresa M. Ellis, and Brenda J. Turnbull. 1997. A conceptual framework for an evaluation of the comprehensive regional assistance centers. Policy Study Associates, December.

Lally, J. Ronald, and Peter L. Mangione. 1991. Early intervention research: Building on lessons from the 60s and 70s for programs in the 90s. Paper presented at Conference on New Directions in Child and Family Research: Shaping Head Start in the Nineties, Sausalito, CA, June.

Lawson, Millicent. 1997a. House blocks, while panel settles on, new tests. *Education Week* 17 (November 19): 1, 20.

———. 1997b. Test proposal to be tested by experts. *Education Week* 17 (November 19): 1, 20.

Le Tendre, Mary Jean. 1996. Supporting school reform through Title I. *Journal of Education for Students Placed at Risk* 1 (3): 207–8.

Levine, Daniel B., ed. 1986. *Creating a center for education statistics: A time for action.* Washington, DC: National Academy Press.

Licitra, Annette. 1991a. Cross to direct education for business roundtable. *Education Daily* 24 (May 24): 2.

———. 1991b. Cross to leave ED for private sector post. *Education Daily* 24 (15 May): 2.

———. 1991c. ED asks Congress for flexibility in OERI reauthorization. *Education Daily* 24 (September 4): 2.

———. 1991d. ED's OERI reauthorization plan focuses on expanding NAEP. *Education Daily* 24 (June 14): 1–2.

———. 1991e. House panel offers ambitious OERI reauthorization bill. *Education Daily* 24 (October 4): 3.

———. 1991f. House panel reworks bill that would enlarge OERI. *Education Daily* 24 (December 30): 1–3.

———. 1991g. Independent panel studying federal education research. *Education Daily* 24 (February 22): 1–2.

———. 1991h. No official word on OERI nomination. *Education Daily* 24 (April 15): 2.

———. 1991i. OERI reauthorization locked in backstage negotiations. *Education Daily* 24 (November 22): 1, 3.

———. 1991j. Owens accuses OERI of mixing politics and research. *Education Daily* 24 (May 10): 5.

———. 1991k. Owens: OERI must be at heart of national education reform. *Education Daily* 24 (September 11): 1–2.

———. 1991l. Ravitch nominated to head ED's research division. *Education Daily* 24 (June 27): 2.

———. 1991m. Ravitch says she'll work with House on OERI renewal. *Education Daily* 24 (September 12): 3–4.

———. 1991n. Ravitch seeks money, power to flex OERI's muscle. *Education Daily* 24 (September 4): 1–2.

———. 1991o. Testing provisions delay introduction of Senate OERI bill. *Education Daily* 24 (November 1): 4.

———. 1992. Overhaul, expand OERI, Research Council says. *Education Daily* 25 (April 2): 1, 3.

———. 1993a. Clinton nominates candidates for research, higher ED slots. *Education Daily* 26 (March 31): 1, 3.

———. 1993b. ED's research director seeks dialogue with practitioners. *Education Daily* 26 (July 23): 17.

———. 1993c. House, Senate resuscitate last year's OERI bills. *Education Daily* 26 (February 10): 1, 3.

———. 1993d. NEA official closes in on top OERI job. *Education Daily* 26 (March 23): 1, 3.

———. 1993e. Researchers holding breath awaiting next OERI chief. *Education Daily* 26 (March 4): 2.

———. 1994. OERI negotiators settle on research institutes, advisory board. *Education Daily* 27 (March 31): 4.

Licitra, Annette, David Schumacher, and Joe McGavin. 1991. Alexander, Cross talk turkey; Ravitch nomination seeds sown. *Education Daily* 24 (April 8): 6.

Lightfoot-Clark, Regina. 1997. Clinton taps foundation officer to lead OERI. *Education Daily* 30 (October 23): 4.

Lippman, Laura, Shelley Burns, and Edith McArthur. 1996. *Urban schools: The challenge of location and poverty.* NCES 96–864. Washington, DC: Government Printing Office.

Louis, Karen Seashore, and Matthew B. Miles. 1990. *Improving the urban high school: What works and why.* New York: Teachers College Press.

Mace-Matluck, Betty J., Wesley A. Hoover, and Robert C. Calfee. 1989. Teaching reading to bilingual children: A longitudinal study of teaching and learning in the early grades. *National Association of Bilingual Educators Journal* 13 (3): 187–216.

Martino, Joseph P. 1992. *Science funding: Politics and porkbarrel.* New Brunswick, NJ: Transaction Publishers.

Marzano, Robert J. 1992. *A different kind of classroom: Teaching with dimensions of learning.* Alexandria, VA: Association for Supervision and Curriculum Development.

Marzano, Robert J., and Jana S. Marzano. 1988. *A cluster approach to elementary vocabulary instruction.* Newark, DE: International Reading Association.

Marzano, Robert J., Ronald Brandt, Carolyn Hughes, Beau Fly Jones, Barbara Presseisen, Stuart Rankin, and Charles Suhor. 1988. *Dimensions of thinking: A framework for curriculum and instruction.* Alexandria, VA: Association for Supervision and Curriculum Development.

Marzano, Robert J., et al. 1992. *Implementing dimensions of learning.* Alexandria, VA: Association for Supervision and Curriculum Development.

Mason, Ward S. 1983. Two decades of experience with educational R&D centers. Washington, DC: National Institute of Education.

———. 1988. Regional Educational Laboratory approaches to educational improvement: A descriptive synthesis. Final Report of the Laboratory Synthesis Project, RFQ 108331, December.

McGonagill, Grady. 1981. Reorganization—faith and skepticism: A case study of the 1977–78 reorganization of the National Institute of Education. Harvard University, October.

McGuire, Kent. 1999. Hearing before the Senate Committee on Health, Education, Labor, and Pensions, U.S. Senate, 14 April.

Meranto, Philip. 1967. *The politics of federal aid to education in 1965: A study in political innovation.* Syracuse: Syracuse University Press.

Mid-continent Regional Educational Laboratory (McREL). 1990a. Early childhood education. *Policy Notes* 4 (spring): 1–11.

———. 1990b. Status of education in the McREL region. *Policy Notes* 4 (winter): 1–12.

Miller, Julie A. 1988a. Background of secretary's choice to head research agency draws fire. *Education Week* 8 (November): 14, 16.

———. 1988b. Bennett: Despite reform, "We are still at risk." *Education Week* 7 (May 4): 15, 21.

———. 1988c. E.D. plan to close language-research center draws fire. *Education Week* 8 (April 20): 1, 14, 16–18.

———. 1988d. Man on the move: Bennett road shows blends politics with policy. *Education Week* 7 (April 13): 1, 16.

———. 1988e. Politics pervades E.D. research arm, study alleges. *Education Week* 8 (September 21): 22, 28.

———. 1988f. Senators to confirm Cavazos as secretary. *Education Week* 8 (September 21): 22, 27.

———. 1989. Reagan appoints Hines to head Office of Educational Research. *Education Week* 8 (January 18): 18.

———. 1991a. Congress seeks to restrict use of E.D. research funds. *Education Week* 10 (July 31): 39.

———. 1991b. Congress weighing proposal to rein in E.D. research unit. *Education Week* 10 (June 19): 1, 30.

———. 1991c. Three federal agencies probing Cavazos travel practices. *Education Week* 10 (May 22): 20.

Miller, Julie A., and Debra Viadero. 1989. White House announces resignations of six Education Department officials. *Education Week* 8 (March 22): 16.

Mincer, Jacob. 1989. Human capital responses to technological change in the labor market. National Center on Education and Employment, Technical Papers, no. 9, November.

———. 1990. Job training, wage growth, and labor turnover. National Center on Education and Employment, Technical Papers, no. 19, November.

Mirga, Tom. 1984. Justiz is cleared on most charges of anonymous group. *Education Week* 4 (December 12): 1, 18.

———. 1985. Reagan's charge to reorganize agency could mean merger of research arms. *Education Week* 4 (January 23): 13.

———. 1986. Finn names E.D. research chief. *Education Week* 5 (February 12): 12.

Mitchell, Douglas E., Sara Ann Beach, and Gary Badarak. 1991. Modeling the relationship between achievement and class size: A re-analysis of the Tennessee Project STAR Data. California Educational Research Cooperative, University of California, Riverside, October.

Mitchell, Douglas, Cristi Carson, and Gary Badarak. 1989. How changing class size affects classrooms and students. California Educational Research Cooperative, University of California, Riverside, May.

Moorman, Hunter N., and Thomas G. Carroll. 1986. Peer review and NIE/OERI competition for regional educational laboratories and national R&D centers. *Educational Researcher* 15 (August–September): 16–18.

Musick, Mark D. 1999. Chair of NAGB, letter to Commissioner of Education Statistics, Pascal D. Forgione Jr., February 18.

NAE [National Academy of Education]. 1991. *Research and the renewal of education.* Stanford: National Academy of Education.

———. 1999. Recommendations regarding research priorities. National Academy of Education, March.

NAGB [National Assessment Governing Board]. 1996. Policy statement on redesigning the National Assessment of Educational Progress. National Assessment Governing Board, Washington, DC, August 2.

———. 1997. Schedule for the National Assessment of Educational Progress. National Assessment Governing Board, Washington, DC, March 8.

National Center for Improving Science Education. 1987. A proposal for a national center for the improvement of science teaching and learning. Grant proposal submitted to OERI, July 10, abstract.

National Institute on Early Childhood Department and Education. 1997. *Directory of projects, 1997.* Washington, DC: U.S. Department of Education.

Natriello, Gary. 1987. The role of the school in preparing students for work. Final report to OERI, June.

NCER [National Council on Educational Research]. 1976. Resolution of the National Council on Educational Research institutions engaged in education research and development. NCER Resolution no. 091875-18, July 23.

NCES [National Center for Education Statistics]. 1996. *NAEP 1994 U.S. history report card: Findings from the National Assessment of Educational Progress.* Washington, DC: Government Printing Office.

NERPPB [National Educational Research Policy and Priorities Board]. 1995. Minutes of NERPPB meeting. Washington, DC, March 30–31.

———. 1999a. Attaining excellence: A handbook on the standards for the conduct and evaluation of research carried out by the Office of Educational Research and Improvement, U.S. Department of Education, April.

———. 1999b. Investing in learning: A policy statement on research in education. U.S. Department of Education, April 5.

New research post filled. 1996. *Education Week* 15 (June 19): 25.

Newton, Anne E. 1987. Teacher quality: An issue brief. Regional Laboratory for Educational Improvement of the Northeast and Islands, May.

NIE [National Institute of Education]. 1975. Background report on the "labs & centers." Paper prepared for the National Council on Educational Research, March 5.

———. 1977. *Reauthorization of the National Institute of Education, 1976.* Washington, DC: National Institute of Education.

———. 1978. *Summary of the reorganization plan.* Washington, DC: Department of Health, Education and Welfare, June.

———. 1979. Long-term special institutional agreements with the seventeen existing laboratories and centers, January 15.

———. 1983a. Transcript of hearings on a national competition for regional educational laboratories and R&D centers. Chicago, June 20.

———. 1983b. Transcript of hearings on a national competition for regional educational laboratories and R&D centers. Kansas City, June 22.

———. 1984. *Regional educational laboratory institutional operations: Request for proposals, 1985.* Washington, DC: National Institute of Education.

NIE Laboratory Study Group. 1983. Expanding and strengthening NIE's regional laboratory services: Needs, issues, and options. Washington, DC: National Institute of Education, October 3.

OERI [Office of Educational Research and Improvement]. 1990. *Technical evaluation form: Regional Educational Laboratory Competition.* Washington, DC: Office of Educational Research and Improvement.

———. 1994. Strategic plan, April 25.

———. 1995. Regional educational laboratories for research, development, dissemination, and technical assistance, RFP 95–040: Statement of work. U.S. Department of Education.

———. 1997. *Bulletin* (summer).

———. 1999. Interim reviews of the National Education Research and Development Centers, September 16.

OERI bill bogged down as deadline nears. 1992. *Report on Education Research* 24 (July 22): 3–4.

OERI reauthorization hanging with only weeks left. 1992. *Report on Education Research* 24 (September 16): 7.

OERI Review Team. 1999a. National Center for the Study of Adult Learning and Literacy (NCSALL), OERI, February 3.

———. 1999b. Interim evaluation of the National Center for Research on Education, Diversity and Excellence (CREDE). OERI, January 29.

———. n.d. Interim evaluation of the National Center on Early Development and Learning (NCEDL). OERI.

———. n.d. Interim evaluation of the National Center for Improving Student Learning and Achievement in Mathematics and Science. OERI.

———. n.d. Interim evaluation of the National Research Center on English Learning and Achievement (CELA). OERI.

Office of the Assistant Secretary, OERI. 1994a. The fifteen statements as agreed to by the reinvention team facilitators at the August 10, 1994, retreat. August 10.

———. 1994b. Note to OERI staff. May 13.

———. 1994c. Office of Educational Research and Improvement. October 20.

Office of Research, OERI. 1990. *Application for grants under the Educational Research and Development Center Program.* Washington, DC: U.S. Department of Education.

Olson, Lynn. 1999. NRC seeks new agenda for research: Proposal calls for year-long dialogue. *Education Week* 18 (April 14): 1, 27.

Owens, Janice. 1997. *Learning and earning: Analysis of HEA Title II-B graduate library fellowship program recipients, fiscal years 1985–1991.* Washington, DC: U.S. Department of Education.

Owens, Thomas, and Carolyn Cohen. 1991. Northwest entry-level work study. Northwest Regional Educational Laboratory, September 30.

Panel for the Review of Laboratory and Center Operations. 1978. An interim report to the director of NIE: Review of long range plans of the educational laboratories and the research and development centers. January 20.

———. 1979. *Research and development centers and regional educational laboratories: Strengthening and stabilizing a national resource.* Washington, DC: U.S. Department of Education. Final report, National Institute of Education.

Payer, Elizabeth T. 1995. Chronology of OERI reinvention activities. OERI, March 8.

PES [Planning and Evaluation Service]. 1999. Response to Maris Vinovskis' paper critiquing the longitudinal evaluation of school change and performance. August.

Peterson, Penelope L., and Michelle A. Comeaux. 1990. Evaluating the systems: Teachers' perspectives on teacher evaluation. *Educational Evaluation and Policy Analysis* 12 (spring): 3–24.

Phillips, Gary W. 1997. Technical, methodological, and operational issues in the implementation of the NAGB redesign of NAEP. Presentation at the Forum on the National Assessment of Educational Progress (NAEP) Redesign, OERI, June 3.

Pickett, Paul C. 1967. Contributions of John Ward Studebacker to American education. Ph.D. diss., University of Iowa.

PIP [Programs for Improvement of Practice]. 1990. *Regional educational laboratory request for proposal.* Washington, DC: U.S. Department of Education.

Pistorio, Carol, Russell H. Jackson, and Debra Newell. 2000. *Interim evaluation of the regional educational laboratories: Executive summary.* Vol. 1. Houston: Decision Information Resources.

Pitsch, Mark. 1993. Action on reform bill seen unlikely by year end. *Education Week* 13 (November 24): 11.

———. 1994. Next stop for Goals 2000 bill: House-Senate conference. *Education Week* 13 (February 16): 18–19.

Pitsch, Mark, and Lynn Schnaiberg. 1994. Senate amends, then nears vote, on Clinton's Goals 2000 measure. *Education Week* 13 (February 9): 18–19.

Pogrow, Stanley. 1996. Reforming the wannabe reformers: Why education reforms almost always end up making things worse. *Phi Delta Kappan* 77 (June): 656–63.

Porter, Andrew C. 1998. Chair of ACES, letter to Secretary Richard W. Riley, November 3.

Price, Kendall O. 1984. Creating and disseminating knowledge for educational reform: Policy management of the National Institute of Education's regional educational laboratories and national research and development centers. Final report to the National Council on Educational Research, U.S. Department of Education, January.

Pritchard, Ivor. 1990. Memorandum to Milton Goldberg, Director, Office of Research. OERI, January 2.

Public Law. 1994. Title IX: Educational research and improvement. 103–227.

Radin, Beryl A., and Willis D. Hawley. 1988. *The politics of federal reorganization: Creating the U.S. Department of Education.* New York: Pergamon.

Ragin, Charles C., and Howard S. Becker, eds. 1992. *What is a case? Exploring the foundations of social inquiry.* Cambridge: Cambridge University Press.

Randall, Robert, et al. 1970. A developmental process adopted by the Southwest Educational Development Laboratory, July 14, 1970. Southwest Educational Development Laboratory.

Randolph, Jennings, Thomas F. Eagleton, Richard S. Schweiker, Gaylord Nelson, and Alan Cranston. 1977. Letter to Harold L. Hodgkinson, Director, National Institute of Education, January 27.

Ravitch, Diane. 1993a. Enhancing the federal role in research on education. *Chronicle of Higher Education* 39 (April 7): A48.

———. 1993b. The state of the agency. *OERI Bulletin,* no. 1: 2.

————, ed. 1995a. *Debating the future of American education: Do we need national standards and assessments?* Washington, DC: Brookings Institution.

————. 1995b. *National standards in American education: A citizen's guide.* Washington, DC: Brookings Institution.

————. 1999. Hearing before the Senate Committee on Health, Education, Labor, and Pensions, U.S. Senate, April 14.

Reeves, Andree E. 1993. *Congressional committee chairmen: Three who made an evolution.* Lexington: University Press of Kentucky.

Reform bill dies in Senate, focus now on reauthorization. 1992. *Report on Education Research* 24 (October 14): 7.

Research Priorities Planning Team. 1995. Research priorities plan. OERI, June 1.

Resta, Paul E. 1988. The depoliticization of educational research. In *Higher education research and public policy,* ed. Manual J. Justiz and Lars G. Bjork, 157–73. New York: Macmillan.

Riles, Wilson C. 1973. Resolution of the National Council on Educational Research Institutions engaged in education research and development. NCER resolution no. 091875–18 (amended July 23).

Robinson, Sharon Porter. 1979. An analysis of administrator discretion and its impact on black student suspensions. Ed.D. diss., College of Education, University of Kentucky.

————. 1994a. Job preference selection for the new OERI. OERI memorandum, September 8.

————. 1994b. The new OERI structure and staffing plan. OERI memorandum, October 26.

Robinson, Sharon Porter, Kenji Hakuta, and Ted Sanders. 1996. *Building knowledge for a nation of learners: A framework for education research, 1997.* Washington, DC: Government Printing Office.

Rossmiller, Richard. 1975. U.S. House. Subcommittee on Select Education, Committee on Education and Labor. *National Institute of Education: Hearings before the Subcommittee on Select Education.* 94th Cong., 1st sess.

Rothman, Robert. 1988. Dismissing rumors of a rift, Bennett sets September exit. *Education Week* 7 (May 18): 1, 15.

————. 1991a. New O.E.R.I. head sees top priority ways to marry research and practice. *Education Week* 10 (July 31): 37.

————. 1991b. Panel chairman joins call for larger-scale research. *Education Week* 10 (April 17): 23.

————. 1992a. Academy panel urges wide-ranging effort to "rebuild" O.E.R.I. *Education Week* 11 (April 8): 1, 23.

————. 1992b. Historian outlines project to assess federal research agency. *Education Week* 11 (February 19): 6–7.

————. 1992c. House passes compromise O.E.R.I. reauthorization. *Education Week* 12 (September 30): 25.

————. 1992d. With death of O.E.R.I. bill, reorganization put off. *Education Week* 12 (October 14): 22.

————. 1993. Study cites need to improve E.D. research efforts. *Education Week* 13 (May 5): 1, 24.

———. 1995. *Measuring up: Standards, assessment, and school reform.* San Francisco: Jossey-Bass.

Rowan, Brian, and Larry F. Guthrie. 1988. The quality of Chapter 1 instruction: Results from a study of 24 schools. Far West Lab, March.

Rowan, Brian, Larry F. Guthrie, Ginny V. Lee, and Grace Pung Guthrie. 1986. The design and implementation of Chapter 1 instructional services: A study of 24 schools. Far West Lab, November.

Sashkin, Marshall, and J. Kiser. 1993. *Putting total quality management to work.* San Francisco: Berrett-Koehler.

Saylor, J. Galen. 1982. *Who planned the curriculum? A curriculum plans reservoir model with historical examples.* West Lafayette, IN: Kappa Delta Pi Press.

Scates, Shelby. 1997. *Warren G. Magnuson and the shaping of twentieth century America.* Seattle: University of Washington Press.

Schaffarzick, Jon. 1979. Federal curriculum reform: A crucible for value conflict. In *Value conflicts and curriculum issues,* ed. Jon Schaffarzick and Gary Sykes, 1–24. Berkeley, CA: McCutchan.

Schnaiberg, Lynn. 1993. In clearing O.E.R.I. bill, Senate backs more funding. *Education Week* 13 (November 10): 21.

———. 1994a. Fiscal 1995 spending bill affirms reorganized research office. *Education Week* 13 (July 13): 15.

———. 1994b. O.E.R.I. compromise strikes balance on who will control research agenda. *Education Week* 13 (March 23): 17.

———. 1995. Riley appoints independent board to set research agenda. *Education Week* 14 (March 8): 15.

Schneider, E. Joseph. 1984. Letter to Manuel J. Justiz, April 12.

Schultz, Thomas W. 1988. Behind closed doors: Peer review in the NIE research center competition. Ed.D. diss., Harvard University.

Schwab, R. G., Sylvia Hart-Landsberg, and Karen Reed Wikelund. 1991. Implementation strategies for innovative literacy practices: A regional depiction. Northwest Regional Educational Laboratory, April.

Segal, Judith W., Susan F. Chipman, and Robert Glaser, eds. 1985. *Thinking and learning skills: Relating instruction to research.* Hillsdale, NJ: Lawrence Erlbaum.

Shokraii, Nina H. 1998. Why Congress should overhaul the federal regional education laboratories. *Heritage Foundation Backgrounder,* no. 1200 (July 2).

Sieber, Samuel D. 1972. *Reforming the university: The role of the social research center.* New York: Praeger.

———. 1974. Federal support for research and development in education and its effects. In *The seventy-third yearbook of the National Society for the Study of Education,* ed. C. Wayne Gordon, Pt. 2, 478–502. Chicago: University of Chicago Press.

Slavin, Robert E. 1997. Design competitions: A proposal for a new federal role in educational research and development. *Educational Researcher* 26 (January–February): 22.

Slavin, Robert E., Nancy L. Karweit, and Barbara A. Wasik. 1991. Preventing early school failure: What works? Center for Research on Effective Schooling for Disadvantaged Students, report no. 26, November.

Slavin, Robert E., Nancy A. Madden, Lawrence J. Dolan, and Barbara A. Wasik. 1996. *Every child, every school: Success for all.* Thousand Oaks, CA: Corwin Press.

Slavin Robert E., Nancy E. Slavin, Nancy L. Karweit, and Nancy A. Madden. 1994. *Effective programs for students at risk.* Boston: Allyn and Bacon.

Smith, Darrell H. 1923. *The bureau of education: Its history, activities, and organization.* Baltimore: Johns Hopkins University Press.

Sniegoski, Stephen J. 1994. John Eaton, U.S. commissioner of education, 1870–1886. Manuscript.

Sperling, Melanie. 1991. Dialogues of deliberation: Conversation in the teacher-student writing conference. Center for the Study of Writing and Literacy, report no. 48, May.

Sperling, Melanie, and Sarah Warshauer Freedman. 1987. A good girl writes like a good girl: Written responses and clues to the teaching/learning process. Center for the Study of Writing and Literacy, report no. 3, May.

Sproull, Lee, Stephen Weiner, and David Wolf. 1978. *Organizing an anarchy: Belief, bureaucracy, and politics in the National Institute of Education.* Chicago: University of Chicago Press.

Sroufe, Gerald. 1991. Educational enterprise zones: The new national research centers. *Educational Researcher* 20 (4): 24–29.

———. 1995. Emerson Elliott: Proud to be a federal bureaucrat. *Educational Researcher* 24 (7): 29–33.

———. 1997. Improving the "awful reputation" of educational research. *Educational Researcher* 26 (7): 26–28.

Sroufe, Gerald, Margaret Goertz, Joan Herman, Sam Yeager, Gregg B. Jackson, and Sharon P. Robinson. 1995. The Federal Education Research Agency: New opportunities and new challenges for researchers. *Educational Researcher* 24 (May): 24–30.

Stalford, Charles. 1991. Conduct of the 1990 laboratory competition. Office of Educational Research and Improvement, June.

———. 1992. Analysis of laboratory budgets. Memo, Office of Educational Research and Improvement, May 21.

Stiggins, Richard J., Philip Griswold, and David Frisbie. 1990. Inside high school grading practices. Northwest Regional Educational Laboratory, September.

Stolberg, Sheryl Gay. 1997. Keeping track: Top health vacancies. *New York Times,* September 22, C14.

Tan, Hong, Bruce Chapman, Christine Peterson, and Alison Booth. 1991. *Youth training in the United States, Britain, and Australia.* Santa Monica: RAND.

Thompson, James R., and Patricia W. Ingraham. 1996. The reinvention game. *Public Administration Review* 56 (May–June): 291–98.

Timpane, P. Michael. 1988. Federal progress in educational research. In *Higher education research and public policy,* ed. Manuel J. Justiz and Lars G. Bjork, 17–31. New York: Macmillan.

———. 1998. National directions in education research planning. National Educational Research Policy and Priorities Board, December.

Title, David. 1989. The critical role of teacher incentives in the northeast states. Regional Laboratory for Educational Improvement of the Northeast and Islands, March.

———. 1990. Pension portability in the northeastern states. Regional Laboratory for Educational Improvement of the Northeast and Islands.

Toch, Thomas. 1983a. Cuts made despite push for educational reform. *Education Week* 3 (October 12): 16.

———. 1983b. Research agenda faces funding cuts, political pressures. *Education Week* 3 (12 October): 1, 16.

Tomlinson, Tommy M. 1988. *Class size and public policy: Politics and panaceas.* Washington, DC: Government Printing Office.

———. 1990. Class size and public policy: The plot thickens. *Contemporary Education* 62 (fall): 17–23.

Turnbull, Brenda J. 1991. Laboratory evaluation: A technical proposal. Policy Studies Associates, 2 August.

Turnbull, Brenda J., and M. Bruce Haslam. 1994. Decision making in regional educational laboratories. Policy Studies Associates. Washington, DC, February.

Turnbull, Brenda J., Heather McCollum, M. Bruce Haslam, and Kelley Colopy. 1994. Regional educational laboratories: Some key accomplishments and limitations in the program's work. Policy Studies Associates, Washington, DC, December.

Tushnet, Naida C. 1992. Synthesis and translation: Will it be easier for users to discover meaning, truth, and utility in research? Paper presented at the AERA annual meeting, San Francisco, April.

U.S. Congress. 1971. *Congressional directory, 92nd Congress, 1st session.* Washington, DC: Government Printing Office.

U.S. Department of Education. 1992. *Education department general administrative regulations (EDGAR)* (34 CFR, parts 74, 75, 76, 77, 79, 80, 81, 82, 85, and 86). Rev. July 8, 1992, paragraph 75.253. Washington, DC: Government Printing Office.

———. 1995a. Riley appoints first research policy and priorities board. *U.S. Department of Education News,* February 27.

———. 1995b. *Standards for the conduct and evaluation of activities carried out by the Office of Educational Research and Improvement (OERI): Evaluation of applications for grants and cooperative agreements and proposals for contracts* (34 CFR, part 700). Washington, DC: U.S. Department of Education.

———. 1997. *News.* 9 September.

U.S. GAO [General Accounting Office]. 1987. *Education information: Changes in funds and priorities have affected production and quality.* Washington, DC: GAO. GAO/PEMD-88-4.

———. 1994. *Management reforms: Examples of public and private innovations to improve service delivery.* Washington, DC: Government Printing Office. GAO/AIMD/GGD–94–90BR.

U.S. House. 1965a. Committee on Education and Labor. *Elementary and Secondary Education Act of 1965.* 89th Cong., 1st sess. H. Doc. 143. March 8.

———. 1965b. General Subcommittee on Education. *Aid to elementary and secondary education, Hearings on H.R. 2361 and H.R. 2362.* 89th Cong., 1st sess. January 22.

———. 1966. Special Subcommittee on Education. *Hearings.* 89th Cong., 2d sess.

———. 1967a. Committee on Education and Labor. *Study of the United States Office of Education.* 90th Cong., 1st sess. H. Doc. 193.

———. 1967b. Special Subcommittee on Education. Study of the United States Office of Education. 89th Cong., 2d sess. H. Doc. 193.

———. 1967c. Subcommittee of the Committee on Appropriations. *Hearings, Departments of Labor and Health, Education, and Welfare appropriations for 1968.* Pt. 3, 90th Cong., 1st sess.

———. 1968. Subcommittee of the Committee on Appropriations. *Hearings, Departments of Labor, and Health, Education, and Welfare appropriations for 1969.* Pt. 3, 90th Cong., 2d sess.

———. 1971a. Committee on Education and Labor. *To establish a National Institute of Education: Hearings before the Select Subcommittee on Education.* 92d Cong., 1st sess.

———. 1971b. Select Subcommittee on Education. *To establish a National Institute of Education, Hearings . . . On H.R. 33, H.R. 3606, and other related bills.* 92d Cong., 1st sess. February 18, 24; March 17, 20, 23; May 11, 14; June 14.

———. 1971c. Subcommittee of the Committee on Appropriations. *Hearings on Office of Education and related agencies appropriations for 1972.* Pt. 1. 92d Cong., 1st sess.

———. 1972. *Hearings on Departments of Labor and Health, Education, and Welfare appropriations for 1973.* Pt. 2: *Office of Education, special institutions.* 92d Cong., 2d sess.

———. 1974. Subcommittee of the Committee on Appropriations. *Hearings on the Departments of Labor and Health, Education, and Welfare appropriations for 1975.* Pt. 5: *Office of Education.* 93d Cong., 2d sess. H. Doc. 836–839.

———. 1975a. Subcommittee on Appropriations. *Hearings on Education Division and related agencies, fiscal year 1976.* Pt. 1. 94th Cong., 1st sess.

———. 1975b. Subcommittee on Select Education. *National Institute of Education: Hearings before the Select Subcommittee on Education.* 94th Cong., 1st sess.

———. 1976a. *Hearings on Departments of Labor and Health, Education, and Welfare appropriations for fiscal year 1977.* Pt. 1. 94th Cong., 2d sess.

———. 1976b. Subcommittee on Select Education. *Hearings on the National Institute of Education, 1975.* 94th Cong., 1st sess.

———. 1976c. *The vocational education and National Institute of Education amendments of 1976 report.* 94th Cong., 2d sess., H.R. 94–1085.

———. 1980a. *Conference report on higher education to accompany H.R. 5192.* 96th Cong., 2d sess. H.R. 96–1251.

———. 1980b. Subcommittee on Select Education. *To extend the authorization of appropriations for the National Institute of Education.* 96th Cong., 2d sess. February 5.

———. 1980c. Subcommittee on Select Education. *To extend the authorization of appropriations for the National Institute of Education.* 96th Cong., 2d sess. February 6.

———. 1981. *Omnibus Budget Reconciliation Act of 1981: Conference report.* 97th Cong., 1st sess. H.R. 3982, H. Doc. 97–208.

———. 1983. Subcommittee on Appropriations. *Hearings on Departments of Labor, Health and Human Services, Education, and related agencies appropriations for 1984.* Pt. 6. 98th Cong., 1st sess.

———. 1986. *Reauthorization of sections 405 and 406 of the General Education Provisions Act.* 99th Cong., 2d sess.

———. 1988a. Subcommittee on Select Education. *Oversight hearings on the Office of Educational Research and Improvement (OERI).* 100th Cong., 2d sess. H. Doc. 100–77.

———. 1988b. Subcommittee on Select Education. *Preliminary staff report on educational research, development, and dissemination: Reclaiming a vision of the federal role for the 1990s and beyond.* 100th Cong., 2d sess. September.

———. 1989. Subcommittee on Select Education. *Oversight hearing on the Office of Educational Research and Improvement (OERI).* 101st Cong., 1st sess.

———. 1991a. Subcommittee on Select Education. *Hearing on the Office of Educational Research and Improvement.* 102d Cong., 1st sess.

———. 1991b. *To establish the national institute for the education of at-risk students.* 102d Cong., 1st sess. H.R. 2467. May 23.

———. 1992a. Committee on Education and Labor. *Report on the educational research, development, and dissemination excellence act.* 102d Cong., 2d sess. H.R. 102–845.

———. 1992b. Subcommittee on Select Education. *A bill to improve education in the United States by promoting excellence in research, development, and the dissemination of information.* 102d Cong., 2d sess. Committee Print. H.R. 4014.

———. 1992c. Subcommittee on Select Education. *Hearings on reauthorization of the Office of Educational Research and Improvement (OERI).* 102d Cong., 2d sess.

———. 1994a. Committee on Appropriations. *Departments of Labor, Health and Human Services, and Education, and related agencies appropriation bill, 1995.* 103d Cong., 2d sess. H.R. 103–553.

———. 1994b. Committee on Appropriations. *Hearings on the Departments of Labor, Health and Human Services, and related agencies appropriations for 1995.* Pt. 5: *Department of Education.* 103d Cong., 2d sess.

———. 1994c. Committee on Conference. *Conference report: Making appropriations for the Departments of Labor, Health and Human Services, and Education, and related agencies, for the fiscal year ending September 30, 1995, and for other purposes.* 103d Cong., 2d sess. H.R. 103–733.

———. 1995. Committee on Appropriations. *Hearings on the Departments of Labor, Health and Human Services, Education, and related agencies appropriations for 1996.* Pt. 5: *Department of Education.* 104th Cong., 1st sess.

———. 1996. Committee on Appropriations. *Hearings on the Departments of Labor, Health and Human Services, Education, and related agencies appropriations for 1997.* Pt. 5: *Department of Education.* 104th Cong., 2d sess.

———. 1997. Committee on Appropriations. *Hearings on the Departments of Labor, Health and Human Services, Education, and related agencies appropriations for 1998.* Pt. 5: *Department of Education.* 105th Cong., 1st sess.

U.S. Senate. 1965. Committee on Labor and Public Welfare. *Elementary and Secondary Act of 1965.* 89th Cong., 1st sess. S. Rept. 146. April 6.

———. 1970. Subcommittee on Appropriations. *Hearings on Office of Education appropriations for fiscal year 1971.* 91st Cong., 2d sess.

———. 1971. Subcommittee on Appropriations. *Hearings on Office of Education and related agencies for fiscal year 1972.* 92nd Cong., 1st sess.

———. 1975a. Subcommittee on Appropriations. *Hearings on Education Division and related agencies, 1976.* Pt. 1. 94th Cong., 1st sess.

———. 1975b. Subcommittee on Education. *Hearings on higher education legislation, 1975.* Pt. 2. 94th Cong., 1st sess.

———. 1976. *Education amendments of 1976 report.* 94th Cong., 2d sess. S. Rept. 98–882.

———. 1983a. Committee on Labor and Human Resources. *Nominations.* 97th Cong., 2d sess., December 9, 1982.

———. 1983b. Subcommittee on the Committee on Appropriations. *Hearings on Departments of Labor, Health and Human Services, Education, and related agencies appropriations for fiscal year 1983.* Pt. 4. 97th Cong., 2d sess.

———. 1985. Subcommittee on Appropriations. *Hearings on Departments of Labor, Health and Human Services, Education and Related Agencies appropriations for fiscal year 1986.* Pt. 3. 99th Cong., 1st sess.

———. 1991. Subcommittee on Education, Arts, and Humanities. *Reauthorization of the Office of Educational Research and Improvement Act.* 102d Cong., 1st sess.

———. 1992. Committee on Labor and Human Resources. *Report on the Office of Educational Research and Improvement Act.* 102d Cong., 2d sess. S. Rept. 102–269.

———. 1994. Committee on Appropriations. *Departments of Labor, Health and Human Services, and Education and related agencies appropriation bill, 1995.* 103d Cong., 2d sess. S. Rept. 103–318.

———. 1996. *Departments of Labor, Health and Human Services, and Education and related agencies appropriation bill, 1997.* 104th Cong., 2d sess. S. Rept. 104–368.

U.S. Senate Budget Committee Task Force on Education. 1998. Prospects for reform: The state of American education and the federal role. Interim report.

Verstegen, Deborah A. 1990. Education fiscal policy in the Reagan administration. *Educational Evaluation and Policy Analysis* 12 (winter): 367.

Verstegen, Deborah A., and David L. Clark. 1988. The diminution in federal expenditures for education during the Reagan administration. *Phi Delta Kappan* 70 (October): 137.

Viadero, Debra. 1995. E.D. spends time on task of reshaping research efforts. *Education Week* 14 (February 8): 19, 29.

Vinovskis, Maris A. 1988. *An "epidemic" of adolescent pregnancy? Some historical and policy perspectives.* New York: Oxford University Press.

———. 1989a. The role of education in the economic transformation of nineteenth century America. National Center on Education and Employment, Conference Paper no. 9, December.

———. 1989b. The use and misuse of social science analysis in federal adolescent pregnancy policy. Distinguished Lectures in the Social Sciences, Northern Illinois University, DeKalb, November.

———. 1992. Analysis of the research and development centers funded by the Office of Educational Research and Improvement (OERI). Preliminary draft. OERI, May.

———. 1993a. Analysis of the quality of research and development at the OERI research and development centers and the OERI regional educational laboratories. OERI, June.

———. 1993b. Early childhood education: Then and now. *Daedalus* 122 (winter): 151–76.

———. 1994a. Comments on "Regional educational laboratories: Some key accomplishments and limitations in the program's work." Memo to Dick Hays and Bob Stonehill, OERI, December 4.

———. 1994b. Further comments on proposed FIE replication and evaluation of promising practices. Memorandum to Jan Anderson, Joe Conaty, and Dick Hays, OERI, May 20.

———. 1995a. A life course framework for analyzing educational research projects. Paper prepared for OERI, July.

———. 1995b. Comments on draft statement of work for regional educational laboratory RFP. Memo to Margo Anderson, Eve Bither, Chuck Hansen, and Bob Stonehill. OERI, February 12.

———. 1996. An analysis of the concept and uses of systemic educational reform. *American Educational Research Journal* 33 (spring): 53–85.

———. 1997. An analysis of the proposed phase three standards for the conduct and evaluation of OERI activities. OERI, March 26.

———. 1998a. *Changing federal strategies for supporting educational research, development, and statistics.* Washington, DC: National Educational Research Policy and Priorities Board.

———. 1998b. Measuring the interim performance of the regional educational laboratory's educational research and development activities. Background paper prepared for the U.S. Department of Education, October 4.

———. 1998c. *Overseeing the nation's report card: The creation and evolution of the National Assessment Governing Board (NAGB).* Washington, DC: Government Printing Office.

———. 1999a. Do federal compensatory education programs really work? A brief historical analysis of Title I and Head Start. *American Journal of Education* 107 (May): 187–209.

———. 1999b. *History and educational policymaking.* New Haven: Yale University Press.

———. 1999c. Improving federal educational research, development, and evaluation. Joint hearing on the "Overview of Federal Education Research and Evaluation Efforts," U.S. Congress, House of Representatives, Committee on Education and the Workforce, and Senate, Committee on Health, Education, Labor, and Pensions, June 17.

———. 1999d. Improving the analysis and reporting of policy-related evaluations at the U.S. Department of Education: Some preliminary observations about the longitudinal evaluation of school change and performance. August.

———. 1999e. Missing in practice? Systematic development and rigorous program evaluation at the U.S. Department of Education. Paper presented at the conference Evaluation of Educational Policies, American Academy of Arts and Sciences, Cambridge, MA, May 13–14.

———. 2000a. The federal role in educational research and development. In *Brookings papers on education policy, 2000,* ed. Diane Ravitch, 359–96. Washington, DC: Brookings Institution Press.

———. 2000b. Revitalizing federal education and evaluation efforts. Testimony before the hearing on education research and evaluation efforts, U.S. Congress, House of Representatives, Subcommittee on Early Childhood, Youth, and Families, May 4.

Voss, James F., David N. Perkins, and Judith W. Segal, eds. 1991. *Informal reasoning and education.* Hillsdale, NJ: Lawrence Erlbaum.

Walker, Jerry Phillip. 1972. *An analysis of differential perceptions toward educational research and development held by professional staff members of research and development centers and development laboratories.* Ph.D. diss., Ohio State University.

Walker, Reagan. 1989. Temporary appointees named to 6 top E.D. posts. *Education Week* 8 (March 29): 19.

Warren, Donald R. 1974. *To enforce education: A history of the founding years of the United States Office of Education.* Detroit: Wayne State University Press.

West, Peter. 1989. Bush picks Cross for E.D. research post. *Education Week* 9 (September 27): 15.

———. 1995. O.T.A. decries lack of focus on teachers. *Education Week* 14 (April 12): 1, 11.

White, Eileen. 1982. NIE: A failed mission? *Education Week* 2 (December 22): 13.

Wise, Arthur E., and Gerald E. Sroufe. 1990. A response to America's reform agenda: The National Institutes for Educational Improvement. *Educational Researcher* 19 (May): 22–25.

Wong, Jeannie. 1993. Congress seeks overhaul of federal education-research program. *Chronicle of Higher Education* 39 (July 21): A26.

Word, Elizabeth, Charles M. Achilles, Helen Bain, John Folger, John Johnston, and Nan Lintz. 1990. Project STAR final executive summary: Kindergarten through third grade results (1985–89). *Contemporary Education* 62 (fall): 13–16.

Zodhiates, Philip Phaedon. 1988. Bureaucrats and politicians: The National Institute of Education and educational research under Reagan. Ed.D. diss., Harvard University.

Index

Achievement Institute, 141, 148
Advisory Council on Education Statistics (ACES), 163, 198
Alexander, Lamar, 115, 123
American Education and Research Association (AERA), 85, 104, 109, 114, 119–24, 186, 187
At-Risk Institute, 141

Barkley, Bruce, 138, 231–32n. 18
Bell, Terrel, 45, 101–5, 108, 225n. 42, 236n. 5
Bennett, William, 108, 113, 227n. 59
Berkeley Center, 16, 18, 19, 20, 22, 23, 25, 30, 31, 118
Bither, Eva, 65, 118, 149, 168, 232n. 20, 233n. 35
Brademas, John, 77–80, 221n. 12, 222n. 22, 236n. 5
Bureau of Education, 8, 179, 195
Bush, President George, 114, 127
Bush administration, 3, 114–16, 118–20, 122–24, 129, 131, 178, 186, 194, 196, 229n. 77

Campbell, Roald, 13, 88–89, 206n. 13
Campbell panel, 39–43, 46, 88–91
Carter, President Jimmy, 99, 103, 225n. 44
Carter administration, 6, 44, 94, 112
Cartwright, Ron, 149, 232n. 22
Cavazos, Lauro, 113–14, 227n. 63
CEMREL, 43, 98, 107, 113, 216n. 26, 224–25n. 40, 226n. 50
Christensen, John, 168, 231n. 12

Clinton, President Bill, 115, 136, 137, 149, 230n. 1
Clinton administration, 3, 6, 129, 130, 136–37, 149, 154, 157, 162, 165, 167, 175, 178, 183, 185–86, 195, 198, 230–31n. 8, 234–35n. 49, 236n. 64
competition, 156, 184–85, 192, 200
  1985 request for proposals, 13–14, 45–47, 63–65, 105–8
  1990 request for proposals, 49, 63–65, 117, 219n. 54
  1995 request for proposals, 151
  and centers, 28, 145–46, 173, 206n. 20, 212n. 59
  criticisms of, 14, 74, 120, 233n. 32
  fairness of, 28, 63–65, 74, 113, 206n. 20, 212n. 59
  and labs, 48–49, 63–65, 74, 111, 156, 219n. 58
  nonfederal funds for, 79, 90, 103
  suggestions for, 13, 45–46, 104, 105–8
Conaty, Joseph, 30, 118, 146, 232n. 20
Congress
  1976 NIE reauthorization, 14
  1979 review, 205n. 7
  1992 OERI reauthorization, 120–25
  1993–94 OERI reauthorization, 4, 172–74, 204n. 9
  1995 OERI reauthorization, 108–10
  2000 OERI reauthorization, 183–84, 185

46–48, 50, 65–67, 69–70, 84, 91,
118, 139, 150, 158, 173, 177, 197,
213n. 68
Moorman, Hunter, 30, 157–58, 231n.
12, 234n. 40
Moynihan, Daniel, 76–77, 78, 221n.
13

National Academy of Education
(NAE), 2, 186, 190–91
National Academy of Sciences study,
2, 11, 12–13, 14–16, 49, 69, 117,
118, 122, 135, 136, 141–42, 156,
193, 204n. 13, 209n. 35
National Assessment Governing
Board (NAGB), 163, 164–65,
167, 182, 234n. 44, 238n. 25,
239n. 34
National Assessment of Educational
Progress (NAEP), 100, 163, 164–
66, 182, 198, 229n. 77, 239n. 34
National Center for Education Research, 181, 185, 190, 192, 196
National Center for Education Statistics (NCES), 13, 55–56, 108, 110,
116, 117, 127, 129, 132, 133–34,
140, 162–67, 172, 173–74, 176,
180, 182, 193, 198, 201, 203n. 4,
226n. 53, 238–39n. 32
national center for evaluation and development (NCED), 184, 185,
192, 196
National Council on Education Research (NCER), 13, 39–41, 43,
89, 95–97, 101, 105, 108, 114
National Diffusion Network (NDN),
128, 150, 157
National Educational Research Policy
and Priorities Board (NERPPB),
5, 128, 135, 136, 140, 142–43,
144, 149, 160, 167–76, 185–86,
188, 190–91, 194, 231n. 10, 238n.
25
National Education Association
(NEA), 99, 109, 119, 127, 139,
228n. 74

National Institute for the Education
of At-Risk Students, 121, 123,
124
national labs, vs. regional. *See* regional labs, vs. national
National Research Council, 190
national research institutes, 6, 128,
136, 138, 140–48, 150, 163, 167,
176
NIE/OERI, reauthorization of, 117,
192, 200–201
1975, 40, 88–92
1976, 13, 94–95, 223n. 34
1980, 93–94, 98
1986, 108, 117
1990, 49
1991/1992, 122–25, 126, 128, 136,
138–40
1993/1994, 4–6, 119, 126, 128, 135–
36, 148, 150, 163, 167, 184, 188,
204n. 9
1999/2000, 159, 183, 186, 237n. 17
Nixon, President Richard, 76
Nixon administration, 44, 77, 78, 80,
81, 83, 85, 101
Northwest Lab (NWREL), 50, 52, 54,
57, 59, 60, 156

Obey, David, 86, 105, 108, 111, 129–
30, 222n. 23, 226–27n. 54
OERI, reinvention of, 126, 133, 135–
40, 185, 232n. 20
Office of Reform Assistance and
Dissemination (ORAD), 128,
138, 140, 148–50, 162–64,
168, 176, 181–82, 185, 192, 237n.
12
Office of Research (OR), 3, 17, 55,
108, 140, 213n. 70, 226n. 53,
231n. 10, 233–34n. 36
and centers, 1992 review of, 32–33,
68
and centers, monitoring of, 12, 17,
28, 30, 47, 66, 117, 146, 212n. 60
dissolved into research institutes,
134, 141, 147, 148, 194